The Right Kind of Pride:
A Chronicle of Character,
Caregiving and Community

By Christopher Cudworth

First US Edition 2014

ISBN:0692253777

ISBN-13:9780692253779

Human Nature Publishing

DEDICATION

This book is dedicated to all those affected by cancer and other life-threatening diseases, and to all those who offer support in character, caregiving and community.

Special thanks to my children Evan and Emily Cudworth whose insights are a special part of this world. To family, friends and all those who supported us in so many ways, especially Linda Culley, whose care and character inspired us all.

The Cudworth and Mues family: Evan Cudworth, Christopher Cudworth, Linda Cudworth, Diane Mues, Melvin Mues, Joan Mues, Paul Mues and Emily Cudworth. Photo circa 2006.

For family perspective in advance of reading this journey through cancer survivorship, read The Story of Chris and Linda on pages 61-69

Content

PROLOGUE

Linda's handwritten journal

If there was one thing I learned about my wife Linda Cudworth during the first 20 years of our marriage, it was her general disdain for expressing herself in written form. Often when she had a letter or message to write, she would come to me with a legal pad and words composed in the distinctive longhand cursive writing she preferred to typing on a computer.

"Would you take a look at this?" she'd ask.

Then I'd perform the role of editor. She might be writing a letter to the parents of her preschool students or be spelling out a plan for an education program at our church. Usually her writing was quite good. She simply wanted to be confident the words read well and made sense.

We'd sit together and work through the language until she was satisfied. I'd type it up and print out a copy for her to review. She'd proof the work with a critical eye, handing it back to me for revision if she was not satisfied somehow. If we did that once together, we did it 50 times over the years.

It seems most marriages depend on shared skills like that. It was never much trouble to help her out with those letters to parents. It gave a glimpse into her working life.

Pressed into action

Her distaste for putting thoughts down on paper only magnified when my wife was urged by friends and counselors to keep a journal of her thoughts during treatment for ovarian cancer. At their suggestion she obligingly purchased a journal with blank pages. She'd set out to record her thoughts as treatments proceeded, but it was always clear she was not in love with the process of writing down her feelings. You can tell from her words in the following journal excerpts from 2010 and 2011 that writing about her life with cancer was not her favorite thing to do. Yet true to her honest character, she does a wonderful job of communicating her determination and hope.

Sunday, Sept 12, 2010

Here it is, the eve before yet another—3rd— chemotherapy regimen. I have had a summer of escalating blood tests, CAT SCAN (showing large tumor) biopsy (yes, it is cancer) colonoscopy (clean, thank God) and now six rounds of 3-week cycles that will hopefully kill the cancer – –and not me.

We have had really 5 tough years of cancer and job losses, financial depletion, etc…but we are still here and living in our house—thanks to God, family and friends.

I have been through the "I just want to die" phase, so now I will have to do this the best I can. I am fearful about the side effects and my ability to keep teaching mornings.

Chris is also at such an odd position at his job he cannot even "let on" what is going on…insurance issues. So tomorrow he will drop me off at my parents'—who will take me up to Niles—and Mary—to begin this awful infusion of poison. I hope that it works.

Tuesday, June 11, 2011 "Summer"

I look back on other well-intentioned beginnings to a "cancer journal"––but I never seem to get past day 2 or 3. It just gets too hard!

Yet, here I am, again, on another eve of chemotherapy (Cisplatin and Taxotere, again) — and I am finding it hard to imagine how I will feel, taste, hear, smell all those horrible, awful things. My hair is not close to grown back (from Dec. 1) my eyes still tear; neuropathy is BAD and nails are still falling off. How can I do this again??? People—everyone––are so kind and helpful. I will need lots of extra help as mom is now taking care of dad—and his dialysis…and again, Chris is in a tense situation at work regarding health insurance. I pray that his job keeps going well and that they will be understanding and sympathetic—And that I can do this—the best I can and get rid of this cancer!!! It is a very difficult life to live over and over and over—again."

Perspectives

Despite her stated disdain for writing down her feelings, her words stand as a powerful testament to the resolve she showed in dealing with ovarian cancer after it entered her life at age 46.

At that time our son Evan was entering college and our daughter Emily was a sophomore in high school. The initial diagnosis of Stage IIC did not tell us much about her chances for survival. We did what the doctors instructed and prayed that we could find ways to thrive in the challenges we would face together.

Our goal was always to keep cancer in perspective, not let it define our existence. To accomplish that took a combination of self-examination and faith. We worked together to communicate our needs, thoughts and thankfulness to a caregiving community that grew up around us. As a caregiver, this process helped me better understand her thinking while translating our experience into an ongoing dialogue with our caregiving community. This book is a chronicle of that process and what we learned from it.

On the fly

The first thing we learned about cancer survivorship is that it puts you in all sorts of situations where your emotions, attitudes and philosophies are put to the test. That's because there are typically so many variables. As you try to cope with all the changes cancer treatment can bring, it is easy to feel as if you're making it all up as you go along. To some degree, you always are.

As a caregiver there were times when I did not feel like I had a clue why certain emotions were dominating my mind. I know my wife felt the same way because we always talked about what was coming up next. How would we handle everything?

She might be staring out the window of the car and say something like, "I don't know Chris...everything is so...Oh My God, slow down, you're driving too fast!"

See, she was always the cautious one. It was her job to keep things under control. It was my job was to keep things moving. That's the yin and yang of 'couplehood.' It just gets exaggerated when something like cancer comes along to mess with other plans in your life.

Dualities

The events during the year of my wife's initial cancer diagnosis in 2005 sound crazy in retrospect. It seemed like cancer was trying to take over our whole lives. My mother had been diagnosed with lymphoma that spring and began taking an oral chemotherapy. She chose that option because oral drugs caused fewer side effects. It was her goal to stay strong enough to provide daily care for my father, a stroke victim since 2002.

My mother's strategy worked at first because she enjoyed relatively good health during the summer months. She even scored her first hole-in-one at the golf course that June. The club pro gave her a little trophy with a golf ball in it. That made her proud and happy. She also got to tease my father (the formerly avid golfer) that she was the only one in the family that had ever gotten a hole-in-one.

Behind those joys there was a baseline sense that her health challenges were real. One July day she called to ask me to meet her at the bank to become a co-signer on all their accounts. "You never know what can happen," she offered.

As summer weather changed to fall the doctors discovered an underlying case of pancreatic cancer. She was given chemotherapy but it made her very ill.

Frequencies

At the time I was working for a newspaper and had gone into the regional office near our home to check email and touch base with my boss. I was sitting with a laptop near the photography department where the photo department's dispatch radio for police, fire and ambulance could be heard. A voice came over the radio announcing a familiar address, that of my mother's home. I jumped in the car and arrived as the emergency team was carting her out of the house to the ambulance. She smiled quietly and said to me, "I'm too weak to walk."

She came home from the hospital after two days and was excited to spend time with family over a weekend. But early Monday morning she suffered a stroke that robbed her of consciousness and removed her ability to swallow. The only choice was hospice care.

We were present at her bedside alongside my father the night my mother died. That proved to be a gift in many ways. There is closure that comes with being present at the death of someone you love. For my wife it was also an illustration of the preciousness of life. She was determined to keep it.

"I'm strong," she told me in the car on the way home that evening. "I can do this."

Responsibilities

Before we could embark on that journey, there were new responsibilities to consider. My mother's passing meant that I was now directly responsible for my father's caregiving. That had challenges of its own. His stroke in 2002 had resulted in apraxia and aphasia. That meant that his ability to speak was almost entirely compromised. He also lost use of his right arm and leg and required a live-in caregiver. I took over managing all these aspects of his care. These were heady adjustments and the stress of it all was profound.

Closeups

My main concern was the potential impact of my divided schedule on my wife and children. I took them to a family services counselor for a discussion about how to handle such new and profound challenges in our lives.

As it turned out, that particular counselor was not much help. He actually seemed befuddled by a family of people who were in full communication about our lives and able to express feelings in a cogent manner. It was a nice enough visit, but we didn't stay long.

After a lighthearted commentary on the experience, including a quick, funny and accurate psychoanalysis of everyone in our family, my son Evan said what was on all of our minds. "I think our family is strong enough to get through anything."

That was all we needed to hear at that moment. Going forward, the kids had one simple request. "Just keep us informed on what is going on."

In fact we elected to use that approach as a guiding principle with everyone who helped us during our eight-year journey through cancer and caregiving. That vision of mutual strength brought us together as a family and served as a foundation for dialogue with a caregiving community that helped us in ways we could never have managed on our own. That turned into one of the most inspiring aspects of our journey together.

The Girl's Club

Early on in my wife's diagnosis the foundations were laid for support. None was more vital and direct than the commitment shown by the preschool staff where my wife worked as a Pre-Kindergarten teacher. The very week of my wife's initial diagnosis, her boss and good friend Linda called me to let us know they wanted to provide aid and support in care giving.

"We're going to let you into The Girl's Club," she told me. "That means we're going to help you. The Girl's Club has One

Rule. You have got to tell us everything going on with you and Linda. Otherwise you're out of The Girl's Club. Got that?"

I assured her that we understood the rules of The Girl's Club, and that our family was fully on board with that philosophy. From that point on—with respect for patient privacy of course—the Girl's Club was our "go-to" source in organizing everything from meals to the caregiving website that served as a communications hub for a network of more than 70 people who signed on to provide rides, in-home visits and other care giving needs. That enclave included a group of women from a Batavia Park District exercise club that had become close friends, fellow church members, longtime personal associates and parents and families of preschool students.

Front lines

Despite the broad scope of assistance available to us, the front-line caregiver and patient are still the primary interface when it comes to covering daily needs. As Linda and I learned what it meant to deal with cancer, my caregiving skills were put to repeated tests. When these efforts fell short in some way, the stress of disappointing her could be difficult to handle.

Fortunately there always seemed to be someone ready to step up with encouragement and advice at just the right time. Often those calls of support seemed to come out of the blue. Or perhaps not.

A few weeks into the first cycles of my wife's chemotherapy, one of my former coaches from high school heard about Linda's cancer and called to offer us support. We talked for a while and then like all good coaches he offered a bit of insight and encouragement.

"Your whole life has been preparation for this," he told me.

It was a compelling notion. Over the years our relationship had grown from athlete and coach to something more. We became friends and even business partners with his corporate fitness company. So sports were never far away from the core of our relationship. His instincts about how athletics prepare you for life were exactly what were needed at the time.

Early lessons

That coach and I had known each other more than 30 years. At the age of thirteen I played baseball for his team and later on this fiery, motivated man would also coach me in high school cross country. We enjoyed thrilling success and also learned how to deal with the challenges of defeat. He'd seen me at my best and worst.

We need people like that in our lives to help us achieve balance and perspective, especially in times of stress or trouble. That is what my old coach meant when he told me "all your life has been a preparation for this." Winning teaches us how to recognize and apply our strengths. Losing teaches us how to live with our weaknesses. The balance of these two teaches us to take pride in the quality of the process as well as the results. That's the right kind of pride.

Teamwork

As life goes on and we meld ourselves with another person such as a wife or partner, things naturally get more complicated. Sometimes you arrive at a point where you cannot tell yourself from the relationships in which you're involved. When something like cancer comes along, you fear for the person who suffers from the disease. You fear for yourself as well. What will become of this person into whom you've evolved, this flesh and soul fused with the life of another person?

The answer is that you have to dig deep to consider the nature of your commitment to one another. When intimate or difficult tasks are required it can be a lifesaver to go back to those statements of mutual yet practical purpose. Things like marriage vows come in handy in those moments.

At one point late in her survivorship my wife required some very intimate assistance in going to the bathroom. She stood naked above me and I could sense her fatigue and frustration in needing to be helped with such tasks. I looked up at her and said, "One flesh, honey. I am you." The message was well received. We were grateful for the bond.

Progeny

Our children obviously depended on us for guidance and strength in the face of difficult circumstances. That was one of the largest burdens to face in some ways. When kids realize their parents are both flawed and human, those can be frightening times for all.

The parental instinct is to protect your children any way you can. Yet truth is often the most potent antidote to fear. Being honest is the best way to give a realistic picture of your circumstance. People of all ages recognize genuine communication because it does not separate them from truth. We elected to be straightforward with our children, not hide information or coddle them falsely.

However, when our kids were away at college and needed to focus on their studies, we kept them informed on treatments and changes but not to the level of daily updates. The kids were where they belonged, and we told them so. We needed to support that. In all cases we chose never to compromise the verity of the information we shared. If anything they tended to push us for more information if they sensed we were being overly protective.

Communicating hope

Outside the family, privacy for the patient always came first, and we were careful not to speculate on what the outcomes might be.

Amid all this respectful caution there was always room in the process of caregiving for sharing and inspiration. Being positive and communicative is quite beneficial because it affirms the good and shares the challenges so they don't feel like solo burdens. Expressing hope is never a lie. Hope is the essence of survival.

In that context we also blogged about our journey because it was our goal to share the blessings as well as the challenges experienced along the way. The core chapters of this book provide a chronological record of an important period in that journey in all its practical and philosophical dimensions.

Having faith

In our case we saw plenty of evidence to believe that some greater force was at work in our lives. We had faith that things happened for a purpose. Of course some discount faith as having any practical value in life. Others cannot imagine trying to get through life without it. These are very personal choices and valid expressions of individuality and worldview. We shall express appreciation for both viewpoints here.

We'd still be selling the truth short if we did not relate how many ways our prayers and trust were fulfilled in both daily and long term ways. We even saw a few miracles come our way.

Miracles happen

For years, a sign bearing the message *Miracles happen* was nailed to a giant maple tree behind our house. It was positioned where we could see it out the kitchen window.

What is a miracle? A miracle is something so profound you might not think it at all possible. You might not imagine it even in prayer. You cannot predict a miracle or define it by solely by scope or scale. Yet when something miraculous occurs it always seems more insightful than mere chance.

Linda and I looked at that sign every day because we'd had both practical and spiritual miracles happen in our lives.

Even before our family faced cancer with Linda, there were moments when some element of divine purpose seemed to be at work. Not all of those experiences were pretty or easy to accept. But they functioned as miracles just the same.

A call to forgiveness

One evening early in our marriage when the kids were still little, I came home angry about a conflict at work. A supervisor had tried to force me to allow him to take credit for all my work. It did not seem right, and it brought about a lot hard feelings.

Upon arrival at home, I told Linda I needed to walk off the frustration and work out the anger in my head before spending time with the family. For half an hour I walked around the nearby high school track trying to figure out what to do. Finally I lay down on the high jump pit, took off my glasses and prayed. The sky seemed to draw closer to my eyes and the word "forgiveness" popped into my head like a voice from outside my body.

I looked around to see if someone had snuck up on me. No one was there. Then I got up and began walking back home. I was still a bit angry, yet I kept turning the idea of forgiveness around in my head. It took three full cycles of re-focusing on forgiveness to fully make the anger go away. By the time I got home there was a peaceful feeling inside me. I acted with forgiveness from then on. Two weeks later that manipulative boss was fired from his position.

At first I felt guilty. Then I realized it was a situation of his own making, not mine. In all, it felt like a miraculous deliverance from a situation in which there seemed to be no better answers. But take note: that former boss and I are still friends to this day. We both learned from the experience.

Weakness as a sign of strength

That powerful lesson of "winning by losing" through forgiveness was real. In fact it is often true that the things we consider our greatest strengths; competitiveness, determination, selfish pride, and many others can turn out to be weaknesses in the end.

Yet to many people it feels counterintuitive to show any kind of weakness, especially during times of stress. It feels like giving up or giving in.

In truth the ability to show weakness is something in which you can take pride because it reveals an honesty necessary to get to real solutions. People trust you rather than having to calculate your intentions or needs.

Refusing victimhood

When you are placed in a situation that feels like a great injustice has been done, such as when cancer enters your life, it's a natural instinct to become angry and ask the eternal question, "Why me?"

My wife rather vociferously refused to allow that type of thinking into her life. I can testify that everyone around her seemed to marvel at the strength in this perspective. Why was that? What inspired her—and ultimately all those around her—to refuse victimhood as a way of thinking?

Freedom from anger and fear

The answer is simple. The idea of seeing ourselves as victims did not square with the blessings we felt at work in our lives. Our insurance policy against victimhood was to focus on gratitude for the work of the doctors, nurses, friends, family and even strangers who helped us. Thankfulness can go a long way in protecting you from anger, anxiety and fear.

That does not mean that shocks cannot come along.

Getting through it

At one point I lost my job the day after informing an employer that my wife had cancer. The situation was complicated and rife with legal and financial repercussions.

Knowing my wife would be upset beyond reason, I called our close friends to join us at our home for support. It was an uncomfortable moment letting Linda know that on top of finding out about the certain return of her cancer that week, we would now have to pay COBRA costs for insurance and cling to coverage until I could find new employment. The costs would be $2000 per month just for the premiums. It was daunting to figure out where we'd come up with money to pay those premiums and cover our family expenses. We still had a daughter in college too.

We talked and we prayed together. Our attitude was to "wait and see" in trust that things would work out. Our friends assured Linda that things would be okay and all was not lost.

Beyond happenstance

As it turned out, bigger things truly were taking place behind the scenes.

The very same week that I lost my job our church was contacted by a wealthy family looking to help out congregants in need. The day that she heard about our situation, the Community Care and Outreach leader contacted us and said, "This timing is incredible. We have money here to help. What do you need?"

Thanks to the kindness of a family with the means to help, we were able to pay our bills on a consistent and timely basis until we got back on our own feet.

Salvation

We had nearly run out of money once before when Linda

needed intensive in-home emotional and physical care and it was vital for me to stay at home with her. With nothing but our last little stronghold of savings left in the bank, it was getting tight to pay the mortgage and other bills. We were acutely aware that bankruptcy from medical costs is one of the most common forms of financial ruin in America.

One afternoon when we came back from a doctor's appointment there was a plain envelope lying on the floor inside the front door mail slot. It held $3500, the exact amount needed to pay our bills that month. We sat at our dining room table and prayed in thanks together while asking, "How did they know how much we needed?"

Then we both broke down and sobbed. We had tried so hard to be proud and strong. It's no use in many ways. People see it in you somehow. At that moment you feel naked and exposed to the world. Yet you feel protected as well. It is truly like a dose of scripture come to life.

If you're not the believing type then credit it all to the goodness of human nature and the sometimes marvelous workings of chance. Whatever works for you. In any case it never hurts to be grateful when your burdens are lifted.

Institutional kindness

Over time we paid plenty of money in insurance deductibles, COBRA coverage premiums, uncovered medical expenses and the lot. Every year our tax filings showed the financial burdens of treating cancer. That medical expense threshold on your 1040? We blew past that every year. Paying for cancer treatment is not cheap.

What helped us greatly during our overall cancer experience

was the institutional compassion of the local non-profit hospital organizations with whom we worked. At one point the main hospital responsible for our care reviewed our financial position and wrote off 90% of our medical expenses after the insurance portion was paid.

When you get that type of notification in the mail it really makes you stop and think. You come to realize how much work it takes for people to accomplish that kind of mercy through fund raising and financial management. In return we tried our best to pay back some of that kindness by directing contributions in Linda's memory to that hospital. It was certainly the right thing to do.

No such thing as perfection

There were moments when institutional kindness needed to flow the other direction. With something so complex and profound as cancer treatment, there is no such thing as perfection. Mistakes can and do happen. Drugs interact. IV lines seize up. In our case, an inter-peritoneal IV port leaked. It caused an acid burn on Linda's stomach and sent us to the hospital on Easter morning. The attending physician took one look at the situation and the concern on his face was evident.

For our part, we could have screamed and yelled or threatened to bring a lawsuit. Instead our primary goal was to get the port fixed, and that happened. So compassion in care works both ways. We were fortunate to have good doctors and 99% of our care went well. For that we were always grateful.

Communities near and far

When we did have questions or challenges, we also looked for support and encouragement from others going through similar experiences. Our gynecological oncologist discreetly put Linda in touch with one of his patients who lived in our town. Those two formed a "chemo bond" and supported each other as mothers.

There was also practical and emotional support available through online groups and discussion boards specific to cancers such as ovarian. If we posted some challenge related to chemo or side effects, informed advice would roll in from people around the world.

Some of those people became communication partners who were consistently involved in offering perspectives on plans of care and dealing with side effects. I'd log on the computer and share the good wishes and advice offered to Linda as we sat together during chemo or recovery stays at the hospital.

We also shared our joy during long periods of remission and the blessings of NED (No Evidence of Disease) to provide encouragement to others as well. Survivorship through months of treatment and periods of remission? It all comes down to simple gestures. You never know when a kind word can help someone else, or when you'll need that kind word yourself.

Something more

We can all speculate about the right things to do when facing cancer, but it is safe to say that most of us do not want to immediately give up and die. There may however be days when that seems like a desirable option.

Through all the ups and downs we came to the conclusion that cancer survivorship is not just about living and dying. It is about developing the fullest way possible to appreciate life.

That means one of the greatest gifts we can give to each other in life is to care, and allow ourselves to be cared for. That is the foundation of cancer survivorship.

So the point of this book is to inspire others to realize that it's worth the effort to build your survivorship the best way you can. Worth the commitment. Worth the caregiving. Worth recognizing your blessings.

What you'll find here is perspectives on the practical truths, philosophy and theology that helped us enjoy 8 full years of cancer survivorship. The core of this book includes the chronological blogs we shared with our care giving community. We hope they inspire you on your journey in life, whatever that may be.

Priorities

Given how much Linda loved her garden and her family, we often kidded about how I ranked among her top priorities in life. Between her love of God, our kids, family and Chuck the Dog, I told her I was happy to make the Top 10 some weeks. We also joked that she might trade me in one day for a husband who could actually fix things around the house.

Of course that fix-it stuff was a pretty simple allegory for the flaws any of us brings to a marriage. As a couple with struggles like anyone else, we tried hard to fix what we could and deal with the rest the best we knew how.

When cancer first came along, we felt shock like anyone else, groping for knowledge as we embarked on the hopeful journey toward a cure. When her cancer came back, or some challenging new aspect of treatment arose, we'd go through the process of grieving over present circumstances as we went along, but seeking hope as well. To give ourselves some space between processes, we'd often utter the phrase that served as our survivorship slogan: "It is what it is."

To us those words were not a mark of resignation or complaint as they are often used. In our case, those words helped us objectively cope with life-changing realities and challenges in dealing with cancer in all its ups and downs. We used that phrase to put cancer in its place and let us get on to living life outside the bubble of treatment and disease.

"It is what it is." Say it with enough conviction and it can put things in perspective, give you control over your emotions and free you to pursue a better path of thoughts and actions.

Diagnosis

Like so many women entering their mid-to-late 40s, Linda had been dealing with severe menstrual and menopausal changes in her body for a couple years. I finally persuaded her to book a visit to the gynecologist. She was legitimately reluctant to go because her friends had shared so many stories about doctors who did automatic hysterectomies on middle-aged women. "I don't want to go to some butcher," she told me.

Against these concerns I encouraged her to make an appointment for a checkup. There rests part of the reason for sharing our story. Cancer does not wait for you to make up your mind about whether you are sick or not. If you have concerns or know someone who does, get checked out. It's worth it.

Toughing it out

There was another reason my wife did not go right away to get checked by a doctor. Her family was of tough German stock. They avoided doctors whenever they could on belief that you should ride it out on the medical front unless you could no longer function. "Most things go away if you wait a week," my father-in-law, Melvin, once said.

The tough-it-out strategy did not always work. Mel once developed sciatica so painful he was forced to lean on a cabinet for weeks on end to remain upright. Finally he consented to see a chiropractor and an orthopedic physician who figured out what was causing the pain. Within days of treatment he was cured. Simply put, he was stubborn about his health.

That was the force of will at work in Linda's family, and also the irony. The stubborn nature that initially kept her from seeing the doctor was also what enabled her to get through treatments that likely would have flattened others. Her stubbornness was a tradeoff; a curse and a blessing. Sometimes it is hard to tell those two qualities apart when you're engaged in cancer survivorship. Those are some of the quirks of character we all possess.

Beating the odds

According to the Centers for Disease Control and Prevention, 1 in 72 women in America will get ovarian cancer in her lifetime. The five-year survival rate is 44%.

Those were some of the first statistics we encountered when researching the disease. They are not exactly encouraging. So much of the publicly available information about cancer can be discouraging. That means you must be judicious in dealing with any cancer diagnosis. Put the publicly available facts aside and get to a point of understanding about your personal situation. Consult with your doctors, cancer resource centers and other people that have faced similar circumstances. Those information sources are the best alternatives to help you determine what dealing with cancer will mean to you.

The fact that Linda Cudworth lived eight fruitful years after her diagnosis is testimony to the open-mindedness with which we engaged in treatment, recovery and remission. I am extremely proud of her and grateful for that. Like a dedicated athlete, she worked hard at it. And like an athlete, she won a few fans along the way.

To Linda's credit, her ability to relax well when given the opportunity was also extremely important. She was mindful. We lived a lot of great life together as a result of her determination not to let the disease entirely control her existence. If you retain any message from these words, let it be this: Cancer may affect you, but it does not need to define you. That is how you can thrive despite the difficulties.

A symphony of hope

As caregiver you can never perfectly know what is going through the mind of a person in cancer survivorship. Even when you ask directly, you're sometimes left to read between the lines. I always respected that my wife's main goal was to find ways to get well, not dwell on whether or not she was worried about being sick.

When things got worrisome we found other ways to cope. Her pleasure in classical music was one of the ways we found solace and inner peace. Our opportunities were admittedly enhanced by the fact that her sister is a violist with the Chicago Symphony Orchestra. Hearing that orchestra play always infused Linda with a new sense of life. She particularly loved sitting in Symphony Center or Ravinia during rehearsals to witness how the musicians and conductor worked together to produce such amazing sound.

Yet I also recall looking over at her face during our children's symphony orchestra concerts. Evan plays cello and Emily the violin. Sometimes I wondered if the music felt bittersweet in any way. Living with cancer was like that for us, a symphony of ups and downs, brightness and darkness.

One of my favorite symphonies is Rimsky-Korsakov's Scheherazade. I love that piece of music for its dramatic story-line of characters immersed in life and death struggles. It would often play on CD during my hour-long commute to work. Sometimes I'd catch the last notes of the elegiac violin solo while parking my car outside the office building. Then I'd sit, waiting for the tears to stop flowing. Some days it is all you can do to make it through the day and keep your hopes up in the face of fears and the unknown. Music can fuel that courage.

A song of gratitude

We talked on occasion about her chances of cure and survival. Usually our "serious talks" would take place on the back porch on summer nights, or socked on the couch holding hands in partial darkness with candles burning in the living room. That's when we were both relaxed enough to discuss our hopes.

It was not her style to speculate, but she did confess that the will to live was at times pressed thin when she was in treatment, especially when side effects became difficult to handle. Yet 99% of the time she never appeared to quit or give up hope. She did pray fervently and those prayers were frequently answered with more abundant results than we could have hoped or imagined. Perhaps that's because we were also included on prayer lists at our church. A dear friend named Bonne wrote each week asking for specific things about which to pray and distribute those to a large group of people waiting to do just that. It was always humbling to realize there seemed to be some force outside our control giving us guidance. We simply needed to take the time to listen.

What do you offer in return for answered prayers? The main thing is gratitude. However, we joked more than once that God always seemed to give us "just enough" to get along in life. "I don't want to be rich," Linda told me more than once. "I just wish we didn't have to struggle sometimes to do things that normal people do." That was both an economic and emotional statement.

While having "just enough" at certain times can be quite humbling, you learn to live with it and give thanks for what you do have. That's the song of gratitude. It is best sung loudly and gladly to drown out potential worries. Then you can fix your mind on positive, practical things that need be done.

Blessed to be a blessing

As a practical method of "thinking positive," I used a Communications feature in a caregiving website to blog about our state of mind to those who chose to help us. Those blogs form the core section of this book and were written in real time. They chronicle the philosophy, theology and determination it took to thrive in the face of challenges. We shared our hopes, fears, inspirations and challenges. In many respects that process turned out to be as important as the practical and material help we received.

Words matter

Before publishing the blog, I'd usually read to Linda what I'd written while she sat getting infusions or was relaxing at home on the couch. She'd listen intently, making comments and edits. If she heard something she did not like, she'd chirp "No, you can't say that!" Usually that was in response to writing that got too medical or such. Sometimes we'd disagree when she thought I was revealing too much or had taken a too-humorous or serious approach on one subject or another. Ultimately we'd reach an approved version. Altogether the blog served the role of uniting us in a common purpose and helped this particular caregiver process all that was going on in life.

Writing about our experience also helped us consider the value and nature of community with a focus on the important things in life. Finally, it served to actualize one of my favorite quotations from the book "Ambiguous Adventure" by Cheikh Hamidou Kane. "The purity of the moment is made from the absence of time." In other words, time expands when you are doing something you love. In our case, that meant living the best way we knew how, with gratitude and a commitment to be a blessing to others any way we could. We share these blog posts in hopes they inspire and encourage others to find their unique form of survivorship.

The story picks up in our 6th year of cancer survivorship. These entries are shared here in the order in which they were written. The narrative functions in that respect, but nothing says they must be read that way. If you are so moved, explore this journey in your own way and from your own frame of reference. The purity of the moment really is made from the absence of time.

CHAPTER TWO
ON THE JOURNEY

Update

Monday, June 13, 2011, 12:30 PM

We all survived the weird winter and strange spring. Now summer's here and it's certainly acting funky, no doubt.

Two weekends ago we went downtown to spend the day with our son, Evan. Linda, Emily and I took the train and had an amazing day in the city, capped by dinner with her sister Diane at Sweetwater, a restaurant right below Evan's apartment.

It was a great day but also a little bittersweet because we're sitting on news that Linda's cancer might be back.

She visited the gynecological oncologist and was admittedly nervous going into the appointment because there were familiar twinges indicating something was wrong. She was hoping it was nothing, but the CA-125 number had crept up to 34. That's not high by any measure, but a possible indicator of active cancer. Some women have numbers as high as 19,000, so Linda is in a very early stage of recurrence, if at all. So the next step was a CT scan. The scan showed a 2 cm possible tumor where the cancer had been before, down low in the abdomen. From September through December last year the chemo whacked the cancer but good. The tumor disappeared after a couple of treatments. So the chemo works, but the cancer is persistent, like one of those damn moles in those kid's games where you have to hit them with a hammer.

Now we use the cancer-whacker hammer again and possibly go back to chemo. Linda's appointment is Wednesday. Her woman doctor is very thorough and rational and we have confidence she will help us map out the next course of action. Again, we don't know for sure what we'll be doing. Linda is understandably disappointed that summer may take a turn much like the weird weather this year.

Getting chemo is like choosing to get sick. Having recently gone through a strange bout of food poisoning, I felt like God was telling me to get prepared for what Linda had to go through. Be sympathetic. Have patience. Being sick in the short term is hard. Being sick for a long period is wearing.

We'll do our best to get prepared. We are likely going to need to cancel our five-day trip to Door County. Wednesday's appointment will tell us more. I'm sort of working with Linda to consider still going on the vacation. After all, research shows there's no real benefit in doing chemo early versus waiting until we're symptomatic. But Linda has been through ascites and that's no freaking game. So she just wants to get going.

We're thinking of setting up a Chemo Party Camp in our back yard with the big white tent we have in the garage from soccer coaching days. Linda bought new bright orange chairs and fun decorations so our patio is a charming place to be.

It will be a while before we need meals or rides or anything. Those of you willing to help are much appreciated when the time comes. That's all for now.

Bien Trucha

Friday, June 17, 2011, 12:15 PM

Last night Linda and I went to dinner at Bien Trucha, the Mexican restaurant in Geneva. During the evening I asked one of the hostesses what the name meant. She said it literally means "Good Trout" in Spanish. In Mexico it is slang for Best of the Best, or something along those lines.

We wanted to have a nice dinner and celebrate our 26th Anniversary this coming June 29th. Since Linda is starting chemotherapy Wednesday, we decided to go celebrate our love for one another while she could still taste the food.

It was both a joyful and tearful evening. The gorgeous weather included clear blue skies and happy little clouds drifting by. The food is unique and wonderful. There were fun drinks. She had a celery margarita. I had a beer spiced with some wild sauce. It all added up to some needed enjoyment. Linda has been promising herself we'd get to that busy little restaurant and so we did.

The tears came through the realization that we're headed into a summer and fall filled with the challenges of chemotherapy. There always seems to be a new twist in the process; some new side effect, or just plain fatigue that comes with treatment and recovery each cycle.

It works like this. Linda will be receiving Cisplatin and Taxotere in three-week cycles with no break in between. This combination of drugs knocked out the cancer last time, but the cumulative side effects made it necessary to quit after four cycles of treatments. The tumor was gone, but more than likely some cancer cells escaped the kill zone and that is why it came back.

So now we're going to try to help Linda get through an 18-week regimen that will basically take us through October. It stinks that she has to do this. She's generally healthy and the cancer has never escaped into other organs. Only once in six years has the cancer itself technically made her sick. That was with ascites, fluid in the abdomen. We beat that too.

Going into treatment when you know you're going to get sick seems like the dumbest thing when you're feeling good otherwise. It runs counter to all our natural instincts. As Linda told the oncologist: "Listen, while I'm sitting here feeling well, I want you to know that I want to live. Because when I'm being treated I may tell you I want to die. Don't listen to me."

That brings up the bigger, more profound question. Will this new round of treatments help her live, long term? Will it make the cancer go away forever? The answers are Yes and possibly No. The gynecological oncologist admitted to Linda that we might never completely get rid of this cancer through existing technology and treatments. That may mean another bash of chemo in a couple years. That's the gamble we now choose to take. Will we beat if forever? There is no such thing, most likely. We must make the most of the forever we have before us. That's all any of us can do.

It means living with that knowledge and going through this

treatment on hope that life can have quality again. We've been fortunate to achieve something near to that after every recurrence. Many of the side effects like numb feet are lingering. Last time it took months for Linda's eyes to stop watering, and for her hair to grow back. I've talked with women around the world through online channels who are going through these same processes. It's pretty much the same with all of them.

The cool thing right now is how proactive Linda is responding. She got a cute new wig at the ACS in Batavia and she looks great. God Bless her.

What does all this mean going forward?

It means your help is without doubt so valuable to us in sustaining Linda through a difficult physical and emotional process. We've had what seem like crazy things happen to us. We have also had blessings we cannot even describe happen in our lives. We stand firm in belief there has been a purpose and a benefit to all these changes and challenges. Six years ago we first heard the word "cancer" and could not believe it. Yet when you assess all that has occurred and realize all we have made it through, there is hope. Always hope. Hope in the things you can do here and now. Hope in the face of whatever the future brings. The blessings have carried us through.

Bien Trucha to all of you.

Chris and Linda

Maybe We're Amazed

Wednesday, June 29, 2011, 11:00 AM

When Paul McCartney found himself separated from the Beatles following their breakup, he hunkered down with his wife Linda and started playing music his own way. They lived on a country farm where Linda took photos of their growing family and Paul came up with his first solo album. You can argue forever about the merits of that album, but I've always liked its simplicity. Its honesty. Even its hope.

One of the best tunes is "Maybe I'm Amazed," a song whose lyrics express the joys of loyalty and provide testament to the power of love in facing life's challenges.

Did you know that Paul and Linda were married a couple decades and yet spent very few nights apart? That's not easy to do. You'd think with all the jet setting and touring they would have split more often or even split up. But Paul (and for the most part, the other Beatles) were pretty keen on their wives. They showed great character.

All this runs through my head as my Linda and I celebrate our 26th Anniversary today, June 29th.

It occurred to me that we've been dealing with her ovarian cancer for 1/5 of our marriage. She was diagnosed in 2005. The first round of treatments included 8 rounds of chemo and 3 rounds of inter-peritoneal chemotherapy. That's where they pour the chemo Taxol in through a port in her stomach. They missed once, causing chemical burns down her stomach. Hmph. But we got through.

Then in 2007 the cancer came back and Linda was not, not happy. The emotional breakdown that ensued took months to heal. We thought we'd got it licked by doing the Gold Standard in chemotherapy treatment.

So it was tough going back into another regimen of chemo in

part because Linda was so heartbroken at the thought that cancer had indeed returned. She did do chemo all over again. Her remission lasted all the way through 2010. Pretty good you might say. Then we had to hit it again last fall. Of course we're disappointed facing cancer anew each time. We've also grown from every experience.

Maybe we're amazed that it's back. Maybe we're not. Maybe we're amazed Linda has handled this several times. Maybe we're grateful she's had the courage. Helps that she's stubborn sometimes.(smile). Mostly (maybe) we're amazed that even through all the challenges and stress we've faced, we find a way to forgive each other's weaknesses and faults. We pray for strength and get it. We've prayed for help and gotten that too. We've prayed in thanks and we've payed in bundles. But holy jeepers we've even had help there. This whole experience has been both uplifting and humbling, which is not a bad thing.

What can you learn? Not everything goes the way you want it to. Not in marriage. Not in life. It's how you process and accept setbacks that helps you appreciate life even more when things get better.

The art of survival

Tuesday, July 5, 2011, 3:45 PM

One of my favorite bird painters is Louis Agassiz Fuertes. I first knew his remarkable talents at the age of 16 when I visited the Cornell University Laboratory of Ornithology in Ithaca, New York. So strong was his grip on my imagination that during college I returned to Cornell for a January term to curate their entire collection of wildlife art. This provided an opportunity to see and hold the artist's work. It was a life-changing experience.

Sadly Fuertes died when a train struck his car on a crossing near his home because in the 1920s there were no electric gates or even lighted crossings to give warning of an approaching train. Fuertes was killed on impact. He was only 40 years old. In something of a miracle his drawings from a recent trip to Africa flew free of the car and survived. These paintings were published in a book titled "The Singular Beauty of Birds" documenting the painter's life. Somewhere in his biography I remember this quote from Fuertes: "Hell to be an artist and have work, but heller not to."

The wisdom of that quote has stuck with me all these years because making art is not easy. Honestly I'm not sure I've ever done it. 100s of paintings and many drawings later in life, the process of "making art" is still the goal. I love the effort.

By comparison my wife Linda is an artful gardener. I love that her flowers brighten our lives, especially now. June was rich and wet and cool. Her lilies fairly burst with color in the cool shadows of dawn. "Look at us!" they screamed in yellow, white, maroon and peach. They called her out into the garden each day. She sat on the patio surrounded by pots bursting with color. It has helped greatly with recovery.

Fortunately we were afforded a grace, that following a difficult first chemo session, the second round was tolerated much better. She goes again tomorrow, and we hope that holds true again. Linda was able to garden and tend to her "babies" in the back yard last week. I might come home preoccupied or fretting over some worry and there Linda would be, focused on her plants with a vision thankful and true.

Van Morrison once wrote in a song that a *sense of wonder* is a source of great pride and insight. It's something we should share. That is the secret, isn't it? Keeping our sense of wonder in the face of all things, It can be difficult at times no matter our circumstances. It truly is a blessing to remind each other to keep our sense of wonder intact.

Much talk is given to the so-called "battle" with cancer. But if it is a battle, it is fought with words, prayer and physical resolve. That is the art of survival. So those of you who send her well-wishes, your encouragement is genuinely appreciated. Linda is now signed up to receive the emails from the blog on the Lotsahelpinghands website and sees your comments as well. Those that land with me are forwarded to her email. When she feels lousy, I bring my laptop over and read them to her aloud. That is the art of survival. Crowdsourcing hope. We appreciate all of you. God Bless.

Chris and Linda

Living in the moment

Tuesday, July 12, 2011, 8:45 AM

These summer days. It is so easy to let them slide by unnoticed. It is important to make note of how far north the sun still rises in July. Look at the long shadows it casts at dawn and dusk. Live in the moment.

Tomorrow is the beginning of the second round of chemotherapy treatments for Linda. That means four to six days of sluggish immersion in feeling ill and not caring a whole lot about anything other than getting up and down for necessities. The rest of the time she pretty much turns inward, finds rest in sleep and tries to eat what she can. Her sense of taste gets mighty weird in this zone. Making food is near impossible.

That's why we appreciate the meals you volunteer to prepare. If you consider that food often looks and tastes bad to her, imagine how nauseating a stack of uncooked chicken can look to a chemo patient.

That is why we certainly never take the meals provided by this caregiving network for granted. Even when she's feeling better (and it has gone smoother than expected on the 2nd and 3rd treatments, a trend we hope will continue...) the fact of not having to prepare meals is such a welcome gift. Since neither of us eats a ton, each meal usually lasts a few days. Our daughter Emily the connoisseur knows how to savor as well.

Emily and our son Evan have both learned to cook a number of things, and they cook with friends as well. They are certainly better at it than I was at that age. Frankly, they are better at it than I am now.

I have worked to become a passable griller. I grilled some salmon for the family on 4th of July. Linda hates fish normally. She's sure not going to eat it now.

Tonight Emily's having her gal pal crew over for cooking, fun and friendship. It's always fascinating to get a glimpse of life in her lane. We consider that a gift, too.
She's now working a nanny job this summer and doing a number of photo gigs. She sure has an eye, which means she knows how to capture the visual meaning of a moment. Once in a while the tables get turned. I snagged a pic of her taken by a friend off her Facebook page. It captures her saucy look at life. I like that picture because she seems to be facing life with a degree of insouciance and a lighthearted unconcern.

It's so hard sometimes, gathering up the meaning in life, and not letting things get you down. Thursday night I'm going to a

Living Well Cancer Resource Center presentation on forgiveness. The point of the talk is that forgiveness is a liberating force in our lives. The ability to forgive others, and the will to forgive ourselves for our shortcomings, is paramount to well being. Forgiveness has accomplished a lot for me in relationships and life. But there's always work to be done, and time for more forgiveness.

That's because forgiveness is the one thing that can help us all live in the moment. Forgiveness doesn't mean giving up in an argument, or not having that argument at all. Arguments happen. It does mean looking past that moment and accepting... that even if you are wrong, or the other person is wrong, you can forgive the difficulty of that moment and not hold it against them, or yourself. It means not living off a stack of regrets or old hurts. It means being strong enough to be yourself even when the world wants to force you to be someone else, which it often does. You need to forgive the world too. It doesn't really know what it's doing sometimes.

There is a lot of injustice in life. Some of us don't make it into the Hall of Fame, while others do. Things like that can make people bitter. Even those who've "got it made" sometimes harbor old grudges as wounds that hold them back from living in the moment, which is really all we have. All we'll ever have. All we're meant to have. Living in the moment.

Something like cancer can take even that away, at least temporarily. Moments can feel like years when you're sick, or fearful, or not sure what might happen next. So we depend on strength from other sources sometimes, and are grateful to have it. Every moment counts, especially when you're paying attention. But we especially thank you for paying attention to us. God Bless. Live in the moment. Learn to forgive. Peace be with you. And love.

My name is Chuck the Dog

Monday, July 18, 2011, 10:15 AM

Chuck the rescue dog.

Hello People. My name is Chuck the Dog. You can see my picture in the Photo Gallery.

I'll be writing this week's blog. Trust me, it's not easy to type with paws. Especially those exclamation points. Way up there in the corner of the keyboard. Hard for a dog to reach.

Bark bark bark bark! Sorry about that. The mailman just went by the window. I do not like that mailman. He is grumpy and always looks like he wants to hit something. Even my People; Linda, Chris, Emily and Evan have to admit that as mailmen go, he's the Grumpiest. All the dogs on our Block do not like him either. It's like dog alarms going off as he walks from House to House.

Perhaps he needs a Dog of his own to learn more about us. Maybe then he would not be so grumpy. Because all we dogs want in this world is a little respect. Don't hit us or abandon us or leave us in hot cars and we'll be your friend for life. Although some dogs are not so nice, I'll admit. There's one kitty-corner (sorry, I could not resist at least one Animal joke) from our house who seems like he's got some issues. He only poops on his half of the block. Talk about doggy retentive.

But I digress. I'd rather talk about My People than some dumb other dog who is too lazy to walk a whole block. I like walking every day. The other day while lazing on the couch watching Jeopardy with Linda I added up how many walks I've taken since coming to live in Batavia and it's probably around 750. That's about 350 miles if my Dog Walk Calculations are correct. I love Walks. It keeps My People healthy too.

Lately though my job has been keeping my Linda People company. She's had a couple tough weeks. That is when I lie down next to her and snuggle in for the afternoon. Sometimes she'll scratch my ears and rub my tummy. And I Like that. But other times she's too tired and just sleeps on the couch. So I sleep with her. But if that mailman comes, look out.

You know what dogs say about People, don't you? It almost seems like they're smart enough to Know when dogs aren't feeling well. Of course we Dogs know that by nature. That's why we come sit with you People when you're sick, or feeling down, or just need someone to talk to.

People tend to think everything has to be communicated in words. But we dogs work with our Nose. You can tell a lot about the world by sniffing around, you know, and watching how People move. We dogs know body language better than people.

But I've decided People are quite all right. Ever since People Evan found me cold, wet and covered with white paint in the brown paper bag on the streets of Chicago, things have gotten better. Living in his Fraternity house was quite fun. Those guys were almost as cool as living with a bunch of Dogs. Running around all the time. Staying up late. Eating off the floor. Well, I did that but I could never quite get the Guys to eat like me.

Then People Evan started to travel and People Emily invited me to come live with People Chris and People Linda. Then I met People Grandma and Grandpa, People Uncle Paul and People Aunt Diane. These are all my favorite People. Sometimes (but not too often) they feed me meat under the table. Yum. And I have developed my Look Cute with Mopey Eyes Routine to perfection. Sometimes it almost works.

Well, it's almost August and Dog Days are almost here. Don't tell anyone though. We Dogs like to keep our National Doggydays a secret.

But if you come to my House we will celebrate. I will jump up and down more than My People like me to do but that is because I have heard you are a Pack of People that is helping my People Linda through a tough time. As her Dog I would like to personally thank you for taking care of People Linda. She Feeds me and that is a very important job. In return she is Queen of My Pack. And that rocks. Take Care, all you Peoples. You know what they say: God is just Dog spelled backwards. At least that's what we dogs say. Looking forward to meeting some of you People. Dog Bless You.

Poetic Give and Take

Sunday, July 31, 2011, 7:00 AM

Greetings all. We didn't want to flood your inbox too often so we held off a few days on updates. The progress so far is that Linda has indeed completed 1/3 of the prescribed treatment program. That means two full cycles of 3 treatments each. We have four more rounds of 3 treatments scheduled.

The first one is toughest with fatigue and Linda not wanting to eat much for 5 days or so. She's been doing well as can be expected. The great meals you provide do the trick.

The next two treatments are usually not so profound but do cause fatigue. The challenge is maintaining Linda's blood counts, which slowly drop as this program continues. It gets a little harder to get "up" for each treatment when you know the routine. Her eyes have begun to water and her hair is thinning too. It is what it is.

But we did get to a fun party last night with a gathering of friends from Chris's high school days, really the core group of guys in cross country and track from St. Charles High School. It's been nearly four decades since we all ran together and we all look like the old guys we are, but the fun memories and laughs never seem to fade.

The party was hosted at the beautiful home of our friends in St. Charles. Linda brought her own tea. You learn to bring what you like when you're in chemo.

It is Sunday morning now. Quiet outside and you can see/feel the heat begin to rise with the day. Linda's garden is growing fantastically with all this rain. Her green thumb has always impressed me.

Way back in the early days of our relationship when I lived in Chicago and she was living in St. Charles and teaching special ed in West Aurora, she would come visit my apartment in Chicago on weekends. Wanting to spruce up the otherwise dry bachelor pad, she once brought me a large cactus plant. It did not thrive in that environment. In fact it didn't survive. It got me thinking at the time: "How do you even kill a cactus?" They're designed for life in the desert and hardly need any water, just some sun. Somehow I knocked it out cold. It struck me that the same thing can happen to love if you're not care-

ful. I this poem, circa 1984, three years into our relationship:
The Cactus

She sits in a reddish pot, glare on her face,

brought by acquaintance to welcome the place,

"Not too much water," the average advice,

"And sunlight a few days a week would be nice."

The plant is a heavy, with horrible spines,

that leave subtle marks in your shirt, little lines—

which I learned upon moving the cactus to light

on the days of the week when I thought it all right.

Yet the thing about cactus that's once and for all

is they're never too good by a door in a hall,

where people can kick them and ruin their bloom

so I moved her all over my small living room.

Those changes in routine and bouts of root rot

put a weakness within her, she leaned in the pot,

so I called up my friend on the right thing to do,

and she said "I should never give cactus to you."

Too late to recover and too sick to transplant,

the cactus expired in her dirt tenement,

and I felt pretty bad for the gift that she'd sent

but I felt even worse for the love that it meant.

Yes, love requires tending, and we're not always perfect at it. Certainly not I. But through it all we somehow try to learn to take better care of the things we love. It takes a lot of spine, for sure.

The Rules

Monday, August 8, 2011, 10:15 AM

Some cycling friends and I enjoy a web site/blog called velominati.com. Basically the site is a humorous take on the "rules" of cycling; how to dress, ride and act. We kid each other about how tough we can be, which is the primary focus of the rules, in a humorous sort of way, along with how to properly maintain your cycling tan lines. A little warning: If you choose to visit the site there are some bad words used to reinforce the rules so be prepared.

So that sets the stage for today's blog.

Saturday morning my little group was scheduled for a ride, but it was raining quite hard at 5:30 a.m. One of my riding partners has always been willing to ride in the rain once you're out there, but is not a fan of "going out" into the rain from a dry house. Unfortunately the Velominati Rules think differently. And I must abide by the Rules.

Circumstantially, the crew had been planning to ride to Lake Geneva on Sunday, the next day. So Saturday's ride was not so important as it usually is. With Linda's health in rough shape the last four days I elected not to join them on the trip to Wisconsin because it is generally an all-day affair.

So I definitely wanted to ride Saturday morning and jumped

on my bike, heading out into the pouring rain at 6 a.m. Because, according to the Rules, that would make me a cycling Hardass. (oops, a bad word slipped in there...)

The rain lasted about an hour. I was wet as a seal by then and felt like one too. Rather than being miserable it was fun to ride with rooster tails of wetness shooting up from both front and rear tires. I was also fabulously alone out there on Saturday morning. Rode up over Campton Hills and down the other side of that glacial hill and headed west for a while. Somewhere out past 47 the rain stopped. Then so did I, to pull off the rather hot rain jacket and wick off sweat in the wind.

It got me to thinking. Being a hardass is not easy, but it can be fun. Of course it can also create problems. It's fine to be tough and there are many situations in life where you must be tough to survive. I'm sure you can name a few. There's also a fine line between being a hardass for the fun of it and being hard-nosed simply because you're selfish. I was a little of both this weekend.

One of the key challenges in life if you are a person of faith is when to trust God (people will tell you...always) and when to take initiative on your own (which we also must do.) How do you separate the two?

Where it gets really tricky is when to be strong and when to be sensitive. How do you forge on without being callous and how do you be considerate without being weak, or giving in, when perhaps you shouldn't back off for the betterment of all involved. Most of all, how do you know when and how to hold up your end of the bargain?

When caregiving a cancer patient, these questions get carved in bold relief. Sometimes I fail miserably by pushing when I shouldn't push or caving when I shouldn't cave. Nothing reminds you of your flaws more than caring for someone else. I mean that in both the physical and emotional sense of the word.

Hopefully my Linda can forgive me these flaws and we can help her recover a bit the next two weeks. That first treatment each chemo cycle (pun intended) is like climbing the Chemo Alpe du Huez, an uphill battle fall the way. 5 days of 18% grade in the driving rain of fatigue and nausea, you might say.

She is the ultimate Hardass. And I need to remember that.

Maybe we need to write down our own set of rules for reference when times get tough. Hopefully we can laugh a little along the way. And work on our tan lines.

Jumping over little health issues

Friday, August 19, 2011, 9:45 AM

Seems like all of us face nagging health issues sooner or later. Whether it is a reddened eyelid or painful cold sore, a cavity in your teeth or a mysterious rash, we all deal with life's humbling physical maladies.

These are only magnified when you're fighting cancer.

So it is with some relief that we found out last week that Linda has been fighting a small, non-threatening background infection that made her feel tired and weak. The effects were magnified by the chemo.

Now it's pink medicine time (or something of that order) for my cutie pie while she preps for the next round of chemo.

Next week is the "big" one that wipes her out a few days so we're thankful this week's was more tolerable so she's not completely dragging. But it took some work to get there.

It is weird how subjects like nagging health problems can circle around you at times. For example, during a bike ride with a newfound friend this weekend, conversation turned to the subject of cycling saddle sores, which can really hurt. Basically they're like a persistent blister that occurs every time you ride. If you don't treat them with caution and some sort of medication they just don't go away. My riding partner explained that his doctor had prescribed an "antibiotic pack" for a saddle sore that cleared the thing right up.

Then he quietly observed, 'Same goes for dental health too.'

He's right about that. In recent years medicine has discovered that dental infections cause all sorts of other problems in your body. A few years back when I had a tooth problem the dentist who performed the root canal told me I would likely feel much more energetic in a few days. He was right. Tooth problems can even affect the health of your heart and other body organs.

I used to make myself so sick from overtraining as a runner that I would get wicked colds and even migraine headaches. The doctors once treated my migraine with a codeine Tylenol regimen that made my arm go numb from the shoulder down. That scared me so badly I made a trip to the emergency room. They took x-rays and found nothing but a little fluid around my lungs. The Emergency room nurses sent me home with instructions to get some rest. But that night I headed downtown to a nightclub with my brothers. That's called having no common sense.

Some people simply prefer to avoid the doctor unless it is absolutely necessary. My wife and her family are those kind of people. Tough German stock with good constitutions. That's part of the reason why Linda has made it through chemo again and again. But there are limits to the effectiveness of resolute denial.

Linda's father has been going through some major health problems since April, and starting to do better. Last weekend I kidded him about their family's tendency to avoid the doctor when they have health problems. True to form, he smiled and said, "Well, if you wait a week most things go away."

We all laughed at that. In Linda's case, the apple certainly doesn't fall far from the tree when it comes to fighting through minor health problems. But we all know the challenge and risk is intensified when you're fighting through chemo as well. So I ride her a bit and she gets irritated. But that's my job.

Linda is now far more proactive when it comes to asking advice and presenting issues to the nurses and doctors when her health is compromised. I'm really proud of her for changing in that respect. She feels much more in control when she gets answers and knows how to address things. Of course, some of the side effects of actual chemo we know too well, and there's not much we can do about some of that. But this recent low-grade infection was a good example of how my wife has learned to address the "little" things as not so little. She's definitely feeling better from the antibiotics. I can hardly describe how low and tired she felt before that. In all, however, the goal is looking ahead. We're officially halfway through treatment. Yay!

That brings to mind a little cement creature sitting on our back patio steps, a small statue of a frog. "Frogs only jump forward," they told us. That's our philosophy right now. Jump

ahead and see what life brings us.
Ever seen a miracle?

Saturday, August 27, 2011, 5:45 PM

As little kids we used to lounge around our living room watching sports and comedy shows as a family. Four boys fighting for carpet space and a line of sight for the TV weren't exactly a good audience for post-modern theology, but my father was never one to hold back despite our reluctance to listen. One night while gathered to watch a boxing match between Cassius Clay (before he became Muhammad Ali) and some boxer overseas, my father walked in the room and said, "Ever seen a miracle?"

We all looked at him a moment and turned our eyes back to the magical athleticism of Cassius Clay, who was floating around the ring as if gravity had less of a hold on him. "That's a miracle you're watching, boys," my father continued. "That picture is being beamed into outer space, bounced off a satellite and back down to earth so you can watch it on the television. I'm telling you, it's a miracle."

Trying to ignore our father, we blurted back, "We're watching the fight, dad." But my father knew what he was talking about. He worked at RCA and Zenith early in his career. He had a hand in development of the first TV cameras and televisions that could broadcast color pictures. If you're old enough to remember that NBC peacock logo you'll likely recall how miraculous color TV really seemed after years of watching black and white.

Of course we've now moved onto Blu-Ray and HD and television on-demand. Gone are the televisions with dials, semi-circular screens and antennas with a motor on top to point them in the right direction.

All that progress does not diminish the nature of those early miracles leading to the technology we now enjoy today. Miracles never get old, you see.

Taking the miraculous for granted is a common human flaw. We get spoiled by the nature of our miraculous existence. It's been stated by a few friends of mine over the years: "What would our Founding Fathers think of America now? Do you think they'd be amazed at airplanes and TV and computers?" I think not. Those were people accustomed to thinking in terms of progress. The better question is this: Are we just as capable of looking back to see how far we've come, to appreciate the miracle of our daily existence?

Of course if you're talking about miracles that break the laws of science, physics and chemistry in the manner some people see miracles in the bible, those don't seem to happen anymore. Did God just get bored with miracles of that type? Or were descriptions of miracles a necessary device to explain the amazing spiritual principles that can be life transforming if we let them into our lives? Big questions, I know.

I have had a number of personal experiences that convince me that miracles do happen in modern times. These experiences could also be explained as amazing coincidences. But that still does not change the miraculous, sometimes life-changing nature of their occurrence.

Here's one example. A bit intense, but true.

In 2005 when my mother was dying from a stroke brought on by an attempt at chemotherapy, there came a point where it was necessary to place her in hospice. That was not an easy time. The hospice workers failed to show up the next day to help in transition. My mom's stroke had taken away her ability to swallow. The terms of hospice meant that we could not give her anything to drink. Just swabs of water with a little pink sponge on a blue stick. But, barely conscious, my mom kept gesturing she was thirsty. That tore my heart apart.

Headed home in near panic, wondering why the hospice nurse missed her appointment when support was needed most, I cried and could hardly drive. At home my wife was already in bed because she had just started her first rounds of chemo treatment. My father was not able to help much because he was still fairly compromised from the effects of a massive stroke three years earlier.

Once home I bent over the kitchen table and prayed, asking God what I should do. No sooner had I finished praying did the phone rang. It was my oldest brother. "Hey," he said. "We're driving across Indiana on our way to mom and dad's. Me and Greg were just looking at the stars in a perfect black sky and decided we ought to give you a call? How's it going?"

From there the conversation covered all that had transpired. The stroke. The hospice. Mom wanting water.

Trying not to wake my wife, I started to cry quietly over the phone. "Hey," my brother consoled me. "You're doing the right thing. She can't swallow or eat. It's okay."

To me, that phone call was a miracle. It gave us all strength to carry on. My mother died peacefully a few days later. We were there with her, my wife and I, along with my dad. And say what you will, we considered that a miracle too. Two days later I went for a walk at Dick Young Forest Preserve. I was thinking about my mom's life and looked up to see the shape of two trees perfectly reflected in the clouds in the sky. And felt peace.

There are other times I've prayed for help and gotten it. Perhaps not as dramatically, but still there have been realizations that what happened did not feel entirely like coincidence.

Notice the difficulty in parsing out the difference between taking action and listening for guidance? Sometimes when we ask for miracles they don't come. Often when we take a step and ask for hope and guidance and support in time of need, help often arrives in one way or another.

Of course the opposite of miracle is tragedy. That too is a matter of perspective. It felt tragic the day Linda and I found out she had cancer. We thought our world had ended. But really, it hadn't. That was more than 6 years ago. The world we knew has certainly been changed. In some miraculous ways, it has changed for the better. It's just tough to hold onto that realization some days.

We never really knew the full grace of people's kindness, for instance. You can hardly appreciate that until you are defenseless. It is humbling to realize the goodness that can come from so many people. Faith is not always required. But it certainly can't be ruled out either. Our best hope is to remain open to that sense of the miraculous and give back any way we can.

I think back to what I used to consider a miracle. Those biblical moments when seas part and skies rumble or flash with the voice of God and everlasting light.

Then I think of the sense of comfort and gratitude in the intuition of my brother calling that night when I was so in need. That didn't really constitute a miracle. Or did it?

As my father might have said: "The cell phones alone are a

miracle!" So who's to decide what is miraculous or not?
Maybe my prayer bounced off a satellite to find them in Indiana. Whatever, dude. I hope that satellite feels like following us around. It sure seems to sometimes. Thank you for the miracle of your support, everyone. And never be afraid to call.

Numb and numb'er

Tuesday, September 6, 2011, 2:00 PM

Seems like all of us face nagging health issues sooner or later. Whether it is a reddened eyelid or painful cold sore, a cavity in your teeth or a mysterious rash, we all deal with life's humbling physical maladies.

Which are only magnified when you're fighting cancer.

So it is with some relief that we found out last week that Linda has been fighting a small, non-threatening background infection that made her feel tired and weak. The effects were magnified by the chemo. Now it's pink medicine time (or something of that order) for my cutie pie while she preps for the next round of chemo. Next week is the "big" one that wipes her out a few days so we're thankful this week's was more tolerable so she's not completely dragging. But it took some work to get there.

It is weird how subjects like nagging health problems can circle around you at times. For example, during a bike ride with a newfound friend this weekend, conversation turned to the subject of cycling saddle sores. Those can really hurt. Basically they're like a persistent blister that occurs every time you ride. If you don't treat them with caution and some sort of medication they just don't go away. My riding partner explained that his doctor had prescribed an "antibiotic pack" for a saddle sore that cleared the thing right up. And then he quietly observed, "Same goes for dental health too."

He's right about that. In recent years medicine has discovered that dental infections cause all sorts of other problems in your body. A few years back when I had a tooth problem the dentist who performed the root canal told me I would likely feel much more energetic in a few days. He was right. Tooth problems can even affect the health of your heart and other body organs.

I used to make myself so sick from overtraining as a runner I would get wicked colds and even migraine headaches. The doctors once treated my migraine with a codeine Tylenol regimen that made my arm go numb from the shoulder down. That scared me so badly I made a trip to the emergency room. They took x-rays and found nothing but a little fluid around my lungs. The Emergency room nurses sent me home with instructions to get some rest. Instead I headed downtown that evening to a nightclub with my brothers. That's called having no common sense.

Some people simply prefer to avoid the doctor unless it is absolutely necessary. My wife and her family are those kind of people. Tough German stock with good constitutions. That's part of the reason why Linda has made it through chemo again and again. But there are limits to the effectiveness of resolute denial.

Linda's father has been going through some major health problems since April. He's starting to do better. Last weekend I kidded him about their family's tendency to avoid the doctor when they have health problems. True to form, he smiled and said, "Well, if you wait a week most things go away."

We all laughed at that. In Linda's case, the apple certainly doesn't fall far from the tree when it comes to fighting through minor health problems. But we all know the challenge and risk is intensified when you're fighting through chemo as well. So I ride her a bit and she gets irritated. That's my job.

Linda is now far more proactive when it comes to asking advice and presenting issues to the nurses and doctors when her health is compromised. I'm really proud of her for changing in that respect. She feels much more in control when she gets answers and knows how to address things. Of course we know the side effects from chemo all too well. There's not much we can do about some of that. Yet this recent low-grade infection was a good example of how my wife has learned to address the "little" things as not so little. She's definitely feeling better from the antibiotics. I can hardly describe how low and tired she felt before that.

In all, the goal is to continue looking ahead. We're officially halfway through treatment. Yay!

That brings to mind a little cement creature sitting on our back patio steps. Some friends of ours recently gave us a small statue of a frog. "Frogs only jump forward," they told us. That's our philosophy right now. Jump ahead and see what life brings us.

Shadows and Light

Thursday, September 22, 2011, 8:00 AM

The light can play weird tricks on your brain when you're driving in late afternoon and the sun flickers so strongly through the trees your visual senses can barely process the sudden changes.

That's what it's been like lately, with shadows and light of life flickering through our lives. Chemo, then recovery. Work, then relax. Rainy days, then bright clear sun. All happening so fast, it seems.

The last "big" chemo for Linda was like diving under the sea. She literally submerged for a couple days. She just about got the bends coming back up. We have one more of those to do, on October 5, then a couple more "medium" chemos the 12th and 19th and we're done with the regimen this fall. It will take months for her to recover. Her eyes keep watering. Her feet are numb. Her fingertips have lost feeling. Of course her hair will have to grow back.

Going through that big chemo again last week was tough for her. Then our son Evan came home on Saturday, and daughter Emily on Sunday. Looking forward to their arrival brightened Linda's spirits. Our kids' paths even crossed in the living room for about an hour. Linda healed much more quickly in their presence and Chuck couldn't believe his good fortune in having all his "peoples" there at once.

Shadows. Then light. It can make your head spin.

All you parents know how much it can mean to see your children when they've been away for a while. Even a day apart sometimes can seem like an eternity. Or, they might be away at camp or something and you get used to the quiet for a bit. When they come home all of a sudden you realize there was a hole in your existence. That's the irony of family, children and friends. Shadows and light.

As caregiver to my father it has been instructive to realize that while my visits sometimes seem obligatory to me, to him they are anything but. He had a stroke years ago and is no longer able to speak. But he has taught himself to write again with his left hand. Sometimes communication is difficult and there can be disagreements in which he flares up and gets angry. Old wounds surface. But then, peace returns. He makes a joke. We laugh. We move on. In some form, we do forgive.

We've gotten better at getting the issues on the table early and communicating in different ways. He has expressed concern for Linda because he knows what it is truly like to go through difficult health. He's not always an easy man to get along with, but being his executor has been a gift in working through old hurts yo focus on the present and future. Shadows and light.

Having you all commit to sharing in this journey is a ray of light in our lives. We have not known what this treatment would bring, or how much help we'd need. To Linda's credit she has been able to be self-sufficient in some ways, even driving herself to chemo some days. We just don't know how any of this will proceed. So we carry on.

We still have a ways to go and do not really know what the near future will bring in the way of needs and such. But we certainly appreciate the light at the end of the tunnel. You are holding our symbolic hands along the way.

Don't be afraid to send Linda a little note via email. She's doing really well overall, teaching her preschoolers on days when she is able. That is so fulfilling. We really do thank God for the preschool. It's such a motivator for her and the help and guidance of its director has been so amazing. Thank you also to her assistant and everyone that subs and lends a hand. Thanks so much. It has certainly "lightened" the burden. God Bless.

The Story of Chris and Linda

Monday, September 26, 2011, 10:15 AM

At Morton Arboretum

In October 1981 the couple that became Christopher and Linda Cudworth had met once but never knew it. Chris had agreed to attend a party somewhere in the backwoods wilds of Lisle and wound up playing volleyball in a scrubby open field against a group of laid-back hippie guys and gals. One woman in particular was tall with long blonde hair. She wore a lacy white top with long sleeves and well-worn jeans.

It would be another 10 years or so before the subject of that volleyball game came up in conversation between Chris and Linda, who suddenly realized they had stood across the net from each other that summer day. By the time that fact was known the couple were married with two children, Evan and Emily.

For it had seemed like simple chance that night of October 23, 1981 when Chris turned his chair around at the Scotland Yard bar at 2:00 in the morning. He was there with his one of his closest friends Greg, as well as a mutual college friend Chuck. They had shared quite a few beers at the restaurant where Greg was a waiter. By the time 2:00 a.m. rolled around Chris decided it was either time to quit drinking or accept that the next day would be an entire waste. Just then his two friends got a little rowdy and one smashed a glass on the floor in fun. Chris spun his chair around to face a trio of people seated at the next table. It was Linda and friends Randy and Debbie. "I don't want to be with them," Chris pointed at his buddies, and joked to Linda. "I want to be with you."

And so it began. They exchanged numbers but Linda bet her friends a bottle of wine that Chris would not call. That bet was paid off on their wedding day four years later.

Chris showed up a night early for their first date. "What are you doing here?" Linda asked.

"I'm here for our date," Chris said.

"That's tomorrow night," Linda replied. They went out anyway before Linda had to head back for teacher conferences at West Aurora High School.

Their next date was on Halloween. Chris showed up dressed like the Greek god Mercury in silver face, tights and real duck wings on his ankles. Linda still went out with him, demurely dressed as a cowgirl.

And so it went. Linda put up with remarkable antics from her prospective beau and the relationship grew. One night after dinner in St. Charles the couple went for a walk in an evening fog. Chris felt lightness as he held her hand, as if his entire being was being lifted up. He wondered if he was starting to love the woman.

And then, a challenge for Linda. At 23 she went to the hospital to have benign ovarian cysts removed. Chris showed up (with flowers?) to check on his new girlfriend. She pulled her gown aside to show him the bikini cut in her abdomen. "This must be a serious relationship," he thought to himself after the hospital visit, realizing he cared deeply for Linda.

Then came camping trips to the Wisconsin woods, cross country ski trips and a wild driving trip to Colorado to visit Linda's sister Diane in Aspen. All that togetherness helped seal the deal for Chris and Linda.

But not before Chris was shipped off to Philadelphia in August 1982 when the investment company where he worked consolidated the marketing department. Chris was forced to move. Linda traveled to Philly a couple times, including Thanksgiving, when Chris was barely able to score the last turkey in the freezer case in time for dinner the next day.

Then the investment company gave up on the idea of marketing consolidation and let the entire department go. In the late spring of 1983 Chris moved back to Chicago to live with his friend Greg in Lincoln Park, Chicago.

Linda was still teaching at West Aurora. Chris decided to try running full time with sponsorship and a part-time day job at a running store. Chris set all his PRs in running that year but soon enough realized it was time to move on in life. That next winter he managed the Norris Sports Complex where Linda also worked the desk. People commented they made a good couple.

By then Linda was getting frustrated, asking his brother Jim whether Chris could get serious about marriage or not. "Give him six months, and if he doesn't commit, dump his ass," Jim Cudworth said.

They got married on June 29, 1986.

The couple honeymooned in Glacier National Park, and then came home to jobs that fall. They decided at 27 and 26 years old to try to start a family. It didn't take long as Linda gave birth to Evan Paul Cudworth that following October 30, 1986.

Evan said his first word at 6 months old, uttering the word "bird" while looking at house sparrows on the back steps of a little brick bungalow in Geneva. Evan's wonderment, musicality and astute sense of the world constantly amazed Chris and Linda.

Three years later they conceived their second child, Emily Joan Cudworth, named for her two grandmothers Joan Mues and Emily Cudworth. Emily's keen sense of observation and exceptional recall were early attributes that teachers, pastors and friends would affirm.

As the kids grew and developed their interests, Chris and Linda looked for more space than the 750 sq. home in Geneva. They found a classic ranch For Sale By Owner in Batavia and moved there in 1996.

It turned out to be a good move for everyone. Evan made fast friends and Emily finally learned to ride her bike on the wide-open streets of Batavia. Chris worked in marketing and Linda began teaching full time at St. Mark's Preschool after serving as an aide several years.

Middle school and High school years for both children were filled with plays and concerts. Evan became a cellist and Emily a violinist, initially playing the very same instrument her grandmother Emily Nichols Cudworth had once used.

When graduation came for Evan he had applied to several good schools but literally leaped into his mother's arms when the acceptance letter arrived from the University of Chicago. Chris and Evan had visited the school and it just seemed to "fit" everything Evan was about; inquiry, critical thinking and the urban environment all seemed to call to him. Linda's mother and father had often visited the campus out of interest in the school's history and culture. Evan enrolled in fall of 2005.

That spring and summer of 2005 brought a series unsettling events, however. In spring Linda had gone to a gynecologist for a checkup and the doctor found a small lump on her ovary. The physician performed laparoscopic surgery to biopsy the lump and broke it up in the process. Tests and visits to a gynecological oncologist revealed ovarian cancer, Stage IIC. Surgery ensued, then chemotherapy. It was difficult but Linda kept working with support of staff at the preschool. Friends rallied around the couple too, and people of faith at St. Mark's Lutheran prayed and helped in many other ways.

Chris was also busy taking care of his father Stewart and mother Emily that year. Stew was a stroke victim in need of constant care. His mother Emily was fighting a low-grade case of lymphoma, for which she was taking an oral chemotherapy in order to avoid being too compromised to care for Stew. In late summer it was discovered that Emily also had pancreatic cancer. Doctors tried chemotherapy but her body was not strong enough to take it. One October morning at the St. Charles office of the Daily Herald, Chris heard the police scanner call out his mother's address. He arrived to find them carrying her off in an ambulance. Delnor sent her home a week later, whereupon she suffered a stroke and was committed to hospice care. But not before meeting with family, visiting with her four sons, and hearing granddaughter Emily play her new violin. Chris and Linda were present with Stew when Emily Nichols Cudworth passed away in November 2005.

The events of that year were difficult to comprehend. It

seemed like everything at once was up for grabs. Yet the family pulled together; Chris, Linda, Evan and Emily. Linda underwent additional chemotherapy that spring, including an interperitoneal regimen with chemo directly injected into the abdomen. The nurses missed one time and Chris and Linda wound up in Emergency on Easter weekend.

The focus—for everyone—became to simply do their best at what they do because... "It is what it is." Don't overdramatize. Deal with reality. Take each day as it comes. Keep hope for the future.

This philosophy was neatly summarized in Evan's decision that next summer to head to China in 2006. As parents Chris and Linda wondered whether they should be more concerned about the trip. Of course Evan (whose name means "the challenger") knew how to handle himself, surviving threatening China weather and a bout of food poisoning while seeing a big part of the world.

As college graduation neared for Evan, it grew time for Emily to choose a school to attend as well. But cancer would intervene again, as Linda went back into treatment in fall of 2007. That was a shocker considering how hard we had all worked to get through the "Gold Standard" regimen of earlier chemo. The emotional cost was heavy, and the physical costs included ascites, a swelling of the abdomen that was difficult to manage. But chemo did fight back the effects and Linda was in remission after 8 more rounds of chemo.

All that preoccupation made it difficult to get Emily oriented for college. Columbia in Chicago was her first choice, but the school offered no financial aid. Emily enrolled in a practical yet interesting alternative for her schooling, choosing the Honors Photography Program at College of DuPage. It required a bit of commuting, but the Toyota Matrix purchased that fall had a sunroof, 6-CD changer and all-wheel drive, so she made the best of it. She attended quite a few concerts as well and even invited a few touring rock bands to the Cudworth house. All good.

After 8 great years Chris chose to leave the newspaper business in 2007, for the industry was on the brink of a massive downsizing. Chris took a job as CMO for an agency with whom he had been freelancing for 5 years, and also had brought in a new $1M client. However the company was not thriving and let him and others go right at the point when Linda's cancer came back the fall of 2007.

Believe it or not, there were blessings even in that circumstance. Because while out of work, Chris was able to provide the care Linda needed for several months while she was under great emotional and physical duress.

Yet the day after the prognosis of remission was given once again, Chris accepted a job with an audio visual company as marketing manager.

As the economy continued to sour, much of life felt unpredictable. Even though Evan graduated from one of the most prestigious colleges in the country, jobs were hard to find. Yet he wisely worked with Admissions as an undergraduate and helped transition their publications department into the digital age. That meant he'd proven himself capable of helping in many ways, which is how he earned a position in Admissions with the University of Chicago.

Linda returned to teaching at St. Marks Preschool (now 15 years) where remarkable support through all her cancer treatments has included kindness from student families as well as staff. Through Linda's example many people have learned that it is possible to thrive through cancer. But the help Linda and Chris received was always key. The notion of family began to expand in the minds of Chris and Linda to include so many other people.

The job adventures were not over for Chris by 2010, however. When the economy truly tanked he was laid off from the audiovisual company. Yet he managed to find opportunities, working freelance in spring 2010 and landed a job with a marketing firm that June. But by fall of 2010, when Linda's cancer returned a third time, the company suddenly let him go and attempted to cut off insurance to the family as well.

Through legal wrangling and advice from his close friend and attorney, Chris kept the family insured while working a full-time freelance job with a public relations firm in Libertyville.

It became a family joke that God always seems to give the Cudworth's what they need, even if it is not always what they want.

Then in February 2011 Chris landed a position a marketing communications and public relations near home. His work there produced a number of awards for the company, but they let him go the day after he informed them his wife's cancer had returned.

Through it all, Emily completed her degree at College of DuPage and began looking for schools to continue her education. University of Wisconsin was inviting but Augustana in Rock Island won out, where she enrolled in the communications program, shooting pics for the Photo Bureau and newspaper and expanded her leadership and friend network in many ways.

In 2011 another health challenge impacted the family as Linda's father had a heart episode requiring surgery followed by complications that have made 2011 a tough one for him. Yet close family bonds provide the foundation for his return to better health.

Now it is September, 2011. It will be 30 years since Chris and Linda (officially) met on October 23, 1981.

The story of Chris and Linda is still being written. The couple now worships at Bethlehem Lutheran and Linda is excited to be working with a great new class of children at St. Marks Preschool. Evan is traveling the country in his work and Emily is thriving at Augustana. Despite many challenges, blessings abound. They do abound.

And that, dear friends, is the message of this story.

Update

Tuesday, September 27, 2011, 8:00 AM

Would appreciate prayers for Linda today as she heads up to the gynecological oncologist's office to check out the CT scan taken earlier this week. We pray the chemo is working and that progress is made on fighting the tumor. We're fortunate there have not been direct effects of the cancer this time. The side effects from chemo are enough to handle! Linda is doing her best to deal with that. Thanks again for your support. We have a treatment tomorrow, then next week starts the last cy-

cle. One "big" chemo and two middle ones to go.
Reality Show

Monday, October 3, 2011, 2:00 PM

This past weekend we drove to Rock Island to see our daughter Emily at Augustana College. She was excited to show us the house next to campus she and two future roommates will be leasing. They were under pressure to find a house because the good locations near campus go fast. The house is super cute and well kept. She'll also have a place to live next summer as she's planning on finding a job and enjoying the community of friends living in the area.

We all know these types of decisions can take a little out of you, especially when you're up to your ears in current commitments and studies as Emily is doing with four courses this term at Augie. It's like she shifted from 1st to 5th gear going from College of DuPage last fall to Augustana this year. She's doing great though and it was fun for us to go see her.

On a lark we tooled over to Le Claire, Iowa, just upriver from Augie. Our mission was to visit the home base for a reality TV show called American Pickers. If you haven't seen the show (History Channel) it is centered around two antique hunters who travel the country "picking" rare and unusual items from mainstream and backcountry contacts. It's just goofy fun.
Since it was so close to Emily's college, it seemed like a neat idea to go see their store. After all, how many times do you know about something like that and say "You know, we should go there..." but never do?

It wasn't a long trip, nor was it that big a deal. But it sure was fun pulling up to the store we see on TV every week. There were dozens of people walking around the place. We took pictures of the storefront and the truck and even a few interior shots where all kids of odd and interesting antiques are piled on the shelves.

The whole notion of "reality TV" is mostly an illusion, of course. These shows plan episodes and set up takes. Nothing is as spontaneous as it seems.

Yet these shows do impact lives. A friend of ours was once featured in a personal makeover program. They literally threw away her clothes (mostly from the 80s) and made her change her hairstyle (big and fluffy, also 80s) recruiting a couple friends from work to critique the changes. It turned out to be a traumatic experience for the makeover subject. She broke into real tears on the air.

Of course truth is almost always stranger than fiction. Many of us live lives carefully constructed to meet the needs of our varied realities. The persona we create and show to others is the often the one we can most consistently manage. Some of us even (by necessity) manage multiple personas. There's the "work" person and the "church" person and the "other job or volunteer" person. Sometimes these personas don't even seem to meet within our daily selves. It's a lot of work, but we keep these personalities up because the real us needs shelter from the storms of life. We keep that private little person to ourselves. That's the Comfortable Couch us.

It all works until something comes along to force us to let down our guards. Then we have to reveal aspects of ourselves that we might not like to share. Necessity is an insistent journalist. When Linda was first diagnosed with ovarian cancer, her preschool associates called me up and said, "Listen, we're here to help. We're going to let you in the Girl's Club. But there's one important rule. You have to tell us everything that's going on."

I've never gotten a little silver pin or a membership certificate to the Girl's Club, but we must assume that there was at least an Associate Membership extended because we've gotten so much help from them. In the last week Linda's girlfriends and some guy friends have called to offer rides, meals and morale support (you read that right). We continue to be humbled by the kindness of others.

My wife Linda is a pretty private person. To open up and share all this stuff about her health and life has never been easy for her. Part of my job since the beginning has been to protect her in some ways. That's part of the role of this web site, to serve as a communication portal when Linda isn't up to receiving calls. Or me for that matter. But I tend to be pretty talky. Can you tell?

Recently the invitation to call or email was opened up because we're far enough down the road and so used to the washboard surface of life as we know it that we can handle the bumps a little better. We have just three chemos to go, and that's great. We did find out there might be surgery in Linda's future, to excise the tumor because it did not shrink enough from chemo. It's like we were driving a country road and came to a sign that says Detour: Bridge Out. So we'll have to go the long way around. But we're going.

Not the news we wanted to hear. Last week was a tough one in many ways. We still jumped in the car, hit the road, laughed with one of our kids and dropped in on a reality show of our own making. That's what they say, isn't it? Sometimes you have to make your own reality (show).

Comic relief

Tuesday, September 27, 2011, 8:45 AM

So this morning I received a text from my son Evan that was actually sent last night after I'd gone to bed.

He was curious about some information in the recent blog entry about The Story of Chris and Linda.

"Was that a typo or was I born the same year that you and mom got married? I called Emily and she was like, "Oh no, that can't be."

Well now....Was Evan Paul Cudworth a "love child?"

Fortunately there is no intrigue. Linda and Christopher Cudworth were married on June 29, 1985 and Evan was born on October 30, 1986. I had mistakenly put our wedding date as June 26, 1986 in the blog. Ooops.

Hooo boy. Linda was already miffed at me for writing so much personal history. Now I've got to answer for messing up birthdays? Intimating (no pun intended) a forced marriage?

Certainly did not intend to shed the light of potential scandal on the Cudworth clan. Thank you Evan for pointing out the error.

But it is funny. Sort of. Evan and I laughed about it anyway.

And sorry, kids. Didn't mean to freak you out. There are no such secrets to bear.

Happy Tuesday, everyone. Monday was interesting enough.
Weekend Warrior

Monday, October 10, 2011, 10:15 AM

On Friday Linda announced she was feeling well enough to want to "go somewhere" on Saturday. That was her way of saying I needed to figure out someplace to take her that was nice and pretty but where she could still enjoy herself without it turning into a physical struggle. Husbands are often required to figure these things out. Right now Linda's not into walking too far, so a hike in the woods is kind of out of the question. For a bit I was thinking of going to Starved Rock where we went on our second date 30 years ago this November 1. But that's a lot of walking. Or Moraine Hills, where she even volunteered to sit in a rowboat if I chose to fish. Hmmm.

We went to Shabbona Lake State Park instead. 45 minute drive, straight out Route 30. See America on a rope of sunbeam. Bright, airy October day.

I knew a spot where it was only a 600-meter walk out to the lake from the back parking lot. So we walked there only to have Linda freak out when the tiniest brown snake crawled across the path. She has a morbid fear of snakes. I picked up the snake and let this little kid who was following us hold it too. It was his first time holding a snake. He was thrilled, and then he tossed it down and ran along ahead to see what life would deliver next.

We brought fishing rods but the fishing was dead. I cast the #5 Mepps and if nothing's biting that, nothing's biting.

While we were there, a fisherman across the corner (yes, the corner, the south end is square) of the lake was making lots of loud noise rattling his tackle box like he was drunk or something. The noise was random and intermittent. Finally Linda, ever concerned for the welfare of others, asks, "Do you think he's alright?"

We could only see the top of his head through tall weeds. He was sitting down on the shore rocks, buried amongst the canary grass and reeds.

More noise. More banging. Didn't sound good. "You alright?" I yelled over.

"You'd better go check," Linda said. "I'll carry your stuff up."

This is where the story shifts into present tense, to give you a better sense of things as they happened in the moment.

So I trot around the gravel road to catch the path that circles the south end of the lake. When I reach him by the shore, about 20 yards down a steep hill, he is sitting splay-legged on the rocks with a look of utter frustration on his face. When I bend over to talk he looks up at me with a combination of panic and suspicion. Yet that look is tinged with a raw determination too.

"Can I help you?" I ask.

He shifts his weight around again, not looking at me right off. His tackle box is sitting inside a big Styrofoam cooler tied together with good old rope.
"Can you help me up?" he asks, finally looking me in the eye.

Instinctively I circle around behind him. He's about 5'6" and weighs at least 200 lbs. Sweaty. He's wearing an old brown shirt, plaid Bermuda shorts and the damned ugliest slip-on black shoes I've ever seen. Most likely a Walmart purchase. But not old. They come off easily, I'll find out later.

"Okay," I tell him. "Stand up on the count of three; One, Two..." and up he comes. But there's something wrong. It's like the universe has confused his body. His one arm swings back to his chest. He grabs it with the other arm, pushing it back to his side. I think: not an easy gig.

"Let's just get up this little hill here," I tell him, guiding him as he lurches half sideways up the hill. His feet point out at dangerous angles. His mind and body are not working together. The 12-foot hill is an enormous effort. He leans forward and gasps, "I gotta sit down."

"That's fine. Take your time. There's no hurry here." I glance over to the trail where Linda might be standing. I see no sign of her.

"What your name?" I ask.

"Richard," he says

"I'm Chris."

"Okay, I'm ready now," he tells me after a few minutes resting on the ground. Another lift. This guy is not light. I revise the weight estimate to 210.

After another 20 feet of walking, he sits down again. I look around and wonder, "How the hell did he get here in the first place?"

"Richard, do you have MS or something?" I ask.

"Parkinson's," he says. "And two brain surgeries. Knee replacement. And my legs don't work too well." He has a feverish demeanor. Agitated. Just sitting there is a lot of work for him.

On his head is a bright green cap. It says NAPOWAN on it, the name of an old Boy Scout camp in Wisconsin. I ask: "Were you in Scouting? I recognize the name on your hat."

"I don't know where I got this," he tells me.

"Were your kids... do you have boys who were Scouts?"

The question seems to perplex him. "Nah," he says.

"Okay, Richard, let's go a little farther."

First he has to pull his shoes back on because they keep falling off. I grab him under the arms and give him another hoist. He teeters in the sunshine. At least it's warm out, but not too warm I think. Otherwise I might have found a dead man.

His twitchy long fishing pole quivers every time I walk with him, like an antennae pointing the way. Richard shuffles and stumbles as he goes. Another 30 feet. He sits down in a lump of grass. The sun is bright. A breeze is blowing. It's a nice day for anyone except for Richard at this point.

There is another 30 feet required to scale the next slight hill. I encourage Richard to give it a go. We walk, a little too briskly, so I offer, "Let's slow it down." He makes it to the top, heaving and blowing.

"We made it up the f****** hill," I tell Richard with a laugh.

"The f****** hill," he repeats. But now we're at a crossroads. The trail splits right and left. Left takes us back to my car. Earlier I'd jogged up the little hill and found Linda and signaled to her to head back to the car. Figured she is there now. Waiting. Perhaps she's even called 911.

Richard sits down again, utterly exhausted it seems, by the act of cresting that little hill. I point out the fork in the trail and explain that we should go left. "I went the other way," he insists.

"Well, you're going to have to trust me on this one. I know where this trail goes. I don't know where that one goes. It may go back to the parking lot or it may veer off toward the lodge. If it's okay, we'll go my way. Is your car back in the parking lot?"

"Truck. My truck's there."

"Okay, well this is the right way then."

We gather ourselves for the effort and walk the short downhill to make the turn and get into some shade. Richard stops and I convince him to remain standing this time. He tires though and sits down anyway. His shoes come off. He pulls them back on again. This time he rises on the count of three without so much trouble. Still his legs do not cooperate well. He is at constant risk of going down for the count.

Behind us two fisherman emerge through the woods and look wonderingly at the lurching figure of Richard silhouetted by the late afternoon sun.

"He's doing his best!" I call back to them. They refuse to pass, each trying to figure out what the scene represents. "His

name's Richard," I explain. "He needs a little help."
For some reason the objectivity seems appropriate. This is like nature's version of the HIPPA law or something.

Or, was I trying to distance myself somehow from Richard? A pang of guilt hits me. The two younger men approach slowly and quickly figure out what's going on. This dude needs help, they gather. One wears a Safety First shirt with a construction helmet emblazoned on it. He knows need when he sees it. Richard trundles on beside me, heaving and breathing. They follow behind at a respectful distance.

Earlier Richard muttered some words to me: "It's good you're looking out for your fellow man." Those words seemed to carry off with the wind at the time. Suddenly they register with me. We stand in the shade with the other fellows who are waiting, in their reserved way, to help us out. One holds out a bright orange PowerAde for Richard to drink.

Suddenly it all makes sense why Linda and I were here at this moment, on this day. Why we drove out Route 30 and why the banging noise occurred. Why no fish were biting and why my wife insisted we look into the situation. It all makes sense. We were meant to be here.

Richard makes the long last walk back to his big black truck. We toss his Styrofoam cooler and tackle box and fishing pole into the bed of his Chevy truck and close the gate. Thunk. It's a certain-sounding kind of closure. The whole scene is quite unlike those macho truck commercials where able-bodied men stand around their trucks looking like pillars of American fortitude. Those commercials miss the point. Richard is a real man too. His truck at that moment is home enough for him.

Richard settles into his front seat relieved to be back in moving comfort. We wonder that he can even drive. Obviously he got there somehow, just as he somehow got down to the lake with his tackle box and cooler and fishing pole. Determination. The desire for independence. Real fortitude. Trying to live the way he wants. It can be so hard sometimes.

On the way back to our car with Linda I burst into tears, feeling grateful we were there to help. It strikes us profoundly how much help we've also been given in our lives. People have lifted us up by the armpits in times of struggle of one kind or another. Whether some of us like to admit it or not, we're all struggling up the f****** hill. The f****** hill is always waiting for us. We can all make it with help. We really can.

Parenthood

Wednesday, October 19, 2011, 9:15 AM

So our current favorite TV show is Parenthood. If you haven't watched this program, it is a family drama mixed with humorous events and real-life-feeling situations. The family is far from perfect and that's what makes it so watchable. Sometimes it makes you squirm a little because it reminds you of your own imperfections. But usually they bring you back from the brink to make you want to come back the next week.

One of the funny things about being a parent is hearing, often years later, the realities of what your children were doing and thinking when they were younger. Linda's family often engages in deep discussions about adventures growing up. Silly and serious events combine to make great family lore. Often her parents will sit with jaws dropped learning about sibling rivalry, and the consequences thereof. It's often very funny.

Our own children Evan and Emily sometimes share stories

about near-accidents in the back yard when they were little. Apparently Evan once slipped out of an apple tree in the back yard of our Geneva home but was caught by the strap of his coveralls. The same thing happened in the same tree to one of our friend's children.

Not all these incidents were caught on video, of course, so we run them in the video of our memories. But those moments of parenthood that are caught on video are valuable. We have a cute clip where Linda is videotaping the kids in the back yard when a squirrel shows up. Ever the protective mother, Linda can be heard on tape saying, "Watch out for that squirrel! They've been known to bite people!" We've long since exaggerated this statement to say, "Watch out for squirrels! They've been known to kill people!" Linda huffs in amused disgust at such teasing.

The point here is that in family life, it is often hard to really know what others are thinking. So much of life goes by in separate channels. We assemble our family worldviews from shared stories, clips of videos, photos and direct experience.

That's what makes it hard when one of us is feeling pain, worried or even feeling joy. We want to share and don't always know how to do it. Even in close families, entering each other's worlds can be awkward at times. No one is ever sure where family and friends really are in their psychological cycles.

People have asked me over the years, "What do your children think about Linda's cancer? How are they handling it?" My only real response is, "We try to tell them the truth. When there's news, we keep them in the loop. Otherwise we encourage them to live their lives and keep in touch."

Early on, when we first found out about Linda's cancer 6 years ago, I dragged the family to a counselor at a nearby clinic. We sat in the room together and listened to the counselor, but there were no real insights. As we walked out the door, our son Evan said, "I could have done better than that."

On the way home, he hilariously offered to psychoanalyze all of us. And guess what: He was spot on. It made us all laugh. Later, he offered a more serious assessment: "I think our family is strong enough to make it through anything."

Even squirrels? They've been known to kill people, you know.

Linda's cancer has been like a squirrel, in a way, coming back at times when we didn't expect it. Each time we've been able to chase the evil squirrel away. But it is starting to drive us a little nuts. Ba-domm, teessssh. I'll be here all weekend, folks.

What's most important is that we all support each other by any means necessary. Emily is off at college and keeps track of us with texts, Facebook and the occasional call when she's got free time. She's busy and intensely pursuing her studies while making amazing new friends. That makes Linda and I feel great, knowing Emily is finding purpose and fun.

This month Evan has been on the road recruiting for University of Chicago while managing his Publications work long distance. He travels out east quit a bit. One stretch of days on the road proved dreary and rainy. His texts included "Ugh. 5 hours in traffic today."

As a parent you feel for a child in such circumstances. But Evan is no longer a child. He is a young man with his own life in full swing. There have been days, even weeks when he's been joyfully traveling this past year, visiting friends and making the most of his time...when thoughts might turn to mom and dad, and a wonder or a worry surely enter his mind. But the truth as parents...is that seeing our young man and woman doing their best in the world is the greatest, most sustaining reward there is. What could possibly matter more, or be better than that?

Linda is almost done with this cycle of chemotherapy treatments. She's sick of the side effects and barely able to eat or drink some days, but overall her health is good. We'll find out what comes next very soon. Perhaps some surgery to nip this tumor out and hopefully get her on the road to recovery soon enough. We may need some help around the house from some of you then. We'll keep you posted.

The Razor's Edge

Tuesday, October 25, 2011, 11:45 AM

We all know how expensive shaving razors can be. Ten dollars for four little implements made of plastic and metal. But when you think about the technology that goes into those blades (and the advertising, Mach IV, Mach V, and Venus, etc.) you realize why the price is so high.

Also, it is pretty important that razor blades be manufactured properly. In college my roommate innocently dragged a poorly made disposable razor across his face and cut himself from ear to chin. He wrote to complain to the company and they gave him a supply of free razors. Talk about an equivocal gift.

We take a lot for granted using products like razors, and our own habits as well. While in the midst of a midsummer shave for cycling, I nipped the end off my thumbnail. I sat there looking at the blood and thought, "Well, that was stupid."

Sorry if this message is causing you pain so far, but we all hurt ourselves accidentally now and then. A friend and I recently had a conversation about "accidents" and we both agreed there might be no such thing. Deep in our psychological makeups lurk subconscious activities that might be cries for help. We wonder aloud why we hurt ourselves or even hurt others without thinking. It's the razor's edge, people. It can make us smooth or cut us quick. When we don't allow ourselves to be helped in some way, our deep subconscious mind can take over. We stub our toes. Bump our heads. Forget something at work. It might even be an evolved response to stress. No one said evolution always pushes us forward, or speaks to us in plain language. Evolution and God seem a lot alike in that way.

In all our challenges these past few years I know I've hurt Linda unintentionally at times by saying things at the wrong time or failing to show proper support when needed. At other times I've knowingly forced her to buck up under the circumstances.

It's true. The best strategy can be to toughen up at times. That's the challenge of caregiving, and life itself for that matter. Stress definitely heightens our frailties, but it does not mean we should just give in to circumstance. I'm one of those people who thinks that God gives us gifts and wants us to act on them. The Bible clearly supports that reality. Bad things do happen to good people. The principal thing is accepting the fact that even bad circumstances can help us grow. Into loving more. Trusting more. Accepting help. Giving back. Being a blessing to others when you can.

Sooner or later, all of us get the bad razor blade in one form or another. Despite how mad you might be about the cut you received from a faulty blade, the "company" (we're speaking allegorically here) turns around and sends you more. That's how life works. It's yin and yang. The bad is balanced by the good. Or so we try to live.

Digging into that new bag of razor blades is surely an act of faith, is it not? One can't help but wonder: is there another bad one lurking in the next bunch? Or are you safer than ever to shave? In the book "The World According to Garp," the lead character quickly chooses to buy a house into which an airplane had just crashed because he believes that now, by sheer odds, it must be one of the safest homes on the block.

I've proposed to Linda that perhaps we should try to start out fresh at this point. Six years into treatment for cancer and she's still strong and teaching and gardening and trying to live life as normal as possible. Who knows what can happen next? It's a razor's edge, how we choose to live. Some people call that hope, as in not giving up.

Yet bigger questions loom. There is likely not a person with cancer who has not asked the question, "Why?"

Millions have asked the question, and still there seems to be no why. It is what it is. Cancers are what they are. Linda and I have spent considerable time considering her treatment and what it means as well. We know that it works, but also that we've had to go through it several times. Her last treatment in the scheduled regimen is tomorrow. Hooray! Her counts are back down to normal. That is the goal and we have achieved that. We're going to try to catch our breath, be with family (we're gathering November 5 to see a play, welcome Evan and

Emily home and celebrate Evan's Oct. 30 birthday).

So, thanks to everyone for helping us through. We managed to avoid the bad razors of complications this go-round. We can be grateful for that. Linda is still dealing with pretty compromising side effects. I must keep reminding her how well she's doing overall.

Goofy though. Last weekend we were relaxing on the back patio in the autumn sun when our dog snapped at a bee, got stung on the lip and went into near shock, getting sick and everything. It took almost 3 hours to nurse him back to health with a little Benadryl. So much for a peaceful afternoon.

Again, the meals along the way have been so helpful along with the words of support, occasional visits and driving Linda to treatment. All are so much appreciated. Definitely took the sharp edge off this experience.

La vie est intéressante

Monday, October 31, 2011, 2:45 PM

At least once a season Linda and I jump in our car and visit Morton Arboretum. We are members there and have favorite parts of the arboretum to visit in different seasons.

In fall we often visit the east side where there are acres of bright yellow maples and moody groves of oaks in brown, red and tan.

In winter we take walks through fallen snow or on trodden paths from the Big Rock parking spot. The woods there protect us from the wind. If it is calm and sunny we'll also do a three-mile loop on the northeast side.

In summer we always visit the prairie on the west side. There are insects and flowers and birds that can't be seen many other places. It's really like being a kid again, wandering through the prairie with all its sunny detail.

In spring we visit the daffodil glade, also on the west side. Thousands of bright yellow and pure white daffodils bloom in patches. You can wander around aimlessly from colony to colony. To highlight the April scene, there are bluish-purple waves of squill washing up against the daffodils. It is the season of hope for us. Renewal. The advent of Linda's favorite time of year: gardening season.

This year Linda's garden had a purple and orange theme. In previous years it has been orange and bright green, or some other combination. But seldom do the reds dominate. Red is too easy. She likes combo colors.

She also ranches monarch butterflies. Linda has a keen eye for finding monarch eggs on milkweed. She brings the milkweed stems and leaves inside and places them in jars of water inside an aquarium with a screen over the top. The monarch caterpillars emerge and go through their life cycles from tiny white eggs to large, striped caterpillars. When large enough they curl into a fiddlehead and turn into a bright green chrysalis with golden spots. They remain in that state for 10-14 days. Then the chrysalis turns dark. The butterfly that emerges soon stretches out its wings and hangs helplessly until the wings fill out. You can seem them pulsating with life.

This year there weren't as many monarchs as usual. This may be due to many causes. Lack of milkweed plants was one reason cited in the media. That problem may be the result of the efficiency of farm chemicals in killing milkweeds.

Monarch butterflies move north and south by generations. Disruption of hatching or feeding along the way can kill off the annual brood.

Linda also does her part to help monarchs by protecting them from predation here in Illinois. If she doesn't harvest the eggs on the leaves they either get eaten or wasps sting the caterpillars, which then shrivel up and die. Nature plays a numbers game and Linda increases the chances for each monarch to survive.

Releasing her babies (actually, adult monarchs...) into the wild is a favorite thing of hers to do. It is also something the neighbor children and her husband enjoy doing. Something about releasing a monarch into the air or onto a plant to let it pump out its wings is innately hopeful. Linda has been monarch ranching for years. She's probably released 200 or so into the wild. Perhaps more.

One can draw a parallel between her work with butterflies and her work with preschoolers. Linda has taught at St. Mark's Preschool for 15 years. She's probably helped as many children out that door as she has released monarchs into the wild. Every one is precious in her sight. Even the challenging kids get into her heart in some way.

Some of her former students still keep in touch years after they've left the preschool. One darling girl has for several years written Linda encouraging notes with happy drawings and good wishes. Others have accompanied their parents while bringing us meals. Last fall a preschool family helped us rake leaves because Linda was too tired. This year she's doing better but we're going to have to go out and shake the trees because the leaves are still green on several of them.

It seems like even the seasons sometimes don't even know their purpose under heaven these days, or what their timing should be. So we roll with it.

To get a feel for what's happening in the bigger world we sometimes go to the "Church of the Arboretum," as we call it. Occasionally on Sunday we'll skip church and attend a different kind of service. We walk in the woods or prairie. Then we dine in the Ginkgo room at the Morton Arboretum where Linda particularly enjoys the cranberry goat cheese salad. You'll have to try it to understand. It just seems to complement the visit to nature.

This last Saturday night we sat home watching a documentary on Netflix titled Microcosmos. It chronicled the tiny worlds we really never see. Mating snails. Spiders spinning webs. Ants gathering food. Only the French could make a movie like that. The narrator talked at beginning and end. Other than that, it was the sound of the tiny creatures doing their business. Bees testing their new wings. Dung beetles rolling balls of poo along the ground. All these things make sounds, but humans seldom hear it.

To Linda, shows like these are the ultimate form of entertainment, garnering her highest compliment. She says it with casual conviction. Then I know she's emotionally and intellectually satisfied. "This is interesting." And to quote the French: "la vie est intéressante."

The hardest thing about this whole cancer experience is that life sometimes gets a little too interesting. Health challenges. Financial changes. Emotions. Fears. Even the intermittent joys have their challenges. It's all distinctive. Bittersweet. Humbling. Rare fruit. Life takes place in the smallest of details.

With cancer it is like the seasons are always changing on you, and unpredictably. You finish chemo and find out surgery might be necessary. You get through surgery and try to get back to normal again. The wind of a job change blows. The rain falls. Snow comes. Spring arrives again. Only not always in order. It's everything we can do to keep up sometimes.

Only goat cheese salad seems like the constant, there for us in all seasons. Yet even that treat can be difficult for Linda to eat when her taste buds tingle like battery juice.

It's not like we want life to be boring or begin taking it for granted. But once in a while--it might be nice if life were a little less interesting...in some of the more difficult facets of existence.

In the meantime, we'll keep thinking like the French, studying the microcosms and releasing butterflies. La vie est intéressante. Life is interesting. So bring it on.

Simple request

Wednesday, November 2, 2011, 7:15 AM

Today is a challenging day for Linda and I. She goes for a meeting with a specialist to determine what to do with the tumor that remains. We really don't know very much until they take a look. The chemo went well and her counts normalized. Now we need to figure out where she is and what this all means.

What we do know is that Linda's health (other than a cold that is vexing her now...) is overall very good. Putting a strategy together to address what to do from here is a lot to comprehend. She's been very strong and I've tried to provide emotional support but it gets hard in these transitional periods. So prayers are appreciated.

I'm in process of ramping up for a 2-day sales program in Denver this Sunday through Tuesday. Two solid days of presenting to major international clients, networking and trying to win breakthrough business opportunities.

Emily's been busy wrapping up finals at Augustana and applying for an internship. Evan is coming off the road and getting prepared to get back into his rhythms and responsibilities at University of Chicago. Linda's parents and her brother are coming out this weekend to help celebrate Evan's 25th birthday, which was October 30. Linda's father is still going through dialysis and is thin compared to his normal self. Joan is quite involved managing the caregiving.

So we're perambulating on the fly, you might say. I'm going to go do some pushups and prepare for the day. And pray that we get encouraging news in some way.

Night Train

Friday, November 11, 2011, 8:30 AM

My parents grew up on farms less than 300 yards apart in the Catskill Mountains of Upstate New York. The farms nudged the base of the Susquehanna River valley where a state road followed the course of the river. A set of train tracks followed that same valley, and those train tracks were kept busy in the late 1950s and 60s with transport of coal and other supplies.

Our family would go back every summer and visit those farms. I can remember many nights lying in an upstairs bedroom listening to the sounds of trains moving through the valley. They seemed to express both promise and penitence. The sound of a train in the distance. Everybody thinks it's true.

By 1970 our family moved from Pennsylvania to Illinois. We lived so far away that we stopped visiting the farms in New York. But the sound of train whistles never left my mind. We lived in the town of Elburn when we moved to Illinois. The railroad cut through the heart of town. You could hear freight trains lonesome and determined roaring past day and night..

When I first commuted to the city of Chicago I begrudged the Metra trains the ability to define my daily schedule. Departure and arrival times meant loss of control and youthful freedom. In time my mind falsely melded the sound of freight train whistles with the thought of those daily commutes. Up at 6 a.m. to make the 6:45, the 7:10 or the 7:20, at the latest. Catch the 5:20 home if I hustled. It rankled me to lose those two-plus hours a day.

Over time it dawned on me that trains were not the cause of dissatisfaction in life. Those issues came from within, not without. I began to forgive trains their purpose. The romance of their whistles in the distance began to return. I recalled how train whistles once delivered a sense of place, the romance in being somewhere unique and the promise of going somewhere else if you wanted.

Then came the night train.

We live in Batavia now, the southernmost of the Tri-Cities on the Fox River. There used to be train tracks that ran north and south through along the river, on both sides. Most of them are now gone. But not all. There is a still a train line that skirts the north side of Fermi Lab, cuts through the city and curves down the east side of Batavia to reach the factories along

Route 25. Thanks to laws about public safety, every train that travels those tracks has to blow its whistle at every road crossing. It can sometimes take an hour for those trains to work their way through town. They sound short bursts of the horn as they go.

Even at its closest point, the night train is more than a mile away from our house. It can wake you up and keep you awake even with all the windows of the house closed. On summer nights with the windows open it sounds as if those trains are coming right through your bedroom.

As the train first rolls into town you hear the solemn first burst of that train whistle. Then it moves, ever so slowly, from one end of town to the other. The whole scenario plays through your mind whether you like it or not. Later that night or early the next morning the train comes back again, honking loud and fierce as some demented goose wandering stupidly through the farmyard.

The call of the night train is a form of aural anxiety, pressing into your brain, as do fearful thoughts. It even seems to bring on those types of emotions. When life is difficult already, or in some way challenging, the night train certainly does not help you find rest, nor peace. The sound travels to you as a single note in the night. It seems determined to find the company of other somber notes in the world.

Cancer is like that night train. There have been periods these last 6 years when cancer was not in the forefront of our existence. The night train of anxiety stayed away for a while. We relaxed. Upon return it rolled through our neighborhood honking away, persistent in its intrusion, forcing us to mentally ride along as it passes through our days and nights. Down to its destination and back. Honking. At. Every. Intersection.

We set out to chase away and silence the night train with chemotherapy. Sometimes the train whistle gets softer, even disappears for a time. But the truth is that you are never sure if the train has gone away entirely. We have friends who travel this road with us, who have faced the night train themselves. Remissions quell the noise but the tracks do remain.

For example, Linda has kept a port in her arm for many years. Occasionally I will brush it with my fingertips. It is a reminder that we're still riding the rails. My dear wife lives with it all the time. These are not the romantic tones of the train in the distance, full of promise, hope and romance. These are the calls of the night train, in which we all recognize our mortality.

The Bible tells us to be wise in recognizing the brevity of our lives, to be grateful for the present, for those we love, and the blessings of mind and heart. In some ways these admonitions resonate in popular culture. Carpe diem. Livestrong. That's what all this is about. All of it. Grace appreciated. Seize the day. Seek to thrive.

As for the night train in our lives, we'd really rather tear out the tracks and stop it cold in its tracks. At this very moment, we're still trying. Linda had an MRI this past week to check out this small, apparently inactive tumor that persists. Her CA-125 numbers are back to normal. Where they should be. Those are good-sounding words.

Today she is getting a PET scan. We've never had the opportunity to have that test before. That is good, yet a little scary. So prayers are welcome. The test will help the doctors study whether any cancer persists. There is a chance that it doesn't. We are after the one spot where things have focused during the last rounds and remove it through surgery. Those are all hopeful signs. We want to send the night train away and focus for a while on the sound of the train in the distance. We all hear it. We all know it's true. We just want to hear it on our own terms.

Funny things

Wednesday, November 16, 2011, 1:45 PM

A remarkable woman, my wife. Linda is going through a couple more procedures and waiting to hear results as another week goes by. She's been pretty patient through it all so perhaps it is no surprise that we've been trying to humor each other through the waiting.

Funny things are always good. Here's a few examples of things we have found funny recently.

At a conference last Saturday for her services hours related to preschool, Linda enjoyed a presentation by the Chalk Guy, Ben Glenn. He talks about ADD. She thinks he has helped her better understand a few things about the man to whom she is married.

The conversation following the conference turned out to be very funny in an instructional sort of way. We've kind of arrived at the fact that at the very least I have AADD. Artistic Attention Deficit Disorder. For example: Has anyone seen my keys? Both sets that I lost in a year? Anyone?

So during the conference, one of the class sessions involved a little interaction among the attendees. Instructions were given: "Turn to the person next to you and give them a compliment in some way..." the seminar leader said.

Two women turned to Linda and said, "We love your haircut and the color of your hair!"

To which Linda replied: "It's a wig!" She wiggled her hair with her hands. The two women sat open-mouthed for a moment. Linda assured them it was okay.

So that was kinda funny.

On Saturday night some friends had us over for dinner. Well, it actually started with me asking if I could come over and play guitars and drink beer. But then it evolved into dinner. We never broke out the guitars. So I felt sort of guilty for inviting ourselves over. Our hosts were gracious and seemed to have a good time anyway.

After a few beers, a couple glasses of wine and a really great dinner, nature called. I visited the bathroom and while standing there, noticed a little chinchilla talisman on the shelf above the toilet. (Yes, I put the seat back down. ADD or not).

I went back out to the dining room and asked, "Hey, what ever happened to your chinchillas?" They used to own chinchillas. soft, furry little critters about the size of a softball.

"Oh, man," our host said. "That got way out of control...the chinchillas thing."

"How so?" I asked.

"Well, we had two. We kept them in a closet because they like the dark. We keep our house cool in the winter and it turns out it was the perfect temperature to kick their breeding cycles into action. Pretty soon we had 20 chinchillas and some of them got away, into the walls. We had to gather them all up before they ate the house down. We have no more chinchillas."

That was a very furry, er, funny story. Funny is relative though.

Today I was talking with a friend at work about getting new business and we were both in agreement that it just doesn't work to ask close friends for referrals. It can be so awkward. I related a story I'd just heard about a fellow who lost his job but would not give up his country club membership no matter how tight their expenses became. Some men would rather golf and keep up their pride and appearances than eat.

On the surface it seemed a little warped, the apparent disconnect with reality exhibited by the man who had to have his country club. "That's sick," my friend said. Then we thought about it and agreed that sometimes going against logic is really important in life. Maybe keeping the country club membership was what could get him another job? One man's luxury is another man's necessity. That's funny in that life is funny sort of way.

Indeed there are many kinds of funny. Day to day we're looking for every kind of funny or we'll just go whacko waiting for this test or that result. I know my wife has always liked to laugh and sometimes I try to make her laugh but it's not easy, even on a normal day, because she's choosey about what she laughs about.

I see it as a challenge. She has very refined tastes in humor and interests. She will not laugh at funny if depends on stupid. Whereas I find stupid humor hilarious at times. Anyone who knows me can testify to that fact. I'll laugh at the goofy stuff that happens on *The Office* or *Parks and Recreation* and Linda does like those. She prefers the subtle teases and biting humor of shows where the humor is much more subtle.

My own humor can be stupid at times, and my kids picked up on certain dad jokes. My son had an interview for a graduate program and they asked him to cite a piece of personal advice he'd received and how he'd expound upon it. "You're only young once," he replied. "But you can be immature forever."

He learned that from me. It's one of the things I used to say, only partly in jest. It really isn't a bad life philosophy to follow, within reason. Bringing youth along you as you grow older? Calculated immaturity. Is that even possible? I dunno. I keep tryin'.

Of course there are times when it is not considered appropriate to act with immaturity or be funny. There are also times when it is absolutely vital to shoot for a laugh in order to keep your sanity in the face of absurd or difficult circumstances.

Ever seen that painting of the laughing Jesus? Perhaps it is accurate. I can't believe he went through life without a little laughter. So what if the Bible doesn't mention it? The Bible doesn't mention a lot of things. That doesn't mean they didn't happen, or never will. Even God must laugh once in a while. I figure he gets a chuckle out of watching me now and then. The moral of the story is that sometimes the more serious life gets, the more we're supposed to laugh at it all. Funny how that works.

Peak experiences

Tuesday, November 29, 2011, 9:45 AM

Climbing mountains is a literal "peak experience" you never forget. In 1984, when Linda and I were dating a couple years, we planned a camping trip to the Colorado Rockies.

We hiked from our campsite at Maroon Bells near Aspen, Colorado up to a mountain saddle at 12,800 feet. I was in the physical shape of my life, lean and fit during the most competitive period of my running career. By contrast, Linda had just had bunion surgery on her foot earlier that year. She's always been game for challenges, however, so we embarked on a trail that wound through aspen groves and then climbed on switchbacks up to the rocky saddle in the sky.

One of the reasons Linda was so eager for the trip west was to take a break from one of her roommates, who owned cats as I recall, and that was one strike against her in Linda's book. The woman was also difficult to live with in other ways. So the trip out West was a momentary break from life with Miss Bitchypants. That is, until we crested the mountain saddle, looked down the other steep precipice and saw, to our amazement, her roommate hiking up the opposite side of the mountain. We had no idea she and her boyfriend were headed the same place that summer.

We said a cordial if dumbfounded hello to her roommate, and then Linda and I shook our heads wondering out loud how that could have possibly happened. So our peak experience at reaching the top of the world--in our books anyway--was tempered by the realization that no matter where you go, reality lies in wait.

Up there in the thin air we also encountered a precocious fellow who for some random reason took a liking to us and snapped our photo up there in the mountains. Though the photo is now faded to the point you can hardly see the mountains in the background, we still have it. And what are pictures for? So you can remember peak experiences like climbing a mountain. Both photos and memories can fade. Yet depend on them for inspiration of a life beyond the mundane.

Linda and I had a little lunch at 12,800 feet and started the hike back down to our campsite. And hiked. And hiked. It was a long way back. Soon I noticed Linda was acting a little funny. She was walking kind of floppy-armed and starting to weave on the path. I gave her my water because she had already finished what she had. Then we kept on going. Pretty soon it was clear that Linda had altitude sickness. The kind that makes you not care about anything at all.

"C'mon, sweetie," I cajoled. "Let's keep going." We were basically alone hiking along a mountain stream. I was hoping to get her back to the campsite where she could recover.

"No, let's just sit here a while," she said. She looked more than a little relaxed and way more than a little dizzy.

"No, you get up now," I told her. Then I fed her our remaining water and we kept on moving. Linda barely made it back. It took a while for her to connect with reality again. But we made it. She was a tough girl then. She's a tough girl now.

A day later we were sitting in our tent when we heard thunder to the west and looked up to see cloud banks obscuring the mountaintops. We nearly didn't get into the tent before the skies opened and it rained and rained. We kid you not, it rained solid for the next 7 hours. Not just pittypat rain, either. This rain may have taken the mountains down in height an inch or two. Our tent floor was soaked through and small rivers were passing under us. We perched on our inflatable mattresses because everything else within reach was soaking wet.

We lay in that tent together all those hours experiencing the full range of emotions from laughter to tears to frustration and anger. I recall thinking, "If we can handle 7 hours pinned together in a tent, we can handle anything. Maybe even get married." I proposed the next spring and we were married that summer. That was a peak experience of course.

When the storm finally passed that day in the mountains we came out into the gathering night and watched the stars emerge. At that moment a boy of about 10 or 12 years old wandered over and told us his father and older brother were still climbing in the mountains and had not returned. We tried to assure the boy they'd be back. He did not look convinced.

All that night you could hear rockslides breaking free and crashing down from the mountains with a sinister roar. We knew the boy was sitting in the family van where his father and brother had left him. Finally, toward dawn we heard voices as his father and brother returned to camp. They were greeted by the boy's joyful voice. Yet the father was stern, scolding his son that he should have had faith they would return.

These are reminders that not all peak experiences in life are positive, happy or planned. Sometimes the difficulties in life are what make us feel real, challenged and alive. They teach us what's important, how to have faith despite frightening situations and why commitment is so important to long term success.

Of course you can also become too used to "living on the edge" when life puts you under constant stress. It is well known that soldiers returning from battle can have a hard time adjusting to civilian life. The heightened circumstances of war make everyday life seem boring and insignificant. While most of us never experience something as intense as combat stress, life can still dish it out sometimes.

Our souls are therefore deeply conflicted by the thrills and spills of life. One even wonders if we don't even go so far to subconsciously create our own little dramas at times, just to make life interesting. We seek a passage or path out of the mundane. The human need for stimulation and attention is so strong.

I do know this: My wife is a person who is indeed capable of living in the moment and would definitely have preferred to avoid the repeated dramas we've faced in our cancer journey. But there have been blessings as well.

It is yin and yang. But think; we'd suffered through 7 hours of confinement in a rainy tent, thinking we'd had the worst day possible. Then we emerged to find a young boy fearful that he'd lost his father in the stormy mountains. Can we all say amen to the fact that so often when we think we know suffering, it is mostly a matter of our own, limited perspective?

That is not to say that our problems will all automatically go away if we have a little more faith. It means we have an obligation to think, and pray, have patience and seek wisdom and support in all circumstances, be they joyful or in pain.

So let us visit yet another landscape, that of physical health. Last week we learned that Linda's PET scan and colonoscopy showed that the cancer is confined, so far as we currently know, to a small tumor near her colon. So we do need surgery to remove that remaining tumor. We must hope there is no other active cancer. The doctor will go in and look around to determine if that is the case. If the road is clear he'll remove the tumor, resection the colon and Linda can rehab a while. Hopefully the colon resection can be done and full function restored. If not, we're prepared to address that in other ways. The surgery is December 12. Your prayers and good thoughts are appreciated.

The ideal world would be successful surgery to remove the tumor, which will also give the doctor the opportunity to fix the hernia that developed following surgery a few years. If all goes well that would put us on the road to health and recovery. And that would be a peak experience indeed.

Checkups

Saturday, December 3, 2011, 10:45 AM

It's a dank and rainy Saturday, but I did get out for a run this morning. Actually I like dank weather for running. I used to compete best when it was slightly nasty out. It's like it draws the focus down to what really matters in the moment.

That's always been hard for me in some respects, living in the moment. Or at least, as time has gone by it has become a little more difficult to achieve contentment. It's like there's always something tugging at me. Obligations. If not those, then objectives. It can be hard to tell the two apart sometimes. That's always a challenge in fact.

Many people who get to know their minds a little better as they get to certain points in life, I've realized there was always anxiety at work in my head. Explains a lot of things, really, once you put all the signals together. And thanks to some counseling last fall through Living Well Cancer Resource Center I've been learning to forgive myself a little more. Not put so much pressure on my mind with regrets or lost opportunities. What have you. Like John Lennon once sang, "The one thing you can't hide...is when you're crippled inside..."

I even checked into a research study on anxiety and depression with Rush hospital recently, to see if it would be beneficial to participate in a study on human emotion and such. I don't know if you know anyone susceptible to depression and anxiety, but having served on a committee with the NAMI organization and keeping up with stories in the news about the number of people worldwide who fight depression, it is sobering to realize how much our society struggles with these issues.

In a book I read recently about two world-class runners, Dick Beardsley and Alberto Salazar, it was fascinating to learn that Salazar fought depression for years. When he finally got treatment, it changed his life. For years he'd been unhappy and unable to find contentment in the moment. His running failed. But a light went on for him when he received medication to help manage his depression.

Interestingly, he was one who always competed best in the rain. Sometimes our efforts can be enhanced by a matching mood.

Through our entire journey together, Linda and I have had to work through emotional challenges. We are thankful we have had support in so many ways. Through friends. Through faith and prayer. Through counseling. Through events and acts of kindness we can hardly describe. Miracles small and large. Seriously.

It was interesting to sit through the interviews at Rush and consider the questions they asked. There is after all no solid DNA test for emotional diagnosis. The best anyone can do is ask questions and put together a picture of where you fit on an emotional scale. I did not qualify for any of their studies for a number of reasons. It turns out I'm not likely manic-depressive, although I do get a little enthusiastic about things at times. I'm not bipolar either. That's a most difficult emotional challenge for anyone.

The one depression drug I tried a year ago just about made me crazy. It was not a good scene. 5 days of increasingly fidgety and finally manic behavior taught me that some things just aren't worth it, if not downright bad for you.

Which is what made my ride home from Rush an amazing circumstance. I listened to a radio interview with Dr. Andrew Weil on a public radio station. He talked about how a lot of drugs for depression and anxiety are not that effective. In fact some (the seratonin inhibitors?) actually prolong real depression rather than end it. Yikes. He went on to describe how certain Omega-3 fish oils are better with mood control.

Weil is a real proponent of natural over chemical therapies. He talked at length how one of the main reasons people can't find contentment is that our food and the way our culture works with so much sitting and material focus and lack of contact with nature mix up our poor little brains and make us a pack of discontents. That sounds pretty real to me. I know my happiness surges when I'm out in the woods, thinking open thoughts and not fighting others over who's right and who's wrong. But human society places so much value on those things, and we get sucked in.

Then Weil talked about the importance of thought practice. Not just "positive thinking" but real discipline and setting yourself up to anticipate those thought cycles that can lead to negative thinking and produce (or result) in depression.

But don't get this message wrong. Depression is real. It is emotional pain. It can be chronic and disabling. So can anxiety. Throughout human history many great people have fought these problems, to which some people are predisposed. Seasonally some people grown weary with life. Age can wear the coating off our wiring. Events. Conflict. Fatigue. Poor health. Loss. All these things can result in temporary or permanent depression. My wife had a bout with depression after she found out about the first recurrence of her cancer. She required attentive care and some meds to help her manage the reverberations of emotional shock. But we got through it together.

So acknowledge how you are feeling. It is important to talk about it. You can do something about it. And should.

Those of us who are wired to be anxious from birth often build up a vortex of prior associations that can serve as triggers to bad feelings about ourselves. If those cycles are furthered by difficult family relationships they can become a sort of permanent fixture in our makeup. Overcoming those patterns requires an interesting mix of emotional tools. Forgiveness is one that Andrew Weil mentioned. That has been a major force of change in my life. Forgiving those with whom you might be angry or fearful is an incredible tool for personal growth. Because truly our anger and frustration is our own personal drama, and not necessarily just. We create personal narratives that aren't all that positives. Sometimes we come to believe in these narratives a little too much. Even faith is at risk of being corrupted in that way.

Gratitude is the next biggest force for change in mental health. Andrew Weil said there is strong evidence for "secular spirituality" in the power of gratitude to create better mental health. It is no cliché to say that gratitude produces a much more positive mental framework. It helps you achieve contentment, for one thing. And in this world and this economy, with all those messages of conflict over money and class warfare coming our way, knowing how to be content (which is different than complacent, the two are actually opposites in some ways) is key. If not the key...to happiness, then to manage your life in a way where you are not constantly anxious about tomorrow and tomorrow.

The bible says God tells us not to worry. Is that not the most difficult assignment in the world sometimes? Worry arrives like a shadow. It follows us around. There is always something to worry about if you try. Even if you don't. Worry is like an extra layer of clothes you do not need. It just makes you hot and bothered.

So is the solution to get naked? In a way, yes. We lay ourselves emotionally bare whenever we confess our fears or ask others for help. In a world that tells us we have to be constantly strong, it takes real strength to admit sometimes that you are weak. The Lord loves weakness in us however, because it exposes our soul, our true being, the un-calculated us that God wants to nurture. Friends recognize this need. And we should strive to recognize, but also respect it in others. That leads to trust, which can produce hope, and thus healing. You might describe this process as the ultimate checkup.

So as we head into this surgery for Linda, we're both working on not worrying. There are lots of what-ifs and who-zits. I'm trying to be sensitive and open with Linda, to support her going in and coming through her surgery. We recognize that until the doctors get in there and decide whether the tumor can be removed safely, along with decisions about the practicality of colon resection, we literally don't know what the future holds.

We do know that Linda is healthy (yay!) and in a largely positive (smooch!) frame of mind. That's thanks to all your help, the work of the doctors and effectiveness of chemotherapy. But on the 12th we'll pray they can do the colon resection and then we wait a few months while recovering, Then they'll go back in briefly and hook things back up. That's the plan. God help us out!

It's a bit more than a checkup, for sure. But to these doctors who do this all the time, it's another day at the office. A highly skilled, medically trained office, to be sure. But it's a form of checkup just the same. Here's hoping for good results.

Sharing the island

Sunday, December 11, 2011, 8:30 PM

Monday, December 12 Linda is having surgery to remove the remaining tumor. The procedure will like also involve a colon resection as well as repair of a hernia that has been a progressive problem the last year or so. We pray these procedures and recovery go well.

We hope you understand the value of being able to share our experience through these words. The purpose of this site is twofold: to manage practical caregiving and also to consider the emotional and relational aspects of this journey.

I've always communicated your replies of support to Linda, and we appreciate the upcoming schedule of meals. We may need some visitors as she goes through recovery with a likely sore tummy and more. We'll keep you posted on those requests as group coordinator Linda Culley and I have discussed what will work best. But we're going to play it by ear for a week or so.

Our trips through cancer treatment have been challenging, for sure. Which got me thinking about what it's like to be immersed in this process. It occurred to me that it's a bit like being stuck on an island, the proverbial "desert island" or maybe something a little bigger, where you have to be both resolute and practical to get along.

That led to thoughts of other islands, and one in particular. In 2007, on recommendation of a neighbor, Linda and I started watching episodes of the television serial drama LOST as she went through chemo that winter. The show lasted 6 seasons or so and focused on a set of characters stranded on a jungle island in the Pacific Ocean.

We'd huddle together on the living room couch and enter a world where everyone seemed to have huge problems in life, dire events or circumstances in their past that defined them as people.

But many of those LOST characters had redeeming qualities as well. The swarthy hard-guy Sawyer turned out to be a good husband when given the chance. Murderous Kate turned into a doting mother when she wound up caring for the child of a woman friend who died on the island. The driven physician Jack finally learned to give of himself to others.

My favorite character Juliet struggled with the impact of her choices. Linda's favorite character Hugo tried to reconcile his good fortune with a tortured soul.

Hugo seemed like he belonged on Gilligan's Island, not LOST. His good nature and rotund physique were endearing. He tried to look for the good in people. But of course was sometimes disappointed.

On LOST people did finally get off the island only to find out their lives were no simpler back at home where their flawed natures still haunted them. Others returned to seemingly good circumstances only to be drawn, wistfully, back to the island where they had begun to discover their true selves. Some swore they'd never go back, yet wound up drawn into the vortex anyway.

Ultimately LOST turned into a story of redemption. As the plot unfolded, we saw the redeeming qualities in each LOST character emerge through events that broke them down and in some cases, rebuilt their personalities almost from scratch.

By the time the show ended, it was the bittersweet moments in the life of every character that drove the narrative. The message was that all of us are, in some ways, bound to be broken and rebuilt.

Many characters traveled back and forth through time. Some started a whole new life in another time dimension only to be jerked back into the "present," changed by their newfound knowledge about life. In many respects, LOST resembled the Chronicles of Narnia, the Christian-themed series of children's books in which the decades that passed in Narnia amounted to mere seconds back home.

Fans of LOST deeply analyzed the series looking for hidden clues of meaning and symbolism. It all came back to the idea that the island as a force of attraction and redemption. It was definitely a place where people were forced to find out about themselves. LOST characters also had to keep up with some strange temporal realities, such as the fact that the island literally moved now and then. That part of the plot has symbolic significance if you think about it. There are many things in life that seem fixed or genuine that really are not. There are also times in life when things show up that we simply don't expect. Those "islands" can turn out to be friends with whom we've lost touch, only to be found again. Or they can be traumatic events, such as the loss of a parent or friend.

Many of us will deal with cancer in our lives, or in someone close to us. It is now projected that 1 in 3 people nationwide will face cancer at some point in life. If it shows up, you are essentially forced to live on that island for a while. That can prove to be isolating, or a difficult place to describe to others. Fortunately we've come a long way in how we view cancer thanks to education, advocacy and compassion. But the most important thing we've learned is that it's often possible to live with cancer, even become a survivor. That's where the genuine support of others can really come into play, because it really helps to have help when you need it.

And helping others has its own rewards. That's how the phrase "There but for the grace of God go I…" transforms into "I will go and share the grace (or peace, or hope, or love, the possibilities are endless…) of God with them…"

Even if you are not a religious person, you can understand the importance of "sharing the island" with someone facing cancer. When I was 35 friend of mine aged 25 got testicular cancer. He had surgery to remove one testicle and all his lymph glands. I went to visit him after the surgery. It was a great effort at first for that young man to walk down his sidewalk and back. Then he made it around the block. Then the went on his first run. He went on to father three children and to become a teacher and a coach state champions in track and field. This past year he was the head coach of a football team that won a state championship.

See, it's the small things that sometimes help, to get us started back on the road to recovery. Working together helps us all survive. Lord knows cancer is not the only challenge in life.

Sometimes it helps to sit around on the island of our cares and share a laugh. Even the characters on Gilligan's Island taught us things about loss, love, discovery and tolerance. Not Shakespeare, but life lessons come in many forms.

Perhaps you've also seen the island movie Castaway in which the character played by Tom Hanks winds up stranded on a Pacific atoll with nothing to survive on but the junky remains from a crashed Federal Express plane. Ultimately the Hanks character besmirches and befriends a volleyball he names Wilson. The ball becomes a mute yet needed companion.

Finally the castaway is able to assemble a sailboat out of debris he's collected. He sails the boat through a wall of surf enclosing the island, then drifts in the oceans until a freighter in a Pacific shipping lane rescues him.

When the Hanks character gets back home he finds life has a strange quality to it. Even people he loved had given him up for lost. It is hard for people to relate to this prodigal man. Ultimately the Hanks character is forced to accept a new version of himself and move on. It turns put that the cliché "no man is an island" is not the entire story. It's what you do on the island that really counts. Faith and gratitude really do matter. Even if things do not always go the way you expect them to, having faith and hope can keep you alive, to survive. And even thrive.

Those of us faced with cancer can't claim special insight from the process, but it does teach the value of family and friends, and also honesty, humility, love and hope. Those are good things to have on any island.

Surgery Success!

Monday, December 12, 2011, 3:15 PM

Greetings to all.

Let's just say our prayers have been answered. Linda is in recovery now and will be in the hospital the next 5-7 days. But here is some joyful news.

The surgeons report that the tumor has been taken out and there were no other signs of cancer in her body.

The resection of the colon was performed successfully and reattached. So no colostomy. Linda's hernia has also been repaired. I gotta tell ya friends, there are good days and there are bad days. This is a good day.

Obviously Linda will be working through some pain during recovery. That's a lot of fixing to do on one person. But I know my wife well, and the good news will sustain her through the next few days. We pray there are no complications of any sort of course.

So say a hallelujah with us!

Because in the last few days we were trying to process next steps and come to grips with how life might be changing. We know our situation could be manageable if those changes needed to come. There were no certain outcomes here. We know that people do great under many circumstances... and appreciating life is what matters most. We've always tried to do that. But obviously given the challenges over the last few years we also appreciate that life might be simpler without certain procedures to attend.

So we rejoice. The tumor is gone. The hernia fixed. All these things we dared to pray for have happened.

So many thanks to all of you. Please pray that Linda can work through recovery with success and manage discomfort. They tell me they'll have her up on her feet as early as tomorrow. She always looks so snappy in those compression socks.

Can't wait to share the news with her. And maybe a bunch of flowers. God Bless. Thanks so much. And hallelujah

Abs of Steel

Saturday, December 17, 2011, 8:00 PM

Well, it's Saturday night and I'm happy to report my wife is getting her sense of humor back.

Today while visiting Linda at Lutheran General, Linda held her stomach in with her hands while coughing and my daughter Emily joked, "Mom, you're going to have abs of steel."

Linda glanced at me, recalling the staples that now line the incision up the length of her left abdomen and said, "I already have abs of steel."

That's my girl.

She is also quite the specimen in the eyes of the surgeons and residents who attended her surgery. Apparently the job they did on Linda's colon resection is considered "textbook." So she's sort of a rock star among the residents. The nurses have all loved her fortitude in getting back on her feet so quick.

So it's nice to get some positive feedback at the end of what was definitely a challenging week.

Linda is no fan of pain medicine. It makes her loopy. She doesn't like that. How she puts up with me is a whole different question, but we'll deal with that another day. I've learned to make lists.

But if you don't use the pain medicine it is pretty difficult to recover from surgery. Every move causes you pain, and they don't want you sitting there sedentary. So it's a tradeoff.

So she grudgingly popped the "anti-pain" button before major moveabouts and rehabilitation exercises. The first couple days were some kind of ouchy. The simple act of breathing into a tube to exercise her lungs was sometimes excruciating.

By the time I went home Wednesday morning Linda was starting to sit in chairs and gingerly move about on her own. By Wednesday afternoon her sister Diane was walking the floor with her. The whole goal is to stimulate the internal organs and get them to settle back into place. If you don't know much about abdominal surgery they basically move your intestines out onto the table and put them back in again. So it takes the body a while to get its bearings back. Its been said the gut has a mind of its own. Hence the phrase "gut feelings." We're feeling it.

Beyond that information we'll leave it to your imagination as not everyone has a stomach for medical information.

As Linda increased her walking distance the kind nurses around the corridor spoke encouraging words. Residents checked in with Linda at 4:30 a.m. (don't know how they do it) followed by her doctors at 6:30 a.m. Two surgeons worked on her; one to remove the tumor and repair her hernia, the other to do the colon resection. All wanted to check on their patient. Then the nurses take over again with blood tests, checking heart rate and oxygen levels, and dealing with a fever that cropped up overnight on Wednesday. Blessedly all those transitional problems seemed to pass.

Her colon doctor is a man of firm resolve and he would not let Linda be complacent. "Up and at 'em" is his motto, and so she went.

Linda's brother Paul and sister Diane made visits during the week as well, which proceeded with challenges of an entirely different nature. This week Linda's father Mel encountered problems following a surgery to relieve fluid around his heart and lungs. He's had health problems since last April when he had heart surgery that led to overall fluid buildup in his body, and ultimately kidney dialysis.

On Tuesday following Linda's surgery, her father was still at Elmhurst Hospital following chest surgery to relieve the pressure on his lungs. But he ran into problems and had to be fitted with a breathing tube. That meant severe difficulty all day Wednesday and Thursday. Obviously the emotional concern for her father was tough on Linda.

Of course her family and I wanted to be honest with her, yet not make her worry unnecessarily. So the job was to communicate her father's situation without being melodramatic. And vice versa; it seems her dad was still quite worried about Linda. Collectively we spent a lot of time walking hospital hallways trying to maintain decent cell phone reception to manage conversations as we tried to figure out just what was happening on both fronts.

The double medical challenge made things tough for everyone. But we stuck together and kept communication up, especially to our son and daughter, who were obviously concerned both for their mother and grandfather. Meanwhile daughter Emily was immersed in mid-terms at Augustana while Evan was scheduled to take the GMATs for graduate school on Thursday. We encouraged them to focus on these objectives and promised to keep them in the loop on everyone's health.

Fortunately Linda made rapid recovery going into the weekend. But the kids still wanted to come out and see both their grandpa and mom, so Friday evening Emily drove home and on Saturday Evan took a train to Villa Park on Saturday where we picked him up and headed to Elmhurst on the first stop of the hospital tour.

It was good news on Saturday to see Mel Mues more expressive and responsive. The respiratory therapist even told us his breathing tube was dialed to do less work for him so that he could possibly transition to independent breathing again.

It's going to be a bit of a different Christmas for us all this year. But we're all good. For several years now during the holidays we've been focusing more on the closeness of our family and this week certainly highlighted the strength of those bonds. Linda's mother Joan has had to be strong in spirit, hope and faith to bear up under months of caregiving for her husband. And the family and our friends have lifted Linda and I, Evan and Emily. And so grateful we are for that care.

You might say it takes intestinal fortitude to love life when it presents gut-wrenching challenges. That is why, when you're tested in matters of the heart, it can indeed pay to have abs of steel.

It's likely/possible Linda will be coming home Monday after visiting with the doctors.

Sunday visit?

Sunday, December 18, 2011, 7:30 AM

A last-minute quickie request. If any of you in this community has a little time today or this afternoon, it would be helpful if you wanted to pay a visit to Linda. She's doing very well and is in good spirits, but would probably appreciate a visitor or two.

Lutheran General is on Dempster in Park Ridge. Two ways to get there: From I-88 take 294 north and exit on Dempster east. The hospital is about one mile east.

I'm headed to church, then my dad's house and doing some Christmas shopping. Haven't had time for that.

Coming home

Sunday, December 18, 2011, 10:00 AM

Linda just called...after having breakfast! and said the doctors are sending her home this afternoon. So I'm headed up there at 11:00 because she said, "Come early...." as she's had enough hospital time, thank you.

So no need for afternoon visits after all!

Nurses, literally and figuratively

Tuesday, December 20, 2011, 5:30 PM

Two days after my wife's surgery I woke early to head west and pick up our dog to go home and check on the house. Stepping onto the elevator I encountered two tired-looking nurses leaning on the back wall.

"Shift over?" I asked.

"Yes," one of them breathed, trying not to look too relieved.

"Well, I admire your work," I told them. "Patients can be a pain in the butt, I'm sure."

"You said it, not me!" one of them replied as they headed out the elevator and down the hallway, exchanging knowing glances.

Nursing is no easy gig, of course. Nothing in the medical profession really is.

They see so much, both literally and figuratively. Nursing is the most intimate of all professions. Even more so than being a doctor, in some ways. From inserting catheters to administering shots to washing patients who can't wash themselves, nurses see humanity up close and personal.

There are also broader dimensions. Families in crisis. Human frailty laid bare. The human condition. On those dynamics rest hopes of healing. That is why medicine exists, and nurses carry it out to the best of their abilities.

Of course nurses deal with varied results and varied perceptions of their profession. Not having worked in the medical field, I do not entirely know what the environment is like. But some nurses I've met speak of doctors that do not treat them well, or show respect. Maybe the pecking order at some hospitals is harsh. Yet the good hospitals seem to celebrate every role from orderly to surgeons. And there really are some great hospitals in the area where we live. We can be grateful for that. And this is no paid testimonial.

I'll reiterate: When we think about who provides a great amount of the care and recovery in medicine, we should never forget to thank the nurses, both men and women. There was Allan, and Silvia, Rafaela and Kathy. the list goes on. All with attributes that add up to good care.

Because nursing is basically professional caregiving, it is something to observe when you've been placed in the role of caregiver yourself.

The challenging part is that the tools have advanced but the needs have not changed. The records have gone digital. The ability to monitor patients is so sophisticated. Yet it is still the human responsibility of nurses to read those signs and pass them back along the chain for the doctors and surgeons to study. Front line. First responders. In tune. In touch. That's the role of nurses.

It is a cosmopolitan profession. The nursing professionals in the four or five hospitals with which we have had experience is quite racially diverse. Hospitals seem to hire nurses to match the culture and backgrounds of their constituent populations. But not always.

Language is another important aspect of nursing. For example, at the network hospital where Linda had her surgery, the primary phone greeting is given in several Eastern European languages. Diversity is not some casual thing at a hospital. It really can mean life or death.

Style of communication is also important in nursing. Some nurses excel in this category, with a gift for compassion that is comforting and encouraging. Others are more business-like, and their attributes can be of tremendous value in many circumstances. Linda's chemo nurse this time around was a focused woman whose competency and organization were of great assurance. Success in chemotherapy treatment can depend on the nurse's ability not only to administer the medicine, but also to track and monitor patient response in real time (daily response to treatment, blood counts and side effects) and over the course of treatments (chemo tolerance and patient affect) these attenuations add up. Literally and figuratively.

Getting chemo really is like running a marathon; checking your vitals along the way, taking aid at the proper points and pacing your effort so you don't falter. Chemo is a marathon.

But surgery is a sprint of sorts. Our surgeons fixed a hernia, did a colon resection and removed a 31mm cancer tumor in about 2.5 hours. That's fast, and brilliant work. You can worship athletes all you want. Medical doctors like these deserve real accolades.

It is the nurses however who are the trainers that get you back into shape after the taxing sprint of surgery or the exhausting marathon of chemo. With cancer sometimes you need both to be successful. Fast twitch and slow twitch.

That and a sense of perspective and humor helps. I was really glad the people at the nursing station had a sense of humor when after the first night at the hospital I trundled out of Linda's room at 5:00 a.m. to visit the bathroom down the hall. No one looks dignified at that hour, and I felt a little like a college freshman in a "walk of shame" down the dormitory hall after an all-nighter. But no one said a word. They see weirder things every day. Lucky for me, a bald man seldom has bad hair days.

Nurses see it all of course, the whole range of human foible. Being able to encourage patients with an occasional jest about the difficulties of recovery can break the ice and open channels in working through pain or other humbling issues such as finding ways to go to the bathroom when it is far from easy and convenient for the patient. All this basic stuff,. They have to know when and how to be light about it, and when not.

Nurses are the professionals who get it all going for people again, over and over. Week after week. Year after year. Think of all the focus and dedication it takes to be a nurse for 5, 10 or 25 years. And people do it.

The nurse who checked Linda out of the hospital has been working in the same phase of nursing for 25 years. She was immensely practical and detail-oriented, dispensing instructions so that we would know how to care for the surgical wounds and tend to bathroom matters the right way. That nurse fit her job.

A young nurse named Rafaela checked on Linda regularly during her week in the hospital. She seemed to appear like magic from around the curtain whenever there was a need in the room. That nurse excelled in care.

The first night after surgery, Linda's nurse was a soft-spoken woman who struck up a conversation starting with a compliment about the fact that I was staying overnight with my wife. Perhaps it is not so common for people to stay over. The new Planetree model for health care offers a more humanistic approach to medicine and facilities, especially hospitals. Hospitals now provide comfortable couches that convert into beds so that family or supportive friends can stay overnight with a patient.

I can tell you that's a huge improvement from the night spent next to her bed back in 2007 when the only available place to sleep next to her was something like a Medieval torture device. The vinyl recliner on which I slept formed a pronounced hump approximately the curve of a mature dolphin in mid jump. It was not the most comfortable night of sleep in my life, punctuated as well by beeps and whistles and the bustle of nurses hustling in and out for blood pressure checks and temperature readings. They were just doing their job, yet I felt like it was a tortuous night of sleep deprivation in a black site somewhere in Eastern Europe. I exaggerate, but when you're tired the mind works overtime.

To her everlasting credit, my mother-in-law, who had done overnight duty on the dolphin chair the previous evening tried giving me fair warning without scaring me off completely. Let us simply say that it was one of the 3 worst nights of sleep in my life. The top 2 were surviving a bad bout of the flu and there was one very long night in the late 1980s when a prostate infection made my lower abdomen feel like I'd swallowed an angry serpent. I don't really want finish listing a Top 10. The memories are too painful. The dolphin chair simply had to do in that instance. Such are the duties of caregivers at times. It's like God wants to humble you into sympathy for the patient.

Now I thank God in advance for Planetree.

Still, as a caregiver, I do lose patience in too many situations, grow irrationally embittered by circumstance or fall too quickly into self pity or worse, anger or depression. What is the cure for those selfish emotions? Mostly, it's gratitude. Step back and take a breath. Be a nurse to your own soul. Forgive yourself. Then get back to service.

It's a miraculous little dynamic that when we fix our focus on serving others we wind up serving our own true best interests. That's where we learn we are not alone in our challenges and our minds off our own problems.

People who through simple self-control and a modest demeanor exhibit such patience always amaze me. Admittedly I envy people like that, especially when failing to manage that level of self control myself. Where do some people get such strength of character? Can it be learned? Are some people just natural caregivers?

Probably those questions cheapen the issue. It is of course a complex combination of things that makes people good caregivers, or nurses, or doctors. Or perhaps it is simplicity that makes it possible. Be content. Learn to give. Don't make life harder than it needs to be.

When it comes to institutional compassion, that is a goal much harder to achieve in some respects. The hospital where Linda had her surgery communicates its compassionate values in many ways. If I recall correctly, one of the messages posted on the wall reads, "We welcome all to this place of healing." There's definitely room for a religious message in there, but not an exclusive one. As it turns out, our nation is actually formed on a similar, inclusive ambiguity. So uniquely American. Yet people seem to miss the subtlety in that. Want to turn it into an ideology not in keeping with the Constitution which guarantees freedom of religion and freedom from religion.

We are all equal souls. Nurses probably know that better than most. There's nothing special about any of our functions. We all poop and pee. We all have a heartbeat. Breathe. Think. Cry out in pain. Laugh. Worry. Hope. Heal if possible. All part of the process. Such is humanity.

You know that cynical phrase, "some people are more equal than others..." Well, a nurse cannot afford to think like that. People notice if that sort of thinking creeps in.

When it's your wife or your husband, your son or daughter, close friend or even co-worker, you want the hospital and doctors and nurses taking care of them to do their very best to help them get well. It simply cannot matter whether someone is one race or the other, speaks Russian instead of English, or has no money to pay for the care they need.

I can tell you we have been the beneficiaries of such care, in ways that absolutely flabbergasted our ability to comprehend the many forces working behind the scenes to ensure our welfare. The least we can do in response to this grace and these blessings is what? Give back in any way we can. Pay attention to those taking care of us. Express our appreciation.

And guess what? Opportunities to reach out come up more often than you might think. It is true that when you are in a position of most vulnerability, you are best able to share in the pain and challenge in other people's lives.

Our nurse during Linda's first night in recovery from surgery was so caring and attentive that conversation naturally flowed to discussion of family and friends. It turns out our nurse was a single mom whose husband left her for another woman, leaving her to raise her two children alone. She was frustrated by how hard it was as a working mother--also attending graduate school--to meet someone, a man she could grow to love. She had nearly given up hope, she told us. Even the men on the Christian dating services turned out to be less than honorable.

It's a story quite familiar to my wife who over the years has worked with dozens of families and single moms in her job as a preschool teacher. At one point after checking up on Linda, conversing while she worked, our nurse stopped and stood in the middle of the room, seeming to want to gather herself before moving on to other duties. We'd been talking about how she gave so much time to raise her kids, got them to rehearsals and practices and games. But how it was all worth it in the end because it keeps them busy even if it wears her out.

We talked of God and faith, too. She shared several of her favorite Bible passages with us. We told her we'd recently been in a bible course where we read the entire book in 90 days. "Oh, I don't think I could do that," she sighed.

"12 pages a day," Linda assured her.

I admitted. "I didn't keep up and had to hustle to finish."

We encouraged her that all her work as a mom was worth it. That her children would turn out to be a blessing to her for her dedication. "Yes, I know," she murmured. "But I have had to sacrifice a lot."

Then she stood quietly in the middle of the room, seeming to contemplate her place in the universe,. Standing in front of the privacy curtain and silhouetted by the light from the hallway behind her, our nurse stood and stared across the room, soaking up the relative stillness until she said quietly, "Well, God Bless you guys."

It's impossible to know the exact circumstances people face, or how they truly feel. Linda turned to me after our nurse had left and said, "She reminds me of so many single moms I've met, just "poured out" from having to do everything themselves. Wanting to be filled up spiritually."

We met a veritable parade of nurses the following 5-6 days. All types of people and styles of care. Some were talkative. Others were focused and efficient. All played a brief yet important role in our lives. We can only hope that in some small way we give back to these people who daily give so much of themselves. Nurses literally and figuratively rule as far as we're concerned.

PS: Linda's home and recovering well now. Thanks to those who are checking in on her. Our needs are not many but there are a few things we'll post on the calendar. Merry Christmas and Happy New Year.

Please pray for Linda's father who is at Elmhurst Memorial in continuing recovery from a number of procedures related to breathing, heart function and dialysis. He's a wonderful man who will not likely be at home for Christmas. But his spirit and the traditions he so loves on the holidays will emanate through all we do. God Bless you Melvin Mues.

Hello and Happy New Year

Monday, January 2, 2012, 9:45 AM

Hope you have all been able to enjoy some time with family and friends.

We were able to spend Christmas with our family and New Year with friends with whom we've celebrated the New Year in many fun ways over the years. They were with Linda the night I met her in 1981 and are such fun people. This year after dinner we capped the night with a delicious, amazing cake from a chocolatier in Geneva as well as a nightcap drink called Carrot Cake. Just fun!

Linda's had a challenge with energy at times the last couple weeks but making good progress following surgery. A few days ago we received a call from a "new friend" who made an interesting observation. He told us that he once worked in the operating room and the rule of thumb according to the surgeons was one month of recovery time for every hour you were in surgery. That's a helpful thing to think about in not rushing the process.

We've had some very nice time with our children, Evan and Emily who were home for Christmas. Em has one more week home before heading back to Augustana College. She spent New Year's with Evan in the city and they seemed to have a great time.

We do ask prayers for Linda's father Melvin Mues. You may recall that earlier this year (in April) her father required heart surgery and had severe challenges in recovery including leg swelling and chest fluid that led the doctors to begin dialysis.

His breathing has long been impacted as well, and he's lost so much weight. Fortunately we've have much time to visit him at home and in the hospital. He will be entering palliative care this week. Mel is a caring, loving man who has given of himself to others his whole life. We pray in thanks and love for the gift of his life to all of us, to the church he serves and for everyone that knows him.

Linda has specifically told me to thank you all for your prayers and support through this journey. May God Bless your New Year.

Update

Monday, January 2, 2012, 1:15 PM

Linda's wonderful father and mentor to all of us, Melvin Mues, passed away at 12:20 p.m. today.

Our family will obviously miss this tremendously caring, loving man. His kindness and wisdom runs through all our lives. And while it hurts to know that he will no longer be with us in body, he definitely is and always will be with us in spirit.

I cannot write an obituary for the man here. It would take too long. But he knew how to live life well, and that is the greatest gift of all.

Funeral arrangements are being made and will be announced.

This faithful, strong and sensitive man is now with God, and that is our strength. We will miss you Melvin Mues. And next 4th of July on your birthday we will light up the sky in your honor, as we have always done, and always will. God Bless.

A fitting eulogy for Mel Mues (by Evan Cudworth)

posted by Christopher Cudworth, Friday, January 6, 2012, 6:45 PM

Today we laid to rest Linda's father, Melvin Mues. The funeral followed the wake yesterday where we were busy greeting friends and family members. It has been a privilege to celebrate the life of this gentle, caring man and it is amazing how many great things you learn about someone through others.

During the funeral service today at St. Paul Lutheran in Addison our son Evan delivered a fitting, stirring eulogy for his grandfather. With his permission the words are provided here.

***

"Life can't be all bad when for ten dollars you can buy all the Beethoven sonatas and listen to them for ten years."

This is supposedly a quote by William F. Buckley, Jr., a man of great wit whom my grandfather admired. I say "supposedly" because, despite my repeated efforts over the past few days (including asking a University of Chicago librarian) I was unable to find a hard source linking this quote to Buckley. It sounds like something he'd say--and by He I mean Buckley--but I'm just as content attributing this quote to my Grandpa Mues.

On its surface the quote appears to be about Beethoven. Grandpa loved classical music, and I consider my appreciation for classical music to be among the greatest gifts he gave to me. Between Diane, my sister, and I, how he and Grandma managed to sit patiently through so many amateur performances of Dvorak's "New World Symphony" remains a beautiful mystery to all of us.

But the quote isn't solely about Beethoven's music. It's also implicitly about something else Grandpa loved: economics. And not the economics we hear about these days on TV, but the actual physical production of goods and services; the tiny things we take for granted. From his days on the farm, to radio work in the Pacific, almost every story he told was an opportunity to illuminate for us the intricate yet invisible workings of this world. Even when his stories were about oscillating drill bits that only Paul could understand.

However, when you stop to think about it, the fact that we can buy a CD for $10 and listen to the same performance for 10 years is incredible. Because it's not just the musicians and the record companies bringing us Beethoven--literally thousands of people across the globe have to collaborate to produce and then mold the plastic, encode the disk, design the cover art, deliver it to the store--all for a reasonable price. Grandpa understood and appreciated all of these things. An insatiable thirst for knowledge is the second great gift Grandpa gave me.

Finally, this quote is, miraculously, about time. Ten years of Beethoven. But is ten years enough? 20? 50? I knew my grandfather for 25 wonderful years. With him I spent 25 Christmases, 25 4th of July birthdays, and countless pre-dinner prayers of thanks. Of course there will never be enough time with the ones we love, but we have so many things to be thankful for. Grandpa had a gift for setting the tempo just right--so that every minute we spent together as a family (and even those we spent apart) felt warmly deliberate. This was a marvelous gift.

I owe Grandpa many, many things; and I'll miss him greatly. However, life can't be all bad when for 25 of his 83 years, I had the opportunity to share in the wisdom and love of Melvin

Mues.

Life is life. Let's live it well.

Wednesday, January 18, 2012, 1:00 PM

One of the most interesting aspects of being involved with a person going through cancer treatment is learning how other people view your experience.

Often people are curious and quite kind in inquiring how things are going. Are things okay? Is the patient feeling better? How are you holding up?

Also something rather sweet often happens. Wanting to commiserate, people frequently find themselves moved to share some of their own life challenges. And 9 times out of 10 it seems they finish their stories with, "Of course it's nothing compared to what you guys are going through. I don't know how you do it."

Everyone faces challenges in life in their own way. Some people do seem to have it much worse than others. But every human problem is of legitimate concern. It's no easier or harder in some ways to face financial struggles, relationship difficulties or health problems than it is to go through cancer treatment. Cancer might seem a little scarier than other challenges but there really is no merit in calculating the odds or putting one type of challenge on a higher scale than another. In any case, we try to help each other through.

The week before we lost my father-in-la, a longtime friend texted me with news that his mother-in-law had just passed away. You could feel the emotional pain in his words. He and I had not spoken in a while but I knew it was not the time to catch him up on our situation and its complexity. Later my friend did inquire how things were going and I sent him a quick summary. His response was dramatically simple: "If there's one thing I've learned recently it's that Life is Life."

He meant that difficult things do happen in life, and it's how we respond to them that matters. Which is why we all try helping each other by listening and participating in each other's lives. It helps us make sense of the good and the bad.

As well as the in betweens.

That's where we are right now. Linda is recovering relatively well from her surgery. But there are still side effects from those procedures and from the chemo she's had. Most of us fight a battle with hair where we don't want it to grow. Linda simply wants the hair on her head to come back. Her feet are still numb, and her fingernails are now shedding like fish scales. All the results of chemo. Have I mentioned she's a pretty perseverant gal?

And yet we are indeed getting out to do fun things. We danced like nuts at a friend's wonderful wedding last weekend. It was so fun to see Linda having fun and getting some social time after weeks and months where both of us spent so much time in hospitals between her surgery and then her father's illness.

But it was all part of an important process. His wake and funeral were so meaningful. Such a great life that man led.

Looking ahead, we learned that Linda's gynecological oncologist wants to keep her on some form of maintenance chemo treatment. We're waiting to hear what that might be because one of the recommended treatments for ovarian cancer is Doxil, which acts like a "slow release" treatment rather than a spike and a falloff. But a shortage of that drug nationwide is preventing new patients from being added to that waiting list. So we will be looking at other options and waiting to find out what the doctors recommend. We got into all sorts of conversations about estrogen blockers and this and that. In early February we'll find out what comes next.

In the meantime, we're living life the best way we know how. The little phrase we've used to deal with the ups and downs over the years has always been "It is what it is." In other words: no sense trying to change things we can't control. God tells us not to worry. Do your best and that's that.

Life is life. All we can do is help each other try to live it well

Leap Year

Tuesday, January 31, 2012, 2:00 PM

Remember when you were a little kid, and Leap Year was so exciting? What a novel concept! An extra day in the month of February. Summer Olympics are also held during Leap Year. 2012. 2016. 2020. Guess that gives the athletes an extra day of training.

For Linda it means one extra day before her least favorite month of the year rolls around, which is March. To an avid gardener March is little more than a big tease. 30 days of alternating cold, snow, thaws and mud. How delightful. Linda mostly tromps around looking out the window ruefully at snowflakes falling, waiting for the wind to die down, grumbling, "March sucks."

Of course opposites attract and March happens to be one of my favorite months. Mostly. My least favorite type of weather is 38 degrees and really windy. Good for nothing days. Can't birdwatch. Running and cycling are no fun in those conditions. And the raw wind is simply no joy.

Whoops. I forgot that I like March! It's always been a season of hope to me! Forget that 20 out of the 31 days in March are unforgivingly harsh. In like a Lion, out like a Lamb my foot! But the 11 nice days are often so treasured they make the other crappy days worth it. Of course that's being optimistic, but...

Crocuses come up in March. Usually. And snowdrops. Sometimes. The occasional bold daffodil may bust out in March but usually pays the price of submersion in a snowdrift. Goes to show that you have to have faith when you get your hopes up.

Among wildflowers, you can find skunk cabbage in the woods as early as February. The flowering shoot of an early skunk cabbage actually produces heat that can melt the snow around the plant. With coloration like a trout and a waxy, swirling bloom, skunk cabbage is an oddity in the plant world. That's why I've always liked trying to find it when the snow is melting and the ground is half frozen. It's a reward after winter and an inspiring example of perseverance in the face of a sometimes-cold world.

That's kind of where we are right now. Sticking our heads up a little as winter wanes. Looking hopefully ahead to spring. And getting ready to celebrate Linda's ##th (hee hee) birthday on February 7. (Hint: she's finally catching up to me...) Then Valentine's Day, St. Patrick's Day and suddenly it will be April.

While we wait for spring we expect to hear what the plan will be for continuing treatment. Linda has an appointment with the doctor this Friday, February 3rd. So it will be good to know the plan, in any case.

Come early April Linda and I always visit the Morton Arboretum Daffodil Glade on the west side of the preserve. Thousands and thousands of daffodils in random patches fill the open woods. White and yellow daffodils mix with bright blue squill to light up the woodland floor. We've gone for several years and will post an announcement here in case any of you would like to meet us there in early spring. I'll post a picture on our site page in hopes that it will inspire you to consider making the trip either with us or on your own. It never fails to inspire hope and joy in heart and soul.

That is, if March weather doesn't hold us hostage into April. Did I mention that I like the month of March? Really!

Walking to Orion

Friday, February 24, 2012, 2:30 PM

Of course no marriage is perfect. And despite (or because) Linda and I have gone through so much together, we do fight now and then. This past Wednesday night it was on the way to church. I know, ironic, right? Well, if you never fought you wouldn't need to go to church, so at least we were going for a reason. Even if she wanted to dump me on the curb, it still felt like the right thing to go. And yes, it was my fault.

It was Ash Wednesday, and wouldn't you know it, the pastor focused on issues of our frail mortality and how difficult it can be to realize life itself is a gift. I listened carefully to that message and still felt like crap. My cold was coming back. I'd popped a pill before service and was getting sleepy. My eyes were itching. Linda nudged my arm by accident and I felt like jumping up and screaming. Something was just not right with the world and me. I tried to think about better things...

Linda has been doing well lately. Improving. Getting function back and going for walks. She even tackled her favorite route, a 3-mile walk she invented the first day we moved into Batavia and has followed ever since. She's not quite back to exercise class, but did tell me she noticed how much easier it is to work out without a 6" hernia sticking out in front of her. So there she went in new exercise garb and shiny ASICS shoes, coming back with cheeks so cold they felt like icicle bags. "I did it!" she said happily.

Walking is often a form of salvation in times of great challenge. Things have still been challenging in a number of ways, and we all know they add up. Money. Expenses. Job stress. Sitting there in church all I could think about was that I wanted to get out of there and move.

It wasn't that church was not valuable to me at that moment, or that I could not have learned more by staying. I did make it through the sermon after all. But something about being there among all those people when I was so anxious and disturbed by my own impatience with Linda earlier made me want to get out and go. A wise person once shared advice she gives to people who want to go to church but don't have the energy to face people; "Come late and go early." So I decided it was time to go. Really early. But kinda late.

Linda and I had driven together, so I was sort of stuck. But I took the keys out of my coat pocket and laid them next to her on the pew. "I'm not feeling well," I told her. "I've got to go."

Outside the church I patted both pockets and remembered that I had purposely left both cell phones at home. So I started to walk. The air was calm and moist. The constellation Orion hung above the trees on Delnor Avenue like an image of Christ hanging there in the sky.

Except that constellations don't really exist. They are figments of our visual imaginations. The stars in the constellation known as Orion are not arranged on the same plane like people used to think. It's all an illusion.

Yet somehow it was comforting to have that figure up there in the night sky, right in the direction I was headed, toward home in Batavia. There was no wind. No chill in the air, really. Good walking weather.

The roads and paths between St. Charles and Batavia are so familiar to me after living 40 years in the area that I knew the precise shortest route. But it's different at night, walking alone, with no ride promised and none expected. Hear the footsteps. One shoe in front of the other. Rockports and dress socks. Khaki slacks and LL Bean jacket. Just moving along.

The emotional pain of the previous few days ebbed and flowed in my brain. Anger came and went. Confusion. Regret. Fear and determination. Yin and yang.

Out of the corner of my eye I watched for Linda's car, hoping perhaps she'd see me and stop. Car after car passed by. 45 minutes passed, and at Division Street on Route 25 I had not yet reached the aura of the streetlight when our Chevy Impala went cruising past. Not a pause. She hadn't seen me. Or else she was so mad she didn't stop. That would be worse. Much.

It was 9:15 and the dark passages between streetlights were deep and solemn. Twice a great horned owl was heard hooting in low moans. I'm no longer scared of the dark. That went away some years ago. There's nothing in the dark that is any scarier to me than what you find in the light. Injustice. Lies. Manipulation. All much worse than boogeymen to me.

Plus there was Orion for company.

When I reached the dam in Geneva the water was frothing over and it made me think about the people who've lost their lives in that current. Innocent people. Folks just trying to fish or thrill seekers trying to crest the dam in a canoe. Down they went. Life's over. Just like the church service said. Ashes to ashes. Dust to dust. Muddy ashes on your forehead. Welcome to the afterlife.

In the park south of Route 38 my legs started to tire. I had already run 4 miles that afternoon. It was a 6-mile walk home from church. At least my head cold ebbed in the night air.

Quietly I wished Linda had seen me on the way by and picked me up. Had pity and forgiveness. Would she feel that way when I got home? It was likely she was worried about my dumb-bo head, if for no other reason than walking out of church is something I've never done in 30 years together. Husbands...can't live with 'em...

The last mile was slow trucking. Hips hurt. One toe on a sock had worn through, I could feel it. Walking's almost harder than running in some ways. When I got home and measured the distance from church to home using a map function on my iPhone it said: 6.2 miles. A 10k. Wouldn't you know it? Classic distance. Used to race it all the time. Once covered it in 31:10. My walk home took more than an hour and a half.

So what was learned in the distance, this time? That I'm a dumb head. Impatient. Fearful. Anxious. Foolish. Prideful. Ah heck, sinful too. Doubting God. Doubting Linda. Doubting everything. Except the ability to move, and trying to make sense of things.

Sometimes that's the way it goes. We all need a walk with Orion now and then. At least I do. Just trying to clear the head, that's all.

Church of the Morton Arboretum

Sunday, February 26, 2012, 5:45 PM

The photo on Lovin' Hands website this week is of Chris, Linda and her mother Joan Mues. We met in mid-February at Morton Arboretum to take a 2-mile walk through the east side woods. It's really a beautiful place for a walk in any weather.

That's especially true on a Sunday morning when it tends to be quieter. We always visit the Ginkgo Room for lunch. Linda loves the goat cheese and cranberry salad. It's quite delish.

It's nice how the visits differ by season. There are always some birds to see. This trip we found a couple bright Eastern bluebirds and Robins. Both are sure signs of spring. Not too many plants were sticking up their heads yet, but we're fine with that. Would not expect that in February. This year only a skiff of snow bordered the trails. Some years we've hiked on top of thick compacted snow in February. We love it all.

It's all been a rush of challenges and recoveries this year. Linda is still getting over her surgery and Joan is finding her way following the loss of her husband of 50 years on January 2. We look for life-affirming joys such as trips to the Arboretum to restore our spirits. The sunshine didn't hurt either!

This is just one of our outdoor "churches". We also visit the Church of Nelson Lake and the good old Church of the Dog Walk. Of course we jest a little here, but sometimes it's best to make church in new places or even find church where you can

On laughter and quality frogs

Monday, March 5, 2012, 3:30 PM

"People have a hard time letting go of their suffering. Out of a fear of the unknown, they prefer suffering that is familiar."— Thich Nhat Hanh

"A sense of humor... is needed armor. Joy in one's heart and some laughter on one's lips is a sign that the person down deep has a pretty good grasp of life." —Hugh Sidey

Those two quotes above sort of go together, don't they?

It is easy when you've been through some challenges to forget that it's okay to let yourself feel better again. When you've lost someone you love or been hurt in some relationship the difficult present can become the only reality you know.

Linda and I have been working, together and on our own, on creating a present that is both thankful and forward-looking. Recently we've spent more time making each other laugh. Linda's sense of humor can be quite biting, which I happen to find quite charming. She'll burst forth laughing at the oddest times during TV shows. That is a great joy in our family. Recently the 30 Rock episode featuring Leap Year William tickled her funny bone even though 30 Rock isn't her most super favorite program.

It's been said that laughter is one of the important glues in a relationship. We most certainly believe it.

People that make us laugh help us forget the suffering in our lives. We all need that. Even if you're not going through a period of personal difficulty, there is plenty of suffering to go around in this world. The evening news and tornados and earthquakes and floods and hunger and poverty and upside-down mortgages and divorce and nuclear weapons in Iran all add up to make the world seem like a pretty "bad news" place.

It holds true that we should never forget the suffering of others. That is the reason why this blog began, to thank you for helping us through a challenging time, and to encourage all of you in some way as well.

In a few weeks Linda and I are going to make a trip south to the St. Louis area to see some friends. We wanted to go last year but life and cancer intervened. Linda is still wrestling with some side effects of treatment and surgery but she's also back teaching and feeling good overall. So it's time to roam a little.

One of the funny incidents we had with the friends we plan to visit happened one spring night a year ago. We were outside their home listening to the songs of chorus frogs and spring peepers singing when we decided to take a walk to the pond for a closer listen. As we crested the hill, a different kind of voice could be heard near the water. I recognized the sound from a frog monitoring CD I'd been given by the Chicago Wilderness organization.

"Listen!" I exclaimed. "Those are wood frogs! Those are quality frogs," I said in a serious voice.

Our friends burst out laughing. "Quality frogs?" they chuckled. "What do you mean by that?"

Wood frogs have a low, grubbing voice that sounds like two pieces of wet rubber being rubbed together. There is nothing really quality about the nature of their voices, per se. But what I meant was that wood frogs are not all that common, and they don't sing for a very long period during the spring. So the "quality" to which I was referring was the uncommon opportunity to both find and hear them. Plus they are signs of a relatively healthy environment.

So now the term "quality frogs" almost always comes up in conversation when we visit our friends. Those quality frogs may well be indeed singing when we arrive at the end of March. The joke's on me for affixing something of a too-precious label on their presence, It will be a laugh worth sustaining. Time marked with laughter is time cherished in the moment. We can all use more of that. Hope you find someone with whom to share a good laugh today.

Daffodils and cucumbers

Thursday, March 15, 2012, 10:30 AM

My wife the gardener has been stunned by the early arrival of spring this year. It's been a joke between us for years that she hates March and I love it. Pretty sure my daughter Emily hates March too. It's usually cold and raw, her l. Yet he also shares an intense dislike for snakes with Linda with Linda and Emily so it all kind of fits together in a six degrees of separation kind of way. We're a mixed up family, what can I say?

But I'm the strangest one of all according to them. I'm the one who actually likes the month of March. Always have and always will. In those cold old days of the 1970s and early 1980s when winters were fierce and unforgiving, March was hope that it would all come to an end. Something warm had to get through. Just put your head down from November through February and hope that March might grant you a couple 50 degree days. Slivers of hope. Unthaw your buttocks at least. But this year! Temps in the 70s! Who'da thunk?

Linda is worried that everything will bust open and bloom too early. and then get nailed when a Saskatchewan Screamer comes in April, freezing the tops off everything sticking up out of the ground. Let's hope not.

Yet those long olde winters were good training for life. You figure "If I can get through walking to the parking lot to a frozen car at 10 below zero in a 20 below wind chill, I can survive anything."

And it's true. Midwest winters do teach a certain temperance of spirit. At least they used to.

So what can you say about this past winter? I think I shoveled the driveway two and a half times. That's it. Not complaining. It's just weird.

But I know that Linda looks so forward to true spring, especially when she's spent so much time socked on the couch recovering from chemo and surgery in the heart of dark winter.

Now we're sitting outside on the patio with bright yellow and purple pansies staring us right in the face asking, "What the heck are you doing here?"

And we're like, "Us? What are YOU doing here."? The pansies just smile and shake in the spring breeze. Even though they're called pansies, they are flowers that tend to be pretty tough customers.

That kind of sums up our life philosophy as well. We're no tougher than anyone else, just doing our best. So when people smile at us and say, "I don't know how you do it," we smile back like those pansies. Like a flower in a pot on a cold spring day, you really don't have a choice about some things in life. Sometimes the weather's good. Sometimes it isn't. You gotta take it and look forward to another sunny day.

Now, up come the daffodils. So we're hoping to get over to the Morton Arboretum Daffodil Glade. We invite you all to join us. We planned our weekends not thinking the daffodils would be up so soon! So if by chance we find a slot we'll send out an announcement when they come up. It really is worth the trip.

From the title of this blog you must be wondering what daffodils have to do with cucumbers. Well, nothing really evident, but please give me a moment to explain.

See, spring is the start of cycling season for me. Last Saturday while hustling up to meet some friends I stopped at a quick mart and bought a couple bottles of Gatorade. Didn't check the labels really. Gatorade is Gatorade, right? Just different colors representing slightly different flavors. It's not the world-class stuff they claim it is, but it does in a pinch.

So I filled up one of my (new) water bottles with Gatorade, which by the way was warm because the freezer at the quick mart wasn't working. But when I started riding I took a swig and Yuck! What the heck was that? It tasted like cucumbers?!!

Sure enough, there's a new flavor of Gatorade now called Lemon Cucumber. I'm sorry to say this given all the women-bashing going on out there in the world, but I'm going to blame you ladies for suggesting such a god-awful flavor combination. But maybe not. I shared some with Linda and she spit it out. Literally. So you're off the hook. I would like to say that I will never, ever touch Lemon-Cucumber Gatorade again.

Except that my new water bottle now has a permanent cucumber smell. Which is really not good. Cucumber and hard cycling efforts do not go well together. But then I just tell myself to shut up and quit complaining. Linda went for months during chemo not wanting to eat because everything tasted so bad.

Fortunately she's got her taste back. And we're praying that some other things can get back in order, too. But it's taking time. Linda's a trooper is all I can say.

So we focus on the moment. And it's better to sniff the daffodils than drink the cucumbers. Trust me on that one.

Still, we all need to remember to give credit to those pansies. They are truly an inspiration.

Everything's early, and often

Friday, March 23, 2012, 9:15 AM

First off, apologies for sending multiple messages last week. For whatever reason, the confirmation email that usually goes out to my email address did not arrive until Saturday. And then it arrived, and arrived again. About 36 hours late. My bad.

But it seems like everything else in life keeps arriving early. Like spring. Linda's been walking around the yard trying to keep up with blossoms that burst into flower and then fade away the very next day. Too much early season heat for those tender spring petals. They're not used to that. We're 6-8 weeks early on the arrival and progression of spring.

One weather prognosticator blames it on the debris field floating in the Pacific Ocean after last year's Japanese tsunami. So essentially spring started arriving last summer.

I watched a program on the tsunami event and its impact on the nuclear reactor in Japan. One could not help but be moved by the will and humanity of the people trying to contain the very real possibility of nuclear meltdown and disaster. The whole scene had a very fictional feel thanks to the blurring of lines between "reality" shows and real events in life. But the faces of the people talking about the frightening realities they faced were very real. The expression on the face of a man who had to give up searching for most of his family in the flood rubble in order to evacuate and save his remaining daughter showed the tremendous pain of bridging that gap between letting go and yet holding onto life with all your might.

Our early spring with all its gifts of warmth and flowers glowing in the pre-dawn light is a different kind of reminder that life presses us into reality whether we're ready or not. Sometimes it all seems overwhelming. We're just trying to keep up with the household chores and pay the bills and feed the kids and take out the garbage on time. Then you walk out to get the paper or put a sticker on the garbage can and some bird up in the trees bursts forth in song. Suddenly you remember what it was like to be a child, when all that mattered was that bird or a puddle by the side of the street. You'd float a stick and watch the ripple reflecting the sky. Simplicity.

It begs to us, our sense of wonder. Life. It circles us waiting for moments to break through mental barriers to joy and awareness. I know that sometimes the only thing that feels real is the moment when I place my face close to my wife's neck before she leaves for work at the preschool. The collar on her freshly-pressed shirt skritches my face. And for that moment, I'm truly alive. So you carry that around with you.

Our children noticed her vitality when we traveled downtown to watch her sister Diane play viola in a concert with Yo Yo Ma. Our friend Linda from preschool joined us for the trip, and we chatted with Emily in the car on the way downtown, learning about the challenges that our young woman faces in trying to earn an internship and navigate some political mazes in college life. Emily is so amazing and holds such vivid perspectives.

Then we met up downtown with our son Evan, a young man made for the city. He thrives there. It was a superb afternoon with long shadows plying across Chicago and Michigan Avenue. Yet he's got his eyes on moving sometime soon to New York. Another challenge for the kid who's very name means "the challenger."

Our whole family was there, with Linda's mother Joan and brother Paul as well. So we were ready for something special.

When the music played it was amazing to realize the momentous talent of the players, who make it feel so natural. The music rises up like air itself. When Diane played, her technique is so focused and expressive at the same time, it was fun to see. Yo Yo Ma tried to get her to loosen up. He did that for everyone, players and the audience. We were absolutely in the presence of genius that day,. Take a look. Take it in. Listen. It doesn't last forever.

These moments almost always seem to come too early, before you're ready for them. Yet if you pay close attention, they come more often than you might think. When you discipline your senses to awareness, and your mind becomes prepared to discern what it going on around you all of life comes alive, both early and often.

We're headed to St. Louis this weekend. Next week we may try to make a trip to the Arboretum on the fly, for the daffodils. Talk to you then!

Contact

Thursday, April 12, 2012, 1:30 PM

Most of us seem to live in a world that is part science and part faith. Recently I watched the movie Contact featuring Jodie Foster. The late Carl Sagan produced the script. It deals with the fact that so much of our lives depend on science--yet we feel the need to connect with something more in the universe.

Not being a scientist by training, I'm probably not qualified to make the judgments I seem to make in some areas. But what I learned from trying to become a biologist is that the more you dig, the more mystery you find. Also, the more you discover, the more it makes you want to know in many cases.

Some people are incurious. They only want to know what you already know, and that's that. Again, I'm not enough of a philosopher or theologian by training to judge that position either. But what I've learned from years of sitting in the pews is that deciding in advance what you believe without any form of evidence, and/or denying the evidence right before your eyes, can get you into a whole lot of trouble. That's not my opinion. That's why Jesus taught in parables founded on and connected to this early life. He gave evidence for the structure and wisdom of faith, yet based it on concrete, real and testable examples from creation. Pretty smart.

So we have a choice. We can keep an open mind about the foundations of the science that cures what ails us, or we can lean way to one side or the other and close our minds to anything else.

But at some point our choices can become very real at key points in our lives. We've all heard it said that God helps those who help themselves. Certainly having the fortitude to work through chemo or an operation or some personal difficulty that overwhelms your life can bring the impact of science and faith into stark relief. But how do you tell the difference, and what to trust? There are some things that just seem to "be" happening without falling easily into either category.

Right now Linda is hoping like crazy to grow her hair back. We keep praying it will happen because there aren't many practical solutions available. Despite what the commercials say, the "science" of hair growth has not quite solved the problem of alopecia and other forms of baldness.

As one who has had follicle challenges from an early age, I take the attitude that I don't have many bad hair days. But that's my choice. Some men hate being bald and will do anything, including transplants and toupees, to cure their wounded self-image.

I want nothing more for Linda than to have her hair prayers answered. So if you're inclined, focus those prayers there. On her hair.

Ir sort of seems as if science fixes some things half or part of the way, and then it seems like we have to pray or work the rest into place. Or, it works the other way around. We go through a procedure but it's up to the miracle healing powers of the body to get us back to normal. Everything needs a nudge sometimes. Or two.

Then there are moments of incredulity, when something fantastic happens and we can't tell science from faith. The movie Contact shows the   character played by Jodie Foster reacting with absolute wonder in the moment when she's whisked through time and space. She experiences the truly unimaginable, almost retreating into the human brain for safety. At that moment she stares into the cosmic infinite, and mutters aloud, "They should have sent a poet."

Next she encounters a being that takes the form of her late father. This "father" explains that the opening of awareness has to take place in small, digestible steps or it is too much for each new explorer to get a grip on the vastness that exists. It's simply too much to take in. In that regard, the cosmos is just like God. So we endeavor to personalize this vastness through a being to whom we can relate. In our most mystical moments we make that connection and the world makes a ton more sense than usual. That is known as being spiritual. We can train ourselves to better awareness and spirituality through study of holy texts. Then we have to wake up and wait. It's like traveling through space. And time. And the heart.

It all comes down to this: We all need contact. Through thick and thin, good and bad. It starts with a kind word or an ear of support. When one person has a bad day, the other is there to listen. We need to listen. It makes us human.

Everyone on this earth faces challenges. Sometimes expectations get trashed. Hopes get dashed. But usually, new opportunities open up. Scientifically, that's on the order of random sequence. Theologically, it's what we're called to do, to respect the responsibility of free will, yet break through the artifice of selfish living to give, and to care. Sometimes that's as simple as making someone laugh when a touch of joy is really needed. Other times it is sitting with them while they are in pain. So they know they are not alone. That can be a miracle of sorts, not being alone.

It's all about keeping perspective, which is everything.

So whether you keep perspective through science or through faith isn't the sum issue, is it? You can and should use both. Keeping perspective at some point means offering yourself to help others and that is the issue relevant to all humanity. Call it a symbiotic relationship or an altruistic adaptation. Or call it loving your neighbor. Your spouse. Even your enemy. Nature has some harsh rules and can lead to a feeling of isolation. Breaking them through caring is what makes us human, it seems. We are not alone in the universe.

Love to all.

Chris and Linda

Magpies

Saturday, April 28, 2012, 1:45 PM

I'm sitting in a little Decorah, Iowa diner called Magpies. Just had an ice cream flavor called sea salt caramel nut after a seriously good BLT made from real stuffs.

Love these little diners. Like a refuge from the universe. Except we're wired to it. Wirelessly.

So I'm sending this out into the universe with full knowledge that when the art gallery opening here is over and I get back in the car tomorrow it will be to drive real roads across real states and arrive back home.

Linda went to Morton Arboretum today with friends to pick up an order of spring plants. Our garden already looks good, and the rain helps by putting a shine on things and darkens the ground. It will be fun to see what she got.

A week ago that's all we were thinking about, the garden. Enjoying the lull in early warmth and how the lilacs and tulips and even daffodils were hanging on.

We're still grateful for the color and progress of spring, but it is tempered by the reality that we've got challenges to face in terms of cancer treatment for Linda. Her counts went up after 3 months on Tamoxifen and it appears the cancer is trying to wander some as well. So we're headed back into treatment with Doxil next week with hopes we can head this off.

Obviously not the news or plans we'd mapped out for summer.

To make things really interesting, Chris tried to "come clean" with his company about Linda's cancer the day after we found out the news. The company initially promised all sorts of support that Wednesday morning. We thought we'd crossed a threshold in being open about it. But then strange things transpired and the next morning Chris was fired from his position.

This is a pattern we've seen three, maybe four times before. We're real sick of it but in many ways the good that comes from change has always proven to carry us through.

So we hold to the hope that this is how it is supposed to be.

So I sit in a little cafe called Magpies, chirping out this message to our friends and family to hold us in their thoughts and prayers. We'll get Linda going on chemo once a month (starting Wednesday) and look to the days ahead for signs and blessings.

Much love and grace to all of you.

What it means to have faith

Saturday, May 5, 2012, 2:45 PM

That phrase "what it means to have faith" has been buzzing around my head the last few days as we emerge from what amounted to three weeks of challenging news.

First the initial diagnosis the cancer had returned. Then my job evaporating. Then meeting with the gynecological oncologist to set up new chemo for a cancer that just does not want to quit or stay put.

So Linda had her first treatment with Doxil this past Tuesday. It is a slow-release chemotherapy that was in such short supply last January that it was unavailable to us. But new supplies have been released thanks to orders by President Obama to accept medicine manufactured in India. Now Doxil is back on the market. It is still rationed carefully. Doxil is used most frequently with ovarian cancer and other cancer patients whose bodies either can't take repeated platinum-based chemos like Cisplatin or Carboplatin, or whose cancer is no longer responding to those regimens.

Over the past 7 years of treatment we've learned that you never know exactly how your body is going to respond to each new chemo, or how it will impact the cancer either. The worst part of the first Doxil treatment for Linda wasn't the chemotherapy but the steroids they gave her to help her body manage the treatment. Those made her pretty edgy, to say the least. She knew that reaction was coming but it still makes her feel very aggressive and agitated. She told me she was glad she wasn't driving herself home. That means we may need a driver to get her to and from the next chemo if I'm back working. We'll keep you updated on that.

Needless to say we weren't "philosophizing" much on the way home. Then it so happened that we turned up the Worst Road Known to Humankind, Route 59 between Diehl and 56, and there was construction to boot. So we sat, and Linda stewed, and I just played the dumb nice husband. Because I really like my head where it is. In a couple days we hope the steroids will wear off.

Linda and I got to talking and praying a bit about our situation. Honestly we're both stunned and almost embarrassed to have our lives on a repeat cycle like this. It's enough to make you question what God really has in mind sometimes.

In our case the answer about what it means to have faith has long been clear. It means believing things will turn out alright in the long run, even if not how you expected. It also means being humble enough to know when you need help, and to ask for it.

Because whether you're asking the Lord for strength to get through difficulty or asking your friends for emotional support in a secular sense, it takes a certain amount of faith to trust that help will be there.

A recent issue of Time magazine that I read in the waiting room at the cancer infusion center talked about a new vision of heaven. That is, it is possible that the heaven we get may be at least in part based on the portion of heaven we try to create here on earth. It's like Paul McCartney said, "*And in the end, the love you take is equal to the love you make.*"

Think about it. The Lord's Prayer has that interesting line in it: "*Thy Kingdom come, Thy Will be done on earth as it is in heaven...*"

That means reaching out to one another other in love. As God would have us do? Never mind our circumstance or how people are prone to judge each other. The Kingdom of Heaven really is right here, where we make it. That's how it's supposed to be.

When you think about it, that takes the pressure off that "final" big event of our lives, the day or night when we pass from this earth to another realm. From the perspective of Linda and I, we can tell you that the type of grace and help we have received from others is absolutely an expression of "Thy Kingdom Come." It comforts us, and perhaps that strain of joy is meant to teach us something about our lives here and beyond this world. If heaven is where others care for you, then that is also where it is safe to care back. By those measures we've seen glimpses of heaven. All of us can.

So what it means to have faith is to believe in that potential for creating a bit of heaven on earth. Even through pain and difficulty, that bit of heaven can be near. And as you are blessed, so you should try to be a blessing for others.

The Bible gives us hard examples in which people are given the grace of forgiveness and yet refuse to extend the same sort of forgiveness to others. It also shows that people possessed of great wealth and other blessings often have a hard time giving that up for simpler virtues. It's a challenging fact: even when they are basically virtuous in all other respects, they are asked to give more of themselves, even unto death.

When you are forced to give up those basic foundations of comfortable life, through circumstance or illness or misfortune, you begin to truly understand the nature of grace and what it means to be forgiven, to be helped by others, and to be blessed. Your values change. Your appreciation for life itself broadens a little. The notion of heaven takes on a little different look. It's not so important that the streets are lined with gold. It doesn't matter that we are not really angels flying around on gossamer wings. All those tarted up versions of heaven sound plain silly by the time you are really prepared to except what heaven is, and what it is meant to be. Even in its earthly humility, that kind of heaven is your source of faith.

What it seems to mean to have faith is to understand that sometimes the blessings you receive cannot be repaid in some precise fashion, like a debt. Instead you must try in some way to appreciate that grace and extend it to others in any way you can. The size of any gift is not its glory. Neither is the magnitude of a kind act. Instead its motive is the thing of greatest value, the intention of love. The simplest virtues really are the best, most complete source of faith in the entire universe. That's what it means to have faith.

Even when I was in my early 20s and had little used for organized religion, even less for proselytizing, there was something of faith that still spoke to my curiosity and desires. Back then it was friends that mattered most. That doesn't change, per se, but the definition of a friend can change. That is called maturity. It aligns with the wisdom that comes with age.

In the beginning of adult life you do your best to get along, have a laugh, and find true friendship. It's an art that grows with time. Sometimes it converges with a faith community. You may also experience it alone, through enlightenment.

Moving Day

Saturday, May 19, 2012, 6:00 PM

The trip to Augustana College today to help our daughter Emily move out of her dorm room was blessedly uneventful. Or relatively so. Truly, the events leading up to moving day were enough to keep us all more busy than we'd generally like. That is life of late.

Coming off news in early May that we were looking at more treatment for Linda and that Chris would be looking for new work, it did not seem like much more could happen to make life more challenging in the Cudworth family.

But then we got the call from our daughter Emily that she'd been driving her car in Rock Island and got slammed from behind by another driver. Her 2005 Toyota Matrix was smashed up enough to require a tow truck, leaving Emily shaking and upset of course. She still went along with the tow truck to the body shop of a Toyota dealership in the south part of Rock Island to fill out forms and figure out what comes next.

Being the mature young woman she is, it all went fairly smoothly.

But the next day she felt a little sore. And it got a little worse as the day wore on. So she asked the Augie staff about going to the campus nurse and the college told her, "We don't really have one of those. Go to the clinic."

So Emily's roommate drove her to the clinic where they asked her a bunch of questions, threw her in a neck brace and gave her a CAT scan. Which fortunately proved clear. But her body was sore from the impact of being struck so hard from behind. So it was good not to let that slide.

Then things got interesting in a not so good quiet way. No one from the insurance company called that whole first week. Emily began to worry that she would not have a car to move her stuff back home and the body shop manager was out of town the first couple days and not even able to look at the car. When he did finally get to check out the damage, he called Chris with bad news, "The car is totaled."

"Whaaaah?"

"You could fix it. But you wouldn't want to drive it," he said.

So Chris called the family's insurance company and gave them the policy information from the other driver that Emily had so carefully kept on the forms she'd gotten. That set the real process in motion.

The other insurance company finally called Emily, and a sweet young woman named Amy worked with Emily and tried to set up an appointment to meet with her at the hospital. But it was approaching finals week for Emily. There were a pile of things for her to do, including interviewing for the summer internship that was crucial to her major but hadn't been cemented as yet by her department heads. There were also huge papers due in her classes. And at the end of the week, she was looking forward to attending a spring formal in Utica, IL.

But things dragged with the car. Then the rental car she was supposed to get never arrived. Night after night this went on. In fact the car did not arrive until the night her final term paper was due, and late in the day. That prevented Emily from meeting Amy at the hospital and also delayed completing her final paper until the 11th hour. Actually, 2 a.m. to be exact. Emily still got up early and aced the interview the next morning. She'll be working for a classical radio station in Rock Island doing a variety of communications and promotional projects.

Right after the interview she packed up and headed straight to the formal with her friends from the OZOs, the fraternity that named her their official "sweetheart" this year.

Emily chills at home with Chuck.

Meanwhile, at the end of the week the body repair guy called back and spoke with Chris about the state of Emily's car. The frame was bent, he explained. But there was a delay. The insurance company liable for assessing the car called and said they couldn't even get out to see it until the following Thursday.

Into this maw of uncertainty, Chris drove out to Utica to pick up Emily at the formal on Saturday morning. Fortunately she'd had a great time with all her friends. The plan was to drive back west to Rock Island and move much of her stuff into the room of another friend who was staying in the dorm for the 2 weeks. Then at start of the summer Emily would be back out in Rock Island and move into a house one block off campus. Did you get all that?

She will live in a house she's rented with two friends for the summer and the next school year. However the plans to store stuff on campus fell through for logistical and administrative reasons. So it fell to Chris to jam an entire dorm room of stuff into 1 1/2 cars. The rental car Emily finally received was a cute little black Chrysler 200 with no trunk space. So we put no junk in the trunk. We did jam full the 2004 Matrix driven by Chris as Emily marveled at the packing ability of her father.

It was all Emily could do to pack up and stage stuff from her dorm room while Chris ran in and out. There was only one hour to accomplish the task. The temps outside were in the mid-80s and sweat was the order of the day. At 12:15, a quarter hour past the official Moving Day deadline, we pulled out in our little caravan and headed toward home. By then Emily was mostly recovered, you might say, from the spring formal festivities and ready to drive home.

It was a moving day emotionally as well, bittersweet for Emily to say goodbye to some of her senior friends who are moving on in life.

Her next important goal is to go visit one of her closest friends from Augustana who is in the hospital at Northwestern. He got hurt in a friendly wrestling match a few weeks ago. The injury left him struggling for feeling in much of his body. It was a heartbreaking incident with no one at fault. It has had profound affect on everyone who knows the wonderful young man.

Emily and her friends all anticipate visiting him when they're home in the Chicago area these next two weeks. Their concerns were quietly echoed throughout the formal in quiet conversations amidst the revelry. As Emily said goodbye to her OZOs friends, they all promised to make connections so they could go visit their friend together to encourage him as he is starting to show possible signs of recovery.

Yes, it was a moving day all around, the culmination of a challenging few weeks and the start of new plans at the same time. It was a good reminder that we're all moving through time together, through good times and difficulties. The important thing is to keep in touch. Show support, because that's the most moving choice of all.

Life Tectonics©

Tuesday, May 29, 2012, 9:15 AM

In 1985 when Linda and I were married on June 29, we held off on our honeymoon until mid-July that year. We had reservations to camp and stay in a lodge at Glacier National Park in Montana.

We drove the western states eager to see the mountains to which her mother and father often traveled on their summer vacations. Our first camping stop was the Badlands of South Dakota. Then we stayed a night in the cool canyon of a Wyoming park. Next came a night in Yellowstone and then the drive up the east side of the Rockies to Glacier. There we set up our tents under a mossy rim of a giant rock shelf. Our view to the south and east was mountains, and more mountains. It felt like heaven. Cool air and awesome sunrises and sunsets.

During one of the first hikes we made into the heights, we chanced upon a guide who pointed out a strange rock formation near the top of the mountain. "That is a fossilized algae pod," he explained. "Formed at the bottom of an ancient ocean. These mountains are made from rock and fossils that were pushed up by plate tectonics. In fact the entire section of earth on which this mountain range rests was pushed up like it was one dinner plate on top of another. It's a geological phenomena called 'overthrust,' in which sections of continental crust are shoved around by the force of the earth's tectonic forces."

The fossilized algal pods were three or four feet across. Yet they were remarkable in detail, just like one might find in an algae pod today near the edge of an ocean.

The processes that added up to the fossilized pod at the top of a mountain were mind-boggling. First one had to imagine that algae forming at the edge of an ocean. Then one had to imagine the ages it took for algae formations to be replaced or entombed by sediment-- long enough for that material to become fossilized. Then came the violent yet slow uplift of ocean floor to mountain top, where even the snow and ice glaciers that scoured the mountains at Glacier did not reach it. Those glaciers formed the giant rock bowls for which the mountains are named. They also left eskers and bright green and blue lakes glimmering like flat jewels high in the Rocky Mountains, a wonderful symbol for the solidity and temporal nature of the earth.

It really was a perfect place to honeymoon. A place where love and dreams breathe in the atmosphere.

When we returned to Glacier a year and a half later on a trip with Linda's parents and our baby son Evan in tow, the place we call Glacier revealed its ephemeral side in all new ways. I often carried Evan in a backpack while hiking. And having learned to talk at the age of 6 months, Evan was capable of cogent remarks about all we were seeing. One morning as we set off for a hike into a valley Evan looked up at the mountaintops shrouded in fog and said quietly in my ear, "They look like angels." That constitutes one of his earliest memories.

Life moved on. At the start of the decade when our children were entering middle school and high school, Linda and I determined that it was 'now or never' if we wanted to do a family vacation. You know how it gets. The schedules and teen attitudes and money can all conspire against a family vacation. Yet we worked it out and drove Route 2 across North Dakota to Montana. We found ourselves in the midst of a park still half-buried in snow, traipsed across snowfields marveling at how the pale white and yellow flowers followed the edge of the melting snowbanks. Clear water rushed down the hillsides into the gorges. The sounds and sights of Glacier were wind, water, sun and song, birds singing in the distance, and bears hiding in the huckleberry patches. Glacier keeps you honest with its breadth and intimacy.

Our daughter Emily was just finding her way as a photographer at that time. She was in rapture over the subtleties of a never-ending tapestry of waterfalls large and small. Her eye for detail and love of watching the tiny dramas of water cascading over rocks up close filled her mind in a satisfying way. Zenlike, we hiked long and lonesome trails on the side of the universe. Together.

Joined by mountain goats, of course. They don't give up the trail for anyone. We admired their surefooted, stubborn ways. They seemed to emerge from nowhere like ghosts, little black horns sweeping back over their heads. If they want go somewhere, up or down, front or back, they just go. What an example of determinedly unconsidered living. The way to be.

Then it was back to reality with a long drive home. After one 13-hour day in the car Emily just fried out, jumping around the backseat to work off energy somehow, anyway. "Just get me out of this car," she pleaded. Or something like that. It was a long drive. We should have skipped trying to take the scenic route across northern Wyoming. That took forever.

But soon enough we made it back home. Got on the Interstate and hauled our way back to civilization where the kids could see their friends again and get re-rooted in their lives.

Linda and I floated in the dreamworld of having been to one of our favorite places. That first night home is always bittersweet when you've been somewhere you love to go. The clothes your wore smell like the air of the mountains. There is glacial sand on your shoes, and rocks you quietly collected in memory of the visit make their way into the garden.

Then comes a shocker. The next morning home after the trip, at 7:00 a.m., we received a phone call from my mother informing us that my father had suffered a stroke while out in New York State. They had been staying with friends in advance of a family reunion. My dad collapsed in a bedroom and had to be rushed to the hospital, barely alive. When I hung up the phone I turned to Linda and said, "Well, my life just changed."

Somehow I knew that my mom would need big time help on this one. Whatever it would bring, I knew it would be mine to receive it. For the first few weeks we had no idea if my father would even survive. Then I flew to Syracuse and brought him home on a plane trip that can only be described as anxious and harrowing. My father survived all that and is still thriving with a new caregiver, a new electric wheelchair and a new Volkswagen van he recently purchased to cart them around to garage sales. Who knew all that would come into play 10 years on, long after even my mother passed away? Life is so strange.

Life tectonics. All that felt as if a chunk of our personal continent began lifting up over the life that we imagined, to a life that was to be. A year after that trip came news of cancer for my mom, which took her life in 2005. That left the job of caregiving for dad to me.

That same year came the challenging diagnosis of Linda's ovarian cancer that has kept us busy with chemo and recovery for 7+ years. There have been remissions and fortunate breaks in treatment. We still travel together. Yet it's as if Linda is channeling young Emily when she'd had enough of riding in that car on that long trip home. Being pinned in this journey is too much to take some days. She just wants out.

At the same time it is as if we have been slowly rising to new heights with the help of those who have lifted us up physically, mentally and spiritually. How many times have you been driving along absently in your car when you come around a corner and there lies a vista you could not have imagined just seconds before? That's how life works.

We look at the things we do and the things we once did with a different perspective now. You gaze around and wonder: How did we get here? How did anything get here? What does it all mean?

The best thing you can do at the top of a mountain is to stop, take a moment and look around. The clouds really do look like angels. A small voice in our ears reminds us of that. The sky is clear and blue and the mountain range extends into the distance far as the eye can see. You remain in that spot, because it is both the best and only place you can be. That's how time works. It's true for all of us no matter where we are in life in a physical and spiritual sense. Our mountain is always where we're standing.

Please note: Today is the scheduled second treatment for Linda with Doxil. We'll have tests on progress as well, though a slow-release chemo like Doxil can take time to work. We ask your prayers and good thoughts as we work with the doctors and help Linda through these challenges. God Bless you all.

Father's Day and Other Comedies

Saturday, June 2, 2012, 8:00 PM

With Father's Day coming up in a week or so it occurred to me how much forgiveness we dads require from our spouses, children and family, because can do some pretty dumb and funny things sometimes. I know my own father once attempted to siphon gasoline out of a vehicle using a standard vacuum cleaner. The ensuing explosion blew the vacuum and its parts 150 feet in the air.

But when it comes to household adventures, the apple didn't fall far from the tree in my case. For your entertainment, here are a few incidents that are just about as colorful. For these I still ask my wife's forgiveness.

BEEING A FATHER FIGURE

In a rush to grab something to eat before a Sunday afternoon softball game, I reached for the peanut butter and the honey jar at the same time, dropping the honey jar on the counter where it shattered, leaving a pool of glass and honey in a gooey pile on the counter. Not wanting to be late for the game, I scooped the bulk of the spilled honey onto a baking tray and set it outside. Then I wiped down the shelf with a wet rag and took off for ballgame.

My wife and children arrived home to find a roaring mound of honeybees clamoring on the baking tray outside. Not wanting to endanger the children, my wife took the kids around to the front door and kept the back door closed.

Upon arriving home, my wife tersely explained the situation, and warned me about the pile of bees out back. One could actually see the "bee line" flying from the porch to the opposite corner of the lawn and beyond. Their newfound giant source of honey was big news in the bee world. I called a beekeeper to ask what to do and he told me, "Just pick up the tray and move it."

"No thanks," I replied. So we waited until the bees ingested all the honey and the tray was empty. For days the beeline continued. For years my wife has reminded me of this story.

AN (ALMOST) BARN BURNER

Trouble always seemed to arrive with the rest of my family away on other activities. One afternoon while the kids and my wife were away shopping for school clothes, I decided to finish scraping and painting the last section of a barn-style garage we had in back of our home in Geneva.

The old paint on the barn was so tough it required a blowtorch to scrape it off. It had taken weeks to scrape and paint the whole garage, so I was eager to finish off the job. Hurriedly I put torch and knife to the peak of the eaves and took off the last of the paint. Grabbing the paintbrush I applied a quick coat of oil-based paint to the last few feet of the job. But there was still residue from the scraping I'd just done (that did not look so good) so I grabbed the torch and attempted to flick off the granulized paint. Instantly the freshly applied oil-based paint lit in a thin blue flame, licking over the edge of the roof. Panicked, I jumped off the ladder from 8 feet up and ran for the hose near the house, about 30 feet away. I turned on the hose and took off running for the garage when "duuu-unnnnnnnnggggg!" I ran out of hose. Squirting the hose at the garage had no effect. Glancing up at the peak of the garage, the flames were still evident. Visions of the whole, ancient garage burning down before my eyes flickered through my brain. The structure was more than 100 years old. And tinder dry.

I filled up a bucket with water and did my best to rush up the ladder, heaving the water upward against the peak of the eave. For a second, the flame seemed to go out. Within seconds it came back.

Jumping down from the ladder again, I raced to the end of the hose with the bucket and filled it again, this time to the brim. With all the might I could muster, I heaved that bucket of water against the eave and Thank God, the flames were extinguished. Wanting to be sure, I felt the wood of the eaves with my hand. It was still hot. So I doused it again.

Finally I climbed down the ladder, lay on the lawn and laughed and laughed at my stupidity. None of the neighbors were home. God is indeed merciful at times.

HOLEY, HOLEY, HOLEY

Good dads think they are Superman. That is why I figured I could complete the entire remodeling of our only bathroom in a single weekend.

So I sent my wife and kids over to her mother's house on a Saturday morning and proceeded to tear up the floor tile, scrape off the wall tile, take down the vanity and replace it, and do it all without touching the newly resurfaced family tub. That all went pretty smooth. At midnight, standing there with everything in the bathroom torn out, even the toilet, I suddenly realized with horror that I really needed to go to the bathroom. Staring at that scary black hole in the floor, it occurred to me that it would take a brave man with great aim to accomplish the necessary task.

Suffice to say the next few minutes were enough to humble even the proudest man into future prudence and better planning.

By morning, refreshed with a few hours of sleep, it was possible to tackle the reconstruction and finish the job by the time Linda and the kids walked in at 6:00 p.m. the nest evening. Everything really had gotten done. The Floor tile. Wall tile. New toilet. New vanity. Caulk. You name it. All were clinging together with wet glue and freshly sealed grout. I carried each of the kids in to let them go potty. My wife was not too amused. She gingerly got ready for bed.

Yes, we dads can turn otherwise seminal tasks into a form of fine art if we really try.

Trust me, we don't expect to be treated all that special for Father's Day. Just holding back your laughter at our occasional (or frequent) stupidity is the greatest gift you can give.

That said, the last 3 household projects I have done recently, including replacing a light switch that had conked out, were done functionally and operationally correct. Some of us do learn from experience. Eventually. Or else the memories of our failures drive us to success. Whatever it takes, right?

Blowing in the wind

Monday, June 18, 2012, 3:00 PM

In case you haven't noticed, it's hot outside. And windy. Lying in our backyard hammock, it is fascinating to note the resilience of the trees, blowing and shifting and shaking in the wind. Once in a while a long stick breaks free and falls down. You wonder about that moment. What combination of years and weather and wind and growth contributed to that click of wood breaking free? We can consider it a tragedy or a natural occurrence. It falls and we hear it. Proves we're alive, for better or worse.

At times the wind comes to a halt. Everything is still. It is almost as if you are supposed to be listening for something like a secret, or a piece of wisdom.

It can be hard to find time to place yourself in a hammock and look at the trees. All the events we consider so important call us here and there. Last year with everything going on with work and Linda's treatments and trying to hold things together in one basket it took most of the summer to finally flop in the hammock and look up at the trees. Summer was almost gone already.

There's a telling scene in the movie Phenomenon when the John Travolta character considers the energy of wind blowing through the trees. He realizes there is more to the world than what we see in front of our eyes.

There are also many references in the bible to God's voice as wind, and even God as a being, moving through the trees. We're called to recognize the near presence of creativity and creation. It's hard to be sensitive to all that when we live in a world where our attention can so easily by occupied by events that disengage from inner peace.

The wind comes and goes, we know. We can fear a storm, but after it passes, we revel in the fresh new perspectives of the smell of rain and the green leafy debris it throws around the yard with such joy. It reminds us the world is for our appreciation but not entirely in our control.

The storms of life can also dissipate before our eyes, like a threatening rain cloud that comes from a horizon dark and rife with lightning only to break up and pass over our heads with barely a wisp of rain.

When Chicken Little runs out into the barnyard crying "the sky is falling!' everyone jumps to attention. When the little boy cries "wolf" when there is none, the kinsfolk begin to doubt his verity. Linda and I are all too aware that we must not say the sky is falling when it isn't and never cry wolf when help is not genuinely needed.

So it can be difficult for people engaged in cancer treatment to recognize real emergencies or say what's on our minds without wearing out the trust and help so kindly tendered in the event of need. Those days may come. It's just our hope and mission to keep them at bay. Like a windbreak!

We have been holding our breath for weeks as the Doxil treatments go about their work. But the lag from January to March when the drug again became available on the market did allow some cancer to advance. Now the drug appears to be stabilizing the disease inside Linda, and the doctors say it is no time to "throw in the towel." We go this Wednesday to meet with the gynecological oncologist.

Linda's overall health is good despite side effects such as soreness of hands and feet and some challenges related to the surgery last December. She's been gardening and cooking and visiting her mother and sister. We just hiked up and over the hill at Johnson's Mound with Chuck the dog yesterday afternoon.

The other challenges we face are vexing. Chris has been hunting for a job while fighting legal challenges over the circumstances of his dismissal. He has been networking successfully and caring for his father. He's also busy finding a replacement car for Emily after her Matrix was totaled. That has given us plenty to do. There are stacks of papers for each subject on the downstairs desk. Chris wishes he were a superhero, able to fly out the window to solve problems and whizz around in the wind as if it were a plaything rather than a reminder that we're mere mortals.

We do have faith that despite the wind in our faces some days, we are making progress and God will provide. Though we do appreciate the occasional push or word of encouragement along the way. Especially into the wind. God Bless.

A bit of good news in a short message

Wednesday, June 27, 2012, 4:30 PM

Linda just learned from the medical oncologist at Cadence that her CA-125 (the measure of ovarian cancer activity) has officially dropped more than 500 points, from 835+ to 322. That is a sign the chemotherapy Doxil is indeed working. She just received her 3rd treatment yesterday. So we're hopeful the numbers will drop even further. This is the program; treatments once a month with supporting checkups and shots to maintain her health and blood levels.
She's doing very well overall, working in the garden, getting out socially and looking forward to a trip with her sister and mother later this summer.

We'll be cautiously optimistic going forward, praying that the medication continues to work, remains available and everything else intact. Thank you for your support.

Isla Mujeres (Island of Women)

Friday, August 10, 2012, 11:30 AM

Ah, yes. It's Back to School time. We recall the smell of peanut butter and the sound of clanging lunch pail latches and crinkling potato chip bags jammed on top of apples that somehow never get eaten.

August is a month of tenuous joys. The cool front coming through these last few days is a hint of weather to come. Of course it will get hot again. With a summer like we've had, with days and months of 90-degree weather, it should not surprise us.

In a week-and-a-half Linda will be taking a trip with her mother and sister to the western coast of Michigan near Saugatuck. Those three will stay in a cabin near the lakeshore and rest and relax for a few days together.

There's a history with these three, you see. They took off to Mexico years ago to visit Isla Mujeres. Sat in rickety fishing boats bouncing through waves to tiny offshore islands. The Pescadores lanced barracuda and carved them up for a shore side meal. Fortunately there were margaritas involved as she is not much of a fish eater. Never has been.

This time around the three of them will get to choose their wildness in Michigan. Mostly they will seek peace and rest and perhaps some fun little shopping places.

To go on the trip, Linda will need to push her regular Doxil treatment back a week, but that will present no risk. The current chemotherapy regimen is a slow-acting, time-release medicine. From the point of her highest CA-125 count of more than 800 to now, the numbers over the summer have been slowly dropping; to 500, then 300 and now 160. Those are good signs. The doctors have assured her that means the cancer cells are being cured. But it is still there, as evidenced by some tumors that show up in CAT scans.

Her overall health is so good that her oncologist was very encouraging in this week's appointment. "Look at you!" she said. "You look good. You're active. You're working. Those are all good things." Indeed. Linda's planning to be back at preschool in a few weeks.

The side effects including sore hands are no fun, but they are manageable. Unlike other chemo treatments, Doxil does not result in the profound downtime wrought by Cisplatin or Taxol. Doxil works more like a steady, misty rain rather than a violent downpour.

On the job front, Chris has been interviewing with some really great companies and would appreciate prayers on the work situation, as it has been a lot of networking and tests and interviews and more in this competitive job market. God has been with us throughout.

Is it okay to pray to tell God to hurry up? Perhaps he's been busy watching the Olympics with all those athletes giving him the credit and the glory. Or maybe God is studying the Mars Rover Panoramas with the rest of us science geeks.

Chris isn't likely to pick up his daddy's cue and "make a living out of playing pool," but freelance work is a bit like that. Every shot counts, and leads to another. Or not. Every morning a new challenge. Every day a new opportunity.

Speaking of opportunities. Our son Evan moved to New York recently and has an apartment with two associates on Delancey Street in South Manhattan. He's excited to start this new chapter of his life.

Emily is completing a fab summer internship with WVIK radio, where she's done photography, upgraded the website and done live and recorded reads. It's fun to hear her on air. We stream WVIK live through iTunes, and you might catch Em at 5:00 p.m. if you listen.

Summer's not gone yet! Get out there and enjoy! Perhaps we can all meet up for margaritas and a nice Mexican joint and pretend we are visiting Isla Mujeres together. Who will bring the barracuda?

Summer ends with some joys and a wobble

Friday, September 7, 2012, 4:00 PM

Wow. September 7. Most of you are probably either well into Back to School mode or looking forward to autumn weather when you don't find pools of flesh melting from your body.

What a summer! Hot. Dry. Record-setting temps for weeks on end. The hottest summer in history, did you know? Interesting to be part of history. Doesn't feel too different than regular old time, and yet there it is: You lived through the Summer of 2012!

The rains have come back. The lawn here in Illinois is green again. Otherwise we hardly had to mow all year. The gas in the tank of our Honda mower went bad and the poor machine shut down. It said, "I ain't mowing no more till you give me some good gas." And $75 worth of tune-up.

That is the story on so many things. That which you take for granted will come back to bite you in the butt. So we try to carpe diem. Seize the day. Somehow even when you seize them the days still go flying by.

Well, despite the cooker of a summer we just had, there is good news on our front. From June of this year through the end of summer, Linda's monthly Doxil treatments continued. As a result, her counts fell from over 800 to just over 100. That's seriously good news.

The side effects are weird, like usual. This chemo turns her hand into blister pads. It got so bad last month we had to hit the emergency room at Delnor Hospital to have her wedding ring cut off.

But on the way home, we stopped at Trader Joe's to buy some consolation food and the woman working the counter asked how our day was going. I smiled wryly and said, "Well, we started in the Emergency Room," and Linda chuckled and rolled her eyes.

I'd waved to a tall man I knew from visiting the store frequently. He waved back and walked over to give me a big hug. It was an impromptu gesture. Being enveloped in his big tropical shirt made me feel better about the world. As we embraced, the woman at the counter whispered to him, "Would you go and get these people some flowers?"

And he did, returning with a big smile and another hug for Linda. It was kind of like shopping at Trader God's, for that moment. That's how it continues for us. For every challenge, a blessing in return.

In late August, Linda took 5 days to visit the Lake Michigan shores near Saugatuck with her sister and mother. It was exactly what they all needed. Great weather. Sunsets. Lay low and refresh.

Upon her return (and having survived my 5-day bachelorhood thanks to Bob and Kirsten Snodgrass checking in on me) it was my turn to take a little trip north with friends on Labor Day weekend. We planned to ride a 64-mile event called The Wright Stuff.

Things were going well for 25 miles when suddenly, on a long downhill, my entire bike began to shake as if it were about to come apart. In 20,000 miles of riding I'd never experienced anything like it. Looking ahead, and realizing the bike was not going to come back under my control, I picked out a grassy embankment and tried to aim the bike there. The minute my wheels hit the grass the bike slid out and I flew off shoulders first, striking the ground with a bounce and a long slide into deep grass. There I lay, conscious but stunned, staring up at the blue September sky.

My companions were ahead and behind of me at that point, and did not know I'd crashed. I heard a set of wheels whiz by but was hidden in deep grass out of sight.

A trip to the emergency room was in store after that. Then another trip for a checkup once I was home. There is surgery scheduled Monday, September 10.

It was a phenomenon called "bike wobble" that caused the accident. Look it up on the Internet. You'll see why I went down. Onward we go. Wobbling along. Still moving forward. Our interesting journey continues.

AUTHOR'S NOTE: September 2012-November 2012
During the period of recovery from September through November, com-
munications were taken over by the Group Coordinator as demands in
caregiving, rehabilitation and work demands took Chris out of action
posting blogs. The family communications resumed in November.

It's all about faith

Wednesday, November 28, 2012, 12:00 PM

Those of you who know me realize I'm not a big fan of pro football. More the cycling and alternative sports kind of guy. Recently we've also watching Dancing with the Stars with Linda. Ha ha. Some macho sports fan, huh?

But I do read the Chicago Tribune Sports section every day and keep up on the Bears and the like. I can tell you who's had concussions and when they'll likely be back playing. I also know the Bears lost a couple players on the offensive line (no pun intended) to injury last week and signed a former 5-time Pro-Bowl offensive lineman named Andre Gurode to the team.

This guy has worked out 5 days a week keeping himself fit in hopes of getting another chance to play pro football somewhere. He last suited up for the Ravens in the AFC championship last season, and used to play for the Dallas Cowboys.

Before this gets too pigskin-ish, all that information is the set-up for the reason I'm blogging to all of you today. It was September 7 when I last posted, only 5 days after the big bike accident that busted my clavicle and required surgery September 10. That all went well, as has rehab, although my chesticle is still sort of numb and my right ear wiggles when I raise my left arm. But other than that, everything's normal. (Just kidding about the ear thing.) After all, how normal can I be? Really?

The point of all this documentation is something that the new Bears lineman said in the article about him joining the Bears. "I didn't have a chance to rehab after my surgery last year to really get my body right and in tip-top shape," Gurode said. "I've been working out so when a team called, I would be ready to play."

Well, that quote started a resonance in my head, because in our household we've had surgeries and rehab and have tried to keep the faith through it all. There are scary moments through all that. Every time Linda goes through chemotherapy (Doxil, once a month) we're not sure if she'll be feeling the greatest. There are effects from the steroids that wear off quickly, but fatigue lingers sometimes. She's like an athlete in training, except the goal is more like keeping things as normal as possible. For all the work that the new Bears lineman did in training, this is what he said about what also kept him going: "It's all about faith," he said. "You have to be really centered in God and his word, be really diligent and stay ready because you never know what could happen."

This fellow has kept the faith. He has trained to be ready. He has trusted in that at 34 years of age when he sits on the cusp of being "too old" to play the game of football anymore.

My wife likes football even less than me. But once in a while we'll tune in a game, like the Notre Dame versus USC college game the other night. Nothing else was on, and the spectacle of football is, after all, something to see. It is short attention span theater on steroids. No wonder an America starved for stimulation in the face of all its consumerism loves the game of football so much. It's brain candy with happy names for teams like Eagles and Bears and Cowboys and Ravens. Also

Redskins and Chiefs and Seahawks. But we won't go there.

The point here is that the new Bear exemplifies what it means to be strong and faithful. That is inspiring to me after 6 months of applying and interviewing for jobs, and with good companies like AT&T and Sears. I've ben Oh so close. Right down to the final round. But just haven't gotten that call yet.

It would be easy to lose faith. Andre Gurode admits as much, and the uncertainty still lingers after the call has come. "No one has said anything to me yet about what my role is supposed to be. I am just excited to be with the franchise."

This from a man who played nine seasons with the Cowboys before he was a salary-cap casualty in 2011 just after he had undergone arthroscopic surgery on his right knee.

He kept up hope, people. It can't have been easy going to the gym every day for 10 months wondering if some team might remember him.

If you have not watched the movie Moneyball, let me recommend it to you. It's not about baseball as you might think. Baseball is the setting, but the movie is really about having faith in yourself against a culture that maybe thinks it knows more than it really does about itself.

Cancer patients might feel that way. All those millions of dollars in research money, and still you sit at home feeling like crap? Is this the best the world has to offer? Where's the hope in that?

The hope is in knowing that other people do care about you. It's like sitting at the beach. There's hope in the fact that the love you think might be ebbing away from your feet will come up again and cool your toes, warming your heart. Soothing your soul. You look out and see the waves created out of nothing, it seems. Then they rise up near shore in white-tipped wonder. There aren't always waves, but when there are, you know there is a certain dynamic at work. You can trust the rhythm and the laws of the universe to help you out. The ocean is at once careless and caring, it seems. A terror and a joy to behold.

That is life. We hear the gulls cry in the wind. The waves breaking on the shore. We see footprints in the sand, and start to walk. Faith lives on the edge of such things, where the water glistens in flat sheets and quickly sinks into the sand. May the waves of hop e grace your feet each day. Despite our many challenges, we still walk that shore.

Holiday Greetings

Thursday, December 20, 2012, 6:00 AM

From the Cudworth's

We want to say Merry Christmas to all of you, and Happy New Year as well! With much love & thanks!

Emily, Evan, Linda and Christopher Cudworth. And Chuck too!

(Photo of Evan and Emily Cudworth with the Red Ryder BB Gun made famous in the movie A

Christmas Story with Ralphie)

Mettle on Metal

Thursday, December 20, 2012, 7:00 AM

met·tle [met-l]

1. courage and fortitude: a man (or woman) of mettle.
2. disposition or temperament; on one's mettle, in the position of being incited to do one's best: The loss of the first round put him on his mettle to win the match.

The English language can be confusing at times. Imagine you do not speak English but are learning the language and come upon these two words: mettle and metal. They sound exactly alike. Even their meanings have similar foundations. To have mettle is to be strong or made of tough stuff, to hold up or hold together. Metal is the same way.

If we play with the meanings we also find challenging similarities, at least in terms of describing them to one who is trying to learn English. If we speak of something on the order of metal fatigue, for example, it seems to bridge the gap between physical reality and some sort of emotional state. Yet we know that metal is not a conscious material. It can have no feelings or awareness of itself.

Yet if we coin a term that sounds exactly like, and speak the words "mettle fatigue" we all know immediately what that might mean. "Tired of holding out. Sick of trying. Not wanting to be tough, or need to be." That is mettle fatigue. It is just as real as metal fatigue, which can cause iron or steel to bend or crack. We search for words to describe emotional states because words are our tools for emotional survival. It helps us also to realize we are not alone when someone says to us, "I know how you feel. I get that."

In times of great trouble, it is said, people turn to faith because words and actions somehow seem to fail us. We forgive people their "foxhole faith" because we know that in times of trouble, really desperate or frightening times, it helps to say a prayer.

It helps, it really does. Prayer is the WD-40 of our earthly existence. It is multipurpose oil for the soul. Prayer keeps emotional rust at bay just as WD-40 keeps your bike chain from squeaking and turning into a rust belt.

Worry is the rust of our existence. We worry because the frequent rains of life pelt at the metal of our being. The mettle as well. If we are not careful to maintain our oil somehow, like the Tin Man in Wizard of Oz, we are likely to get stuck in one place, our joints and minds frozen by rust. Creak creak.

Hope is the final quotient in this mix of mettles, chemicals and life tools. Hope is like the maintenance manual. We need to consult it frequently to understand how to fix things when they're rusted, broken or frozen up. Hope can come from many sources. From reason. From Faith. From friends. We need them all.

Consulting the Bible on the subject of hope, we find this passage from Job, where a man beset by eternal troubles questions why so many problems have come his way. It is a plead and a call for help, as much as it is a question.

Job 6:11 "What strength do I have, that I should still hope? What prospects, that I should be patient?"

Of course we know the answer to the question Job is asking.

For those of faith, the strength we have is found in the promise of life that God has given us. When we trust that life to God, which is a difficult path to trod at times, then all our answers lead to one thing. That is love, salvation and trust.

The practical side of this path is an equal challenge. "What prospects, that I should be patient?" Well, I'm going to interject a practical observation at this point because the word "prospects" is the most profound word one might find in the Bible, and in life. Our "prospects" are both symbolic and practical, are they not? We might be stressing over money, or lack of it. We might worry over relationships and their damaged state. We might wish for happiness, and find it lacking even in the things we love the most. Life changes, you see. Whether we want it to or not, life alters our prospects.

But we learn from that because with experience comes knowledge. And knowledge alters our perspective.

That is why we are often advised to be patient and listen for the answers. They may come from friends (expected and unexpectedly) or even our enemies. They may come through forgiveness or tolerance. They might also come through the impatience of others, the angry deeds of the estranged or bitter. We have to process them all and discern what we can learn from every situation.

Because rust never sleeps.

Because our mettle will be tested.

Because metal is only so strong.

Because cancer is like a rust.

We gain healing through many sources. It's proven. Even many doctors believe in the power of hope to heal. They also recognize that sometimes it's the simple fact of being a bastard or a bitch that gets you through. There are many kids of mettle in this world, of different strengths. Sometimes you need a little of both.

What all this has to do with Linda and Chris and Evan and Emily and Chuck is this: Our mettle has been put through some severe tests this year. With Linda, it has been challenging trying to keep ahead of cancer. The Doxil is working in containing her cancer, but the counts naturally vacillate and it is nerve-wracking to say the least.

My job search has been filled with affirmation that I have much to offer the right company, yet there have been near misses. Interviews with great firms. So I'm doing things right. It just takes time to get the offer that matters. I'm working with recruiters and networking and still making progress. I feel like Job at times though. "What prospects, that I should be patient?" Well, the freelance work has kept me hopping for one thing. It also brings in needed $$$!

You know the joke: Two vultures sitting in a tree. One says to the other: "Patience my ass, I'm gonna go kill something." We've all gotta eat.

On other fronts, Evan is busy as heck in his NYC/UC life. He'll be home for Christmas a few days. We thrilled to see him in the playful role of a Gingerbread Man in the Macy's Parade. Who knows why such things happen, but it was a prized bit of levity in a year in which some of our other cookies have crumbled.

Emily is looking ahead to plans after college even as she reads so much for classes it just about makes her makeup streak. Her amazing creativity and logic are such a pleasure to behold in a young woman. And Chuck just keeps us all grounded. He'd love to meet some of you during the holidays, so if you're in the neighborhood and want to stop by for an enthusiastic Chuck greeting.

God Bless, and Merry Christmas.

The Day After Christmas

Sunday, December 30, 2012, 9:15 PM

Our family had a very nice Christmas with our son Evan and daughter Emily home for the holidays. We got together with Linda's family over in Addison to exchange some inspired and happy gifts. It was wonderful watching Ralphie get his Red Ryder BB gun while we sat around eating too many cookies.

The day after Christmas Linda had her regular checkup scheduled with Central DuPage. She and I had met together several times over the weekend to discuss the fact that she was experiencing considerable numbness not just in her feet, where she's had neuropathy for years, but up her leg and even into her shoulders. Everything felt tight and she even went into a form of seizure on occasion.

So it was not a total surprise that when we discussed the breadth of her overall symptoms that the cancer care nurses sent us straight over to Cadence in Winfield where an MRI showed that Linda was not imagining things. Her cancer counts were up slightly. The Doxil just isn't strong enough to knock out the disease completely.

Additionally, a brain scan showed there was a cyst and possible tumor in her brain, which explained the numbness and difficulty on her left side.

So tomorrow she's having that fixed. The MRI showed a possible problem only in that spot, and the doctors plan to drain the spot and hit the possible tumor with radiation. The neurosurgeon is a leading doctor in this area of practice.

After that, we will take a couple weeks between treatments and recovery, we'll be going back to a more assertive chemotherapy regimen. It just takes that to keep this cancer in check. Linda's done well on Doxil and has so been enjoying her teaching this year. That makes it even tougher going through chemo that tires her out more. The doctors have expressed belief that her overall health is good enough to justify this plan of treatment. No reason to give up, in other words.

Yes, it's been a quite a year, and not surprising all this sudden change should wind up on the 31st of December. It's like 2012 had it in for us somehow. We remain optimistic, faithful and inspired by the help of everyone. We may need a few meals in the coming weeks, and ask for a little assistance in other ways, but we'll get to that.

Right now we simply ask for prayers that each stage of this treatment goes well, and that 2013 can be a better year for all of us.

Procedure a success

Monday, December 31, 2012, 1:15 PM

Greetings everyone. My trooper wife is alert and chomping ice chips already following surgery to drain the cyst resultant from a spot of tumor on her brain. The surgeon proclaimed the operation a "smooth" one and Linda looks great. Her family is all here and we've moved back into Room 333, our "home away from home" the past week.

Many thanks for your prayers and well-wishes. The next step is to hit the tumor with radiation, which will probably take place in the next week or so.

Then we'll keep after this persistent cancer in other places with chemo.

We're rather relieved that 2012 is coming to a close. Seems like the Year of Job for us. Yet we hope we have been faithful, not complained (much) and embraced our blessings while meeting the challenges, in good stead. See you all in 2013. (insert sound of cheap horn here...bleaaaahhhhhtttttt)

HAPPY NEW YEAR!

My wife the human (cleaning) whirlwind

Monday, January 7, 2013, 8:15 PM

Who'd have thunk?

Ever since we came home from the hospital my wife has swung into gears unknown in prior months. She proceeded to take down the Christmas tree, ornaments and decorations around the house. In a single day. Cleaned the kitchen and bathrooms spotless the next day. Bought new carpets for the showers and scrubbed everything that is inanimate in the entire place. Even the laundry room.

Chuck has just stared in awe. He sits in her lap when she sits down as if to ask, "What the heck if up with you? Don't you know your first job in life is to pet me?"

We're just thankful she's been feeling so good. I came to bed at midnight this weekend after a writing session and almost jumped out of my skin when she piped up, "I'm so excited to get up and clean the laundry room tomorrow!" She's normally sound asleep by that time, but her new energy and perhaps a little help from the steroids has her going strong. Constantly. She's eating well though she lost a few pounds (she's happy about that) and that's all good.

She's a whirlwind. A buzzbomb. Because she feels so much better.

Tomorrow (Tuesday) we are headed to have a radiation treatment on the noggin'. Get that fixed and hope and pray that's all there is to that. It isn't expected to be a complicated procedure but it will take most of the day, we expect.

The next day (Wednesday) Linda has a follow-up appointment with her oncologist at Central DuPage and she may need a ride for a 10:30 appointment as I have appointments in the morning and early afternoon.

Then we'll be getting a chemo strategy going forward. We are thankful for your prayers to see us through each step.

But be warned: Do not try to lie down if you visit our home. Linda may scoop you up in a dustpan and shake you out on the back porch. It's that real! Really!! Look out!!!

Update

Wednesday, January 2, 2013, 12:00 PM

Linda is home and by her own words is "doing much better." The treatment was successful and we're looking ahead to next steps in the process. It was an "adventure" we had not counted on, but with much help from God and some really great nurses and doctors, the week of profound need has passed.

Our dog Chuck was crazy happy to see her come home last night. We all were.

Thanks for the prayers. Much appreciated. We don't know yet what Linda's schedule will be. Necessary steps will determine that. We've come through challenges before and plan to do so again

Upbeat Update

Wednesday, January 9, 2013, 9:30 PM

Greeeeeetings everyone.

Linda had a positive meeting with the medical oncologist today, who characterized her attitude as 'great' and an inspiration for their team, who don't often get to hear the word "excellent" when someone asks their patients how they feel.

We have a plan now, which is to begin treatment with Topocetan, a chemo drug that is plant-based and good for fighting her form of cancer going forward. It is a monthly treatment that produces some fatigue and other possible side effects, but she is raring to get going and plans to get back to teaching preschool very soon.

Her health really is good, although the few pounds she lost during the hospital stay were not her oncologist's favorite thing about the checkup. Linda's just happy to be a few pounds lighter, have a lot more energy and have essentially full function back. "This is the best I've felt in years," she keeps chirping. Then she goes off to clean and organize something else.

I'm half expecting to find neat creases in the bedsheets, she's so neat.

The radiation treatment went so well this week the doctors were gathered around enthusing about the accuracy and completeness of the readings and applications. That's good news and we are praying that is all we'll need above the neck. The small dents they put in her scalp to apply the radiation guides are healed over already today. Can't tell she's had anything done. Linda was so positive and ready that I think she made the day for many of the nurses and doctors.

The neurologist told us (when asked) why he went into his field, and he told us his grandmother had a brain tumor when he was young and it convinced him to pursue that degree. He is a wonderful man as have been all the physicians. We're lucky to have that quality of health care here in our area. We're always very grateful for that.

We continue to pray for movement on the job front, and I have meetings with people and am getting daily calls from recruiters. Just trying to get that company that wants me or...the right combination of freelance clients to build a business around.

Take care and God Bless.

Note: It appears we're going to work with an interesting group on meals for now. A local dietitian has organized a group of advanced cooking students from area high schools to prepare nutritionally sound and cancer-treatment-supporting meals for cancer families. The program runs six weeks. If treatment becomes demanding or such we'll communicate through this channel about other meals, and about rides or other help. We're so appreciative of your consideration.

One fun note: Our son Evan happened to meet The Dog Whisperer Cesar Millan in the lobby of 10 Rockefeller Center in NYC, where Evan works. Normally he ignores celebrities in the building out of respect, but as Mom's a fan he made the approach and got a great photo with Cesar himself, who was reportedly a very nice guy. As you'd expect. I'll post the photo at www.lotsahelpinghands.com

We're also very excited for our daughter Emily Cudworth because there's going to be an NHL Hockey season after all. She's been in Hjalmorsson withdrawal for months now. Go Blackhawks!

The Magpie Coffeehouse II

Saturday, January 19, 2013, 10:30 AM

Last April I blogged to you from the Magpie Coffeehouse in Decorah, Iowa. That is where I now sit after bringing more new artwork to the Eckheart Gallery where there appears to be a market for my paintings. Yay!

It's a busy place, the Magpie, tucked away on a side street of this little town nestled between cedar-lined bluffs and a national wild and scenic river. Years ago this town is where I attended college at Luther. There are still many people in town who visit the gallery. Even roots worn away by the years still protrude from the soil of life.

It was casually noted in our household that this trip would be a good thing to go on for several reasons. One: Linda needed a break from me. That's not the official reason but like all the great diplomacies of marriage there are other reasons that take precedence. It would be good for me to get out of town a day and that Linda could go visit her mom with Chuck in tow.

Even the closest couples need time apart, of course. We haven't had much of that lately with all the events of recent weeks and months. Having me working in the downstairs office is both a convenience and a bother. But we manage.

The wild thing about being home has been watching the renaissance in energy and hope that Linda is experiencing after her surgery. A touch of steroids and weight loss and reduction in neuropathy has done wonders. We're just grateful she is feeling so good right now.

This week she was shopping for a new wig, because the daily use of a wig wears it out somewhat. So she's looking through a bunch of them online and there's one that features a bit more length and styling than the wigs she's been wearing. At first she was like, "No way," but in the mode of our recent worldview, "Change is Good," she ordered the wig and it looks absolutely great.

The world keeps throwing surprises at us, but our abiding attitude is, "How you respond is what matters. And look for opportunities to change."

She's cleaned out and organized every closet in the house. Stuff that hasn't been moved since we moved in 15 years ago has been assessed, reorganized or tossed. She even purchased new garbage cans. We've used the same ones for 30 years. Guess it was about time.

It's about time for everything. On the way up to Decorah I heard this NPR talk show with a guest who is a "life coach."

Her main message: When you find your passion in life, time expands. Linda's been saying that "I feel like everything's flowing. Falling into place. In teaching. At home. It's everything!" Then she gets up and moves off to another cleanup she's been dreaming about, muttering as she goes: "I just don't know what's happening. I'm so happy."

Last week a friend contacted us about helping out with meals, since Linda starts chemo again shortly. We don't know how or whether it will affect her, but meals take a lot of pressure off both of us. This group of high school students organized by a dietitian cooks meals for families affected by cancer. The first few have been like sitting down in a gourmet restaurant. Obviously we're sort of stunned at this generosity, which extends for 6 weeks. So for now we're kind of covered in that department.

Linda's back to teaching and Chris is getting more writing work with continued interviews through recruiters for full time or contract positions. So we're getting there.

Here, there and everywhere. We're getting there.

Signing off from the Magpie Coffeehouse. Hope you get here someday. Decorah is a nice place to play.

Nothing too simple, or too complex

Saturday, February 2, 2013, 1:45 PM

Coming off the December 26 discovery of the brain tumor and ensuing surgery to drain the cyst and radiation to knock out the tumor, Linda has been doing well.

There's no such thing as a "simple" surgery however. The need to use steroids to control the swelling has given Linda a bit of a hyper month and a swollen face. She's dealt with it well overall, but then a sneaky little ear/throat infection crept in and she's been in discomfort for a couple weeks.

The new chemo also tires her out. So we've decided to have her take it nice and easy for a while as we sort this whole picture out. It's hard to tell the side effects of chemo and steroids (which she just finished) from any ensuing effects from the surgery or this bothersome infection.

We've been to the doctor with her and yesterday she had a helpful transfusion to help her regular blood counts back up where they should be. It's not easy doing anything when you're out of breath and such, and she's been a sleepy girl the last few days.

Her mom is over visiting now and we're all kind of keeping watch to make sure Linda is supported while coming out of this cycle. There are also the aftereffects of all the emotional challenges of life since December 26. Getting through surgery. Having radiation. Recovering from both. She went back to work and the daily energy of the kids, while enervating, was also taxing. So we'll be taking a break for a while and Linda's preschool kids will be placed in the capable hands of another teacher assigned by the preschool director.

Linda was so excited to teach the birds unit this week to this marvelous group of kids in her class. I was planning on visiting the classroom to do my drawing birds thing, but we had to hold off when Linda went to the hospital for the blood transfusion.

On the exciting front, we went to Fox Jewelers in Geneva (they are really tremendous) to pick up Linda's repaired wedding ring. We had to have the ring cut off her finger last summer when side effects from Doxil gave her hands such blisters. The ring was split at the base and looking rather forlorn. Now it shimmers and shines! Better than brand new?

She also ordered a tiny silver cross to place around her neck. We've been blessed with so many touches of the Holy Spirit in our lives. Kindness and thoughtfulness abound.

We need to make a trip out to Rock Island to deliver the Chevy Impala to Emily. We've fixed up the car and are going to be doing the same to the Matrix but one had to come first and she needs a vehicle for her many commitments. Unfortunately she was involved in an accident and her Matrix was totaled out. The insurance company cut us a check...

NOTE

Linda was going to drive out with me in another vehicle and then we'd ride home together. But she's too tired to do the trip right now. That means if it moves someone to help out driving out to Rock Island in drop off the one car and drive back in another, we could use a driver? Call Chris at the group number if the spirit moves you. We'd leave around 10 a.m and get out there at noon. Have lunch with Emily and come back home before 2:00, getting home by 4:00 or so. No risk of missing the Super Bowl, God Willing.

Another Golden Ring

Friday, February 15, 2013, 4:45 PM

We've previously I shared the process of having Linda's wedding ring fixed after it had to be cut off her finger last summer due to side effects from chemotherapy. The ring now looks beautiful on her finger. Wonderful to have that piece of our history back shiny and intact.

There have been many such blessings the last few weeks. Linda fixed things around the house that have been bothering her for years. She ran around changing lights and even added a hanging lamp in our kitchen that we've talked about doing for years. Her energy and happiness in all these errands and fixups has been joyful and fun.

Linda has also been teaching at St. Marks Preschool up until a few weeks ago. However side effects from steroids and other medications were making her feel distracted and it was mutually agreed that she should hold off teaching until we sorted things out.

Following that week she started to feel more fatigued. Coming down off the steroids on the heels of her successful (all clear, they checked) brain surgery was difficult. We tried another chemotherapy but it hit Linda really, really hard. The Doxil had not been working and we needed to switch but her body is tired form all this and the difficult fact is that the cancer persisted throughout treatment with Doxil.

This past Tuesday we met with the medical oncologist and we checked in and out of the hospital overnight. Linda was feeling so fatigued all weekend she was confined to bed for the most part. But you know us. We're faithful pragmatists.

To give her a way to call me around the house, I brought to her room the beautiful golden bell given to her years ago by her "Aunt Doris," a dear woman from Germany who had befriended Linda's mother when they both worked together in a hospital years ago. The bell has this lovely European ring. This is our new way to reach each other through the house if I'm writing or working on a painting. The Golden Ring is a sweet way to put our needs in perspective. It gives off a ring of love.

Unfortunately over the last 2 weeks the fatigue has not left Linda. The mix of side effects has been sorted out for the most part. We're no longer going to throw chemo at the cancer in hopes of winning. We're going to throw love at the fact that she wants to live her life without all that if it isn't going to produce a cure. The doctors say that's the best plan.

We are now working with an in-home nurse who happens to have been the first nurse we met when Linda transferred her chemo care from the hospital in the Northwest suburbs to one closer to home years ago. That nurse now works for a home care and hospice organization. She came to our home and said to Linda, "I know you!"

She helped us set up caregiving so that Linda can be more comfortable day to day. This is better than trips to the hospital. She can rest here far better than running around all the time.

Linda keeps telling me how much she misses teaching. It will not be possible for her to go back to her job at St. Mark's Preschool. That breaks her heart. She loves her "kids" and staff at the preschool so much.

Our near term goal is to bring her quality of life up to a relatively normal level of energy because we are not going to pursue any more chemotherapy. It keeps clobbering her blood counts and that is not helpful to her health.

Through 8 years of chemotherapy and relatively long breaks in treatment at times, Linda has maintained hope, been strong and faithful, and lived a productive and loving life. It's hard to convey the many ways she has stood up to difficulty. We've had challenges of all sorts; health, financial, employment. All have been balanced by grace, caregiving toward our family, seeing our children grow into fantastic people and graduate from college. Evan is busy with his life in New York City. Emily just landed a great internship with an agency in Davenport. And after nearly a year of searching, Chris is accepting a great position for a web marketing agency. Yay! God is good.

We hold up these joys up as testament that this has all been worth it. For 8 years Linda has done everything possible, shirking no chances to get health back again. That has worked. I thank her for it and I'm sure we all appreciate this journey in some way.

Life is changing again, and we will live it fully with Linda in this chapter too. God Bless you all and please keep in touch.

We may ask for some assistance in visitation and in-home caregiving. We may have a nurse on duty with us some if necessary as time goes by. For now we're working with the Golden Ring, family and faith. God Bless and we'll talk to you soon.

Understanding Hospice

Wednesday, February 20, 2013, 8:45 AM

It has been an adventuresome few weeks. The profound fatigue and difficulties Linda faced due to a combination of side effects and ongoing struggles with cancer created an imperfect storm that made it difficult for her to function.

Through a series of meetings with her doctors including a medical oncologist, palliative care and gynecological oncologist we determined that due to sharp drops in her blood counts further chemotherapy is neither practical or desirable. There is too much risk that further chemo could really harm her.

Which of course is ironic, given that chemotherapy has delivered 8 years of pretty full life for Linda. Without chemo she would not have survived from 2005, so we are grateful that however difficult at times it may have been to get through treatment, it has been worth it. We all wish there was a better way to deal with cancer. We've done the best we can.

Without chemo, the future is softer, yet unsure. The physicians do not recommend other forms of treatment such as radiation because that method is either too incisive or too broad. It is likely just to make her sicker. We would also not likely gain much in the way of longer or better quality of life going that route.

There is still life to be lived. Linda is hopeful for improvement in her energy, but nothing is guaranteed. Her body is very tired from so much rigorous stuff this last year. The colon resection. Chemo that didn't work for a bit. Then chemo that worked for a while but ultimately allowed counts to rise and cancer to move. We must accept that her cancer is persistent and in some ways unresponsive to more treatments.

She did have the good fortune of a successful brain tumor drainage and radiation. Then a burst of joyful activity came off all of that, driven a bit by those interesting steroids. it proved a light in a recently dark tunnel. Frankly we're grateful for that.

Finally last week the medical oncology team recommended we set up shop at home to get Linda back to whatever level of normalcy we can achieve and see what happens.

That is how you should understand our current team of hospice care; providing palliative treatment. Linda's on a sound medication program to control a bothersome bit of nerve pain that had made her face hurt so much. The cause might have been from a number of sources, but it's now under control.

Then... the medication stopped her up and we dealt with that now too. In that challenge we had a kindly bit of knowledge-able assistance from our nursing friend Francie. Since then Linda's been up and around more but still feeling weaker than she'd like.

We have a hospice team of a nurse (or two...), social worker, chaplain, in-home bathing and assistance caregiver and of course the physicians to help us plan and improve her day-to-day health.

That's the practical goal. Everything else in this process falls into the hands of God with whom we've found so much comfort, sustaining power, hope and mercy... through his faithful servants and friends who have tended to us.

Our children have both been home for a few days and we've been watching movies together and having some laughs too. Evan played his cello for Linda as she dozed relaxedly. He's missed playing that cello because the big old instrument doesn't fit in his New York City apartment.

Emily's been racing around trying to neaten up the house behind us piggies and she's a saint for that. She's also quite happy that her darling Blackhawks (especially Hjalmorsson, that cute Swedish boy) are doing so well.

I've come to appreciate the benefits of our dishwasher, which I never used to use much. Meanwhile the meals provided to us through our friend Sherri are wonderful. Other people have brought us meals as well.

Me, I just need to get out and run more. The central caregiver feels a bit like a May Pole some days.

We don't know what the future will bring, other than I start my new job this coming Monday.

We may need some people to come visit half days and help Linda around the house and through the day. I'm going to consult with the Group Coordinator and we'll be setting up a schedule not for next week but perhaps the week after. If you might be interested and able to come to our home for shifts that might go 7:30-Noon or Noon to 5:45 p.m., please consider it prayerfully and keep an eye out for the calendar announcement if you're interested.

God Bless and take care.
Christopher and Linda Cudworth, Evan, Emily and Chuck.

Come and Visit

Monday, February 25, 2013, 9:00 AM

Congratulations to Chris, as he starts his new job today. Of course, that means there is a need for a bit more coverage for Linda. The mornings are covered, but help would be appreciated in the afternoons, from about 2-4. That is where we could use your assistance. If you would like to come for a visit in the afternoon this week from Tuesday through Friday, that would be appreciated. The time is pretty flexible and you can work it out with your schedule. This will give Chris some assurance that someone will be there with her and give Emily a little break. No medical care is needed. Just come and visit and maybe share a cup of tea. Linda is a big "Ellen" fan, so be prepared to watch an episode with her. Please see the calendar for the opportunity to sign up to help in this way. They do not need meals or food right now. Tasks will be posted on a weekly basis, as the needs arise. Thank you very much. Group Coordinator

In the Garden

Saturday, March 2, 2013, 7:30 AM

"Then Jesus went with them to a place called Gethsemane; and he said to his disciples, "Sit here while I go over there and pray. He took with him Peter and the two sons of Zebedee, and began to be grieved and agitated. Then he said to them, "I am deeply grieved, even to death; remain here and stay awake with me."

It is no coincidence that toward the end of Jesus' life, he retreated to the Garden of Gethesemane to pray. The events depicted in the Bible; when Jesus acknowledges his mortality, expressing genuine fear and agitation at what is about to come, are some of the most compelling and humane moments in all of scripture. In fact they have always attracted me more than the scene of the cross, in terms of connecting with the person of Jesus.

Think about the individuality of those moments, when Jesus calls some trusted disciples to his side. Of course we know they ultimately failed to remain awake. Few among us have the wherewithal to understand the true significance of the presence. The scene in the garden reminds us of that. Yet that scene is not just about the moments in the garden. The garden represents the Kingdom of God and life itself. We should try to treasure the presence of those we love, and help them when and how we can.

Of course many times we fail. Yet many times we also succeed. In fact if we pay attention, we begin to recognize that life is essentially a miracle a minute. We only fail to recognize that because our attention is pulled away in so many directions, by so many things. We fall asleep, in other words.

The power of a garden is both a practical and a spiritual truth. The personal witness in my life to the power of the garden has been my wife. She is an excellent gardener. Every year when people visit our home they marvel at the arrangement of plants she accomplishes.

Yet what they don't often see are the choices she makes in tending her garden. In some years certain types of plants do not thrive. It is too hot or cool, too dry or wet. So keeping a garden is a matter of choices, sometimes very personal choices. More than once I have heard her lament the loss of one of her favorite plants. She mourns her garden even as she loves it. That is the beauty and difficulty of life. We must make choices that are often not easy to find the beauty as well.

In the moment, Linda loves to sit in summer twilight when the light is soft and the plants around her are still open from the day, but relaxed. With a glass of wine by her side, or one of her famously well-made gin and tonics, the height of summer can be celebrated.

For me, that is also the heart of faith. The last 8 years of working with Linda through so many chemotherapies and surgeries and very intimate moments of cleaning pick lines and tending small wounds has been like tending a garden of sorts. Our personal garden of love and survival. It has not been a "battle" the way so many people characterize cancer survival, but a garden of choices. Loving choices. Faithful choices. But hard choices too.

It's true that some of the things we love, activities we like to enjoy together, have not survived the process. It has been tough at times for Linda to enjoy physical activities she so loves. The walking. Riding bikes. (ha ha, the autofill just tried to turn the word "bikes" into "bikinis", what a laugh that would have been.) Even her gardening has been tough at times to accomplish. Last summer her hands were so wracked from the effects of Doxil she had to wear silky soft gloves just around the house, much less out in the yard and the heat and the weeding and the watering. Yet she did it.

She was Christlike in her devotion to her garden. Tending the plants she loves, even through the drought, which forced such difficult choices as the ferns withered away in June. June! Throughout the summer the dry air forced plants outside the watering zone into submission.

Yet what remained was lovely. Her potted plants on the porch formed a huge array of color and form. The one benefit of drought is that we could sit outside without mosquitoes eating us alive. The previous summer the opposite was true. The garden was rich and lovely but the bloodsuckers would carry you away if you got too deep in the garden or tried to sit and enjoy it. Life is that way. Yin and yang. Mosquitoes annually kill more people than any other natural force on earth.

So we have not imagined life to be some distracted timeline where things just roll along without choices to be made. Some of our choices have been painful. Others were not even choices. The loss of her father the very same week that Linda went through major surgery for a colon resection was not easy for anyone to take.

Yet her focus upon arriving home from surgery was to get over there right away and see her father. So the very next day we bundled up and drove over to Elmhurst Memorial so that Linda could be with her dad. His eyes shone when he saw her face before him.

On the way home we received a cell phone call from our daughter Emily, who had just taken a call on our home phone from Linda's gynecological oncologist. He is the man who has led us through all these years. He possesses a deep, rich voice full of authority. When Emily answered the phone he asked if Linda was home, and could he talk with her? Emily was rightly taken aback. There were no "rules" about where mom should be at that moment. Yet she knew that her mother had just had major surgery, and wondered whether she should divulge to her doctor that Linda had taken off in the car to visit her father in the hospital. Linda's doctor reacted with a bit of an admonishing tone, so Emily was a bit freaked after the call.

"He scared the hell out of me!" she chuckled to her mother on the phone. Her doctor really does sound like the voice of God, Perhaps he is, in some sense.

That's how it is with cancer treatment. The voice of God comes at you from all angles. Sometimes it is the quiet whisper of a caregiver leaning over your bed when you need tenderness and help. Other times it is the voice of a doctor saying "You need more chemotherapy."

The voice of God come at us from all directions. It is also funny. Bittersweet. Strange. Wholesome. Truthful. Kind. Hopeful. Honest. Perpetual. Sad. Happy. Merciful. Intimate. Grand. Perfect. Trusting. Smiling. Frowning. Void of fear. Full of fear. Loving. Steadfast. Crazy. Unconventional. Ghostlike. Sudden. Subtle. Frank. Most of all, frank.

That is where we find ourselves, tending our garden in the season of all seasons. That is love. We find inspiration in the example of Christ, the example for so many millions of people. One can see why it works for the Catholics in the mountains of Guadalajara, believers in the hills of Kenya, Protestants walking briskly to church on the streets of Germany or disciples praying with Jesus in the Garden of Gethsemane. Faith is not defined by a race or a gender of humankind. it is not reduced by seasons or drought or mosquitoes chasing you inside. It is the garden of life, faith is. From our perspectives, much like my late mother the Unitarian, we do not necessarily think that our worldview trumps all others. Linda and I have both had deep discussions about God and people and the faith of others. She was most impressed by non-Christian mothers who brought their children to the Christian preschool where she taught on belief that "many paths lead to God."

One of my best riding buddies is a Unitarian as well. He's not a believer in God, but he is a believer in community. We have many long discussions while on our bikes about what makes us all tick and what it means to have faith.

Despite the difficulties, even unto death, faith is sustaining and also a difficult choice to make. You get to define it for yourself, but you also have to account for what you believe in this world and perhaps the next. We simply can never know for sure. Some might say that it is therefore a strange choice, in the end, that we choose to believe. But we do choose to believe.

Sidekicks

Sunday, March 10, 2013, 7:30 AM

On Saturday nights Linda and I watch a combination of shows on National Geographic's various channels. One of them is the reality show The Incredible Dr. Pol, which features a Michigan veterinarian of Eastern European descent who is one of the hardest-working people you've ever seen. His veterinary practice includes 19,000 clients, many of them farmers. Dr. Pol is always driving around at high speed to rescue a cow or horse in distress. Often this involves shoving his arm way up the back end of the animal. What he pulls out or feels in there is the plot booster for many a show.

Dr. Pol is joined on these ventures by his son Charles, an affable lad with a pudge to his frame and an innocent demeanor. Charles plays the foil to many a kicking cow or bucking horse. Generally he stays safe but once in a while he takes a kick to the groin or head. His pale complexion flushes on such occasions, and his glasses seem to fog over.

Last night Bob and Kirsten Snodgrass were visiting and we all watched Dr. Pol together. Chuckling at the antics of Charles, we all observed that while he is worthless on the veterinary side, he plays an important overall role on the show. Human interest. Sincerity. Taking a kick to the groin.

"He's a sidekick," said Linda.

Wow, I thought. That's yet another example of Linda summing up the situation with humor and insight.

For example, on a family reunion in Minnesota years ago, our cabin sat right next to the lake. It was a Cudworth reunion, which was something of an astrological event given that the family is comprised of Leos, Aries and the lot. I don't believe in astrology but it does describe human characteristics in a colorful way. I reserve the right to make that statement despite its illogical foundation.

So here we were, jammed into a few cabins with simmering family differences bubbling around the dock on a hot summer day, when up rides a handsome young man with no shirt, rippling muscles and a boyishly friendly way about him.

"Look," says Linda. "It's Mr. Boat."

For the rest of the week I chuckled about her comment. Mr. Boat was responsible for bringing our fishing boats to dock or taking us out into the array of boats floating in Leech Lake so that we could go drag perch and pike into the backend of the boat. Like the opposite of Dr. Pol, it was.

Fishing is a strange ritual, resulting in entire lines of stinking fish hung in the hot summer sun while the living ones keep swimming around the giant lake. It's all so random. When you're skimming over the water in a high horsepower boat with the spray flying up in the sun and the water roiling up in the wake behind you it's possible to forget you're anywhere important or real. The fish come up and bite the swiveling lures. You thrill to the catch, slowing the boat as you reel in another trophy or something less, and then move on.

That's how life works. We're on a big lake of existence. We can't see below the surface. We buzz around testing our luck on this spot or that.

That's all changed when you have a fish finder, which ostensibly tells you whether there's big or little fish below the boat. A fishfinder is kind of a sidekick to the avid fisherman. The little screen is a conversation of sorts, a documentary of wishful, fishful thinking. You cast your lure down below and quite often the fishfinder is correct. That's what makes a good sidekick. "Isn't that cheating?" my wife asked when she saw the fish finder.

In a lake 30 miles long, there's no such thing as cheating. That's what I told her anyway, trying hard to believe it. That's what sidekicks do. They both question and encourage the main characters. I'm a sidekick of sorts.

It's been that way since the day the gynecologist turned up cancer on Linda's ovary. I've been her sidekick ever since. We've had many adventures on major holidays like Easter, Christmas and New Years, sitting in hospital rooms trying to solve this problem or that. Usually Linda wryly finds some sort of comment to make about the situation even when she's miserable or uncomfortable. She always identifies the sidekicks too. They might be a tender nurse who finds a solution to a rash or worse. Or it might be the odd doctor who stands before her divining the problem with his or her ample brain and experience.

Then there's always me, the affable dope in the sneakers and stained sweatshirt. I've been Robin to her Batman. Heck, I've even been her Lois Lane to her Superman, but only during the summer months when I shave my legs for cycling. The nylons catch on the hairs otherwise. Just kidding.

Being a sidekick is a big honor. You get to watch and learn a lot from the hero of the story. Of course the hero seldom feels like they are a hero of any sort. Frankly, there are many occasions when the hero would prefer any role other than having to be the hero at the time. Many's the time when Linda has turned to me and said, "I just want my life back."

You can almost hear Spiderman saying that. Tired of climbing walls and casting webs, swinging through the city at night and being forced into grapples with the villain. Spiderman is a reluctant hero at times. In Linda's case the villain has been an invisible yet ever present force in her life. Cancer is most definitely a villain. Random and mean.

But here's another confession: It's not always easy being the sidekick either. Sometimes you make mistakes or say the wrong thing at the wrong time, step on a toe or put a cold hand where it makes the hero jump.

A sidekick might undercook the oatmeal or mess up the order of a pick line cleaning. Sidekicks live and learn. There's always something to learn. We're cathartic dopes, carrying on in the wake of our heroes. It's still an honor being the sidekick. You get to see the hero in their finest and weakest moments. And if that's not an honor, I don't know what is.

Darby O'Gill and the Little People

Sunday, March 17, 2013, 7:30 AM

Today is the day that we all celebrate St. Patrick's Day. Never mind the fact that the tradition started with a priest that chased all the Protestants (snakes) out of Ireland. That's really how it all started, in case you had never heard the facts.

So it's a weird case of reverse political correctness that we all celebrate religious intolerance as a day to get drunk and pretend we're Irish. I mean, how strange is that, really? If the day were invented in modern times, it would be branded as a horrid form of orange and green stereotyping.

That is why the movie Darby O'Gill and the Little People is all the more charming in its Disneyesque form of political incorrectness.

Our family discovered this strange little Disney gem a number of years back. I'm pretty sure it warped our children's minds for a while. There are terrifying scenes of the carriage of death descending from the sky, and Darby O'Gill shrieking at the spirits that accompany the carriage, "It's the Bansheeeees!'

That scene comes toward the end of the movie, long after Darby O'Gill, a generally happy keeper of property for a wealthier man, decides to engage in a game of wits with the Leprechaun King, leader of the Little People.

Little People! How politically correct is that? Yet these are a merry bunch of politically incorrect leprechauns, for sure. The King likes his good whisky, and Darby O'Gill gets the good king drunk as heck and then throws him in a sack to take home. Darby then negotiates the three wishes promised by the king's capture.

As the king sobers up and realizes he's been tricked, Darby totes the sack to the local pub where he brags that he's captured the Leprechaun King. The townspeople are both curious and skeptical, particularly one local mug who's got his eyes on Darby's job.

When Darby finally sets up to reveal his captured leprechaun, the Leprechaun King emerges in the form of a hare (the king being a trickster, too!) that runs off.

Darby is the laughingstock, and the movie proceeds to converge on the love story of his daughter being courted by the local mug and a handsome lad played by Sean Connery.

Well, it all winds up good and happy, but not until Darby is actually being carted off to wherever the carriage of death leads, along with the Leprechaun King. Still, the Leprechaun King has one more trick up his sleeve. He engages in a casual yet loving conversation with Darby O'Gill, recalling their many games and exploits in life. It is one of the most tender scenes you'll ever see, one that captures the wistful nature of struggles and joys in life. The message of the whisky and mirth is that the troubles of life all mix together. In a way, the movie is Disney at its best, even if it commits a measure of modern faux pas by current standards.

The hell with it, we have always said. Let Darby O'Gill be Darby O'Gill! Without the shrieking banshees the movie has no grit. Without the drinking the movie makes no sense at all. The King and Darby have a good time with each other. So what if whisky and gold drive their purpose? The stash of riches the King possesses is stored safely underground where the Big People can't get it. What an allegory! One could equitably say that our true treasures in life are just like that. We store them away where the Big People or the Bad People, whoever they may be in our lives, can't get at them.

We're all just Little People, merry and mirthful in our way, making the best of it. Sure, we don't abide by the political reality of kings anymore, but that's not the point. The King stands for something else. The will to live, and live well.

In the dark moments when Darby and the King are sitting in the carriage being carried to the great beyond, we realize that it's not all black and white when it comes to the transition from life to whatever comes beyond. The terror of dying is replaced by the recollection of all that is good and worth keeping in our hearts. Tenderness is abundant. Joy can abound. We are given a gift to hold.

In a way, that is what happens in the movie. Through gentle conversation, the Leprechaun King gets Darby to issue his third wish, which can't be told or it would spoil the ending.

Yet the message of that wish is one of both mortality and joy. This is how we live life from the moment we are born. The time we share is precious, yet time expands to encompass our most fervent wishes. Our trials forge our spirits. It is the journey we all share, and a treasure we keep once we arrive.

Sometimes we must trick the Leprechaun King to actually get our hands on the gold, however briefly. But that is the fun of the game, and the real reason for St. Patrick's Day. When we are all Irish for the nonce.

In the hills of Wisconsin

Sunday, March 24, 2013, 7:15 AM

Over the past few years Linda and I have joined our friends Randy and Debbie on mini-vacations in southwest Wisconsin. Part of our reason for going is a mutual appreciation for the work of Frank Lloyd Wright, whose architecture we have visited in Chicago at the Robie House and out east at Falling Water and Kentuck Knob in southwest Pennsylvania.

While in Wisconsin we always took in a few of the familiar spots, including House On the Rock. We all found the place boorish and over the top. It is said that when the so-called architect of House on the Rock asked to join the Wright school to work in the field of architecture, Frank Lloyd told him, "I wouldn't hire you to design a chicken coop."

From the looks of House On the Rock both inside and out, one can see why Wright despised the man's worldview. It's an abomination, an ugly curiosity that is a testament not to design but of ego. Of course Frank Lloyd Wright also had a great big ego, but his work supposed that in appearance anyway.

So by contrast, the Taliesin home of Frank Lloyd Wright which sits right up the road from The House On the Rock south of Spring Green, Wisconsin is a study of well-chosen prairie-style sparseness and architecture. The House On the Rock is a comparably a penile work of frenetic energy stuck to a cliff. The two contrast each other in a perfectly Wisconsin sort of way.

Granted: you might enjoy the House On the Rock for its eclectic collections of junk. Others rather like the rambling architecture, if you can call it that. We felt the place to be a strained attempt at originality. And that's being kind. The collections fall just shy of hoarding. Those well-known junk hunters on American Pickers might have ignored the lot.

This is not to be snobbish or superior to anyone. We all have our judgments of life. Some of them are accurate. Some not so much. We might miss something in the construct and miss the message completely. Or we assume our way of thinking is the only way. Perhaps the House On the Rock really is a work of genius. If so, it was lost on us. So be it. We tried.

While in Wisconsin we also rode our bikes a bit. Note that the hills there are not easy for the taking. We rode together up and down those un-glaciated mounds of limestone on several summer trips. The first trip was summer of 2009. Linda struggled a bit on the bike that year. We found out that September the cancer was back. It turned out she'd been riding through the early fog of that physical challenge.

That's why it may have been fate of a sort that led me to ride my mountain bike off on a different venture that year. I wanted to take a tour through Governor Dodge State Park, a place that had been formative in my early adulthood. One summer before college there was an RA Retreat held there, and I put in 80 miles running in those deep, rich hills in August of 1978. That year I moved up to second man on the cross country team and we placed second at nationals.

But it was the nature of the park that I remembered most. It encompasses deep valleys of dark green woods, and jutting ledges of shelf limestone. Fields of bergamot (bee balm) and wild eyed sunflowers burst forth in late summer. Birds are everywhere, and singing insects.

As I rode through the park on my own that day something made me stop on one familiar slope heading back toward the park center. The crickets were chirping. An indigo bunting repeated its mid-day song, persistent through the heat and sunshine. And it occurred to me: "This will keep going long after I'm gone. These birds and crickets and shining leaves were here 30 years ago. They will be here 30 years in the future. And 30 years after that. And I will be gone."

Realization of our mortality comes in bird song, and crickets chirping. At that point we don't need religion to tell us what's going on. In fact my worldview is a pretty even balance of the organic and the spiritual. I'm built that way. Some people depend more on the organic than the spiritual to make sense of the world. And that makes perfect sense to me too. No judgement is important but your own. The bible may tell you differently, and the confessional language of faith as well. But I think it's a balance. Yin and yang. Melody and harmony. Realistic and abstract. Some just see the side of the equation that makes sense. I believe they're blessed as well.

Albert Camus wrote that he would rather live life thinking there is a God and to die and find out there isn't than to insist all of life there is no God and to die and find out there is. On the cusp of life we face this difficult question and many convert. Others hold to a belief in God all their lives only to find the suffering too strange to bear, and lose faith.

I do believe in a God who understands both and all perspectives. When I sat on my bike listening to those crickets in the hills of Wisconsin, I also thought about Linda, and whether the cancer would stay away. Not even knowing at that instant it was already back.

Yesterday she stood up shakily from bed and in both a practical and loving move, placed her arms around me for a few moments. She wanted help walking but this was also a time for being close. That's been hard to find over the last few weeks. We are alternately so close neither of us can see around the other for the things that need to be done. We feel separated by a distance of discomfort and the chirping of a hospital bed in the living room. Like crickets in the hills of Wisconsin. We listen and try to understand. That chirping you hear is both a pragmatic truth and a symbol of our being. It is both organic and eternal. That is where we are.

When we stop to listen, the hills and everything we admire and treasure sometimes talks back to us. Of course we must wade through the strange and acquisitive at times to find what is true and important. Perhaps it is true: we must go through the House On the Rock to appreciate our Taliesin. That is life in all its imperfect strangeness. We suffer our own judgments, and wonder why it is all so damned true.

CHAPTER THREE

Radical notions

Wednesday, March 27, 2013, 8:00 AM

The morning after a wife and mother passes away is a strange amalgamation of joy and sorrow. Bittersweet joy at the manner in which we shared in her passing, together, holding her hands; Evan, Emily and I. Just peace after that. No more of the difficult breathing and suffering she's seen the last couple weeks.

Yet her spirit and personality never diminished at any moment. Linda still had amusing quips even through yesterday noon, some that seemed to characterize the whole of marriage, and of life. While moving her from one bed to another for better care yesterday, she tolerated it as best she could. It was not a comfortable task for her or the people helping us.

When she was placed back in bed and positioned with pillows I bent over to ask if she was doing okay and she glanced up at me with a tired grin and said, "I thought I wasn't supposed to suffer."

What a metaphor for life. None of us likes to suffer. Yet here, the lot of us, are immersed in a life of issues; with financial problems that don't go away by themselves, or a car breaks down. Work wears you out. The kids seem like they're not in tune with reality. On and on.

Suffering through all those challenges is never easy. Many times during the last 8 years people would quietly share some challenge in their lives and then turn to us and say, "Of course it's nothing compared to what you're going through..."

Well, I say, "Who says?" Suffering is one of those emotional spectrum things that is relative. What hurts worse, back pain or foot pain? How would you rather die, by fire or by ice? We can't answer those questions, yet we ask them.

We give answers to these questions but they are all relative and all personal. Such as, what superpowers would you like to have? I always chose flying because from the time I was a kid I wanted to be like Superman. Yet when I put on my Superman Halloween suit and really tried to fly from the lower branch of a maple tree, it didn't take long to hit the ground.

My friend Amy scooped me up off the ground and said, "C'-mon, let's go get lunch."

I've tried diving out of a few more rhetorical trees since then and always Linda was there to scoop me up and say, "C'mon, let's go get lunch."

Food. So symbolic.

Linda was a good cook, you see. Underrated. She made damn good drinks too. We'd share them on the back patio on summer nights while watching fireflies rise up from her garden. That is the meat of our marriage, right there. Shared moments. Not the events, so much, but the shared moments.

They all seemed destined to happen despite my balky bachelor phase when my brother finally took Linda aside and told her, "Give him 3 months, and if he doesn't commit, dump his ass."

Okay, okay. So I had a little commitment fear. But once we tied the knot it did not falter. Through all her recent treatments and intimate needs she'd worry out loud that it was difficult and I'd say to her, "One flesh." Anything she needed, needed to be done. That was that.

It pulled us closer and closer. I felt wired to her these last couple years. While I was home working while "not working" we'd sometimes talk to each other through the living room floor. She was respecting my space and yet we were never far apart.

Can't say we were as devoted as Paul and Linda McCartney, who supposedly spent only one night apart in their whole marriage. When my Linda took to loud snoring during chemo I had no qualms about sleeping the front room. Just me and Chuck, hanging out until morning when we'd both charge back in there and climb under the covers with Linda to sleep a while longer.

I know all that's all changed now. But I'm glad that somewhere along the way when things were not going so well with jobs or other things that she did not dump MY ass. I used to joke, "When are you going to trade me in on a model that can fix things?"

She'd laugh. But I can honestly say that the last 6-7 things I fixed around the house actually worked. She'd say, "I have to give you credit. That actually works."

Of course there are some things you can't fix, no matter how hard you try. Persistent cancer sometimes can't be fixed. It can only be held off while you read more instructions and try to form a plan that will come out all right.

I couldn't exactly fix my wife's cancer, but in many good ways cancer fixed us. It helped us see what was important, and how to act on it. It was also a journey worth taking to experience the kindness, intellect, spirit and gifts of others. Those may be radical notions, but they are our notions. Now that she rests in peace, I hope to honor our radical notions even more.

The right kind of pride

Friday, March 29, 2013, 5:00 AM

Proverbs 16:18 — *Pride goes before destruction, a haughty spirit before a fall.*

We are so accustomed to being lectured about the perils of pride, that when genuine pride comes along it can be hard to recognize its virtue. We have learned through the sayings of Proverbs to avoid hubris at almost any cost, for it can bring us down. Yet there are forms of pride that are worthy of our thoughts and our souls. We should remember that too.

There is pride in our family. It can be hard work maintaining relationships, understanding the needs and wants of others, and supporting their goals in life. But we can be proud in that. There is pride in our work, for there is nothing wrong with doing a good job. My father has always told me "Take pride in your craft." That lesson is re-learned ever day.

There is pride in tradition. Our families have fun traditions that we have maintained over the years. Sometimes the rituals get a little worn but we uphold them. Then we have our memories as well. "Remember when..." is a powerful source of pride. Nostalgia is a constructive emotion when it binds us together in love and spirit.

All those forms of pride come together in time of need, especially in the work of caring for someone you love dearly. These last couple months of caring for my wife Linda took every ounce of focus and pride at times. You too can be proud if you try your best to take care of someone who needs you. There will be failures and shortcomings, forgotten this's and not quite thats. Yet you try, and the rewards when someone you love can relax and take in a moment or share a word of love make it all worth it.

When it was all finished and my children and I had held the hands of my wife as she passed from this world to the next, the opportunity to sit alone with my wife finally arrived. As I sat there looking at her face, I touched her lips with my hand and told her I loved her. Then a deep sense of pride in her life came over me. I sat stunned at the realization of how proud I was of this woman. She had borne up through so many difficult and potentially demeaning circumstances. We persevered together.

Even against the stripped pride and temporal sadness of having to deal with a disease changed our lives, our blessings were fulfilled.

She'd lost her hair multiple times and accepted that it would likely never come back. We sat in front of the computer screen together and looked at new wig styles. I pointed to a little looser look and at first she resisted. Yet it did more closely resembled her "real" hair. A day or two later the wig arrived and she did not tell me at first. Then she walked out into the living room wearing her new hairstyle and said something on the order of, "Look what I got you!"

We joked at times about buying red wigs or other colors, but that was not Linda. She was a fun and sometimes joyfully frivolous person all of her life, but not one to playfully cast off her image. Her proper pride would not allow it. I loved her for that.

We all noted that her real character never left her. Not through the deepest difficulties or even toward the very end of her life in this world. She kept to her character. Her love of solace. Her pride in her children and her work. Her love for friends whom she loathed to burden. Above all, her abiding phrase during all these tough weeks was, "I don't want to be a burden."

Her caregivers would convulse with sympathy when she said that. Of course she was not a burden. There were days in the last few weeks when her body so filled with fluid that it was difficult to help her move. Yet it was no effort for me to get my arms under her shoulders and use my own legs to give her strength. Once up and moving, she'd keep going. That's how it worked.

So when it came time to see her stillness, a great sense of pride and gratitude washed over me. I am so proud of my wife, who lives on in my heart. Though it pains us to lose her, it gains us to feel this pride and keep going.

We will share in this life on April 13 when we hold a service at 10 a.m. at Bethlehem Lutheran Church in St. Charles. Linda's own instructions, written 2 years ago with to me, "This can't go on forever, right?" will form the foundation of the service, followed by a luncheon where people can meet and talk and share. If you can attend, we would love to see you there.

And thank you all over and over again for your abiding support and love. It means the world.

A Goofball's Guide to Grief

Thursday, April 4, 2013, 8:45 PM

When you lose something in life that really matters to you, grief takes over.

The most obvious source of grief is losing a loved one. But there are many types and sources of grief. I maintain it takes a real goofball to deal with them all.

You know those thoughts in your head that come out of nowhere and make you feel like you're a little nuts for thinking them? They multiply like crazy during periods of grief. It's easy to blame yourself for strange thoughts and even cry aloud, "Why do I have these thoughts? Who thinks these things?" Only a goofball, right?

Well, fellow goofballs, we all think these things. Most of us keep them to ourselves lest our friends think we are truly nuts.

Welcome to the Goofball club, in other words. Once you accept that you are a healthy form of goofball and that everyone on the planet is a goofball right along with you in some ways, you are liberated from guilt over your goofball thoughts. That's a good thing.

At times we need to let our goofball thoughts run their course to an illogical end. In fact we don't let our minds wander a little, the absurdity of life and loss will step in and start your goofball brain thinking weird thoughts anyway.

Early in marriage my wife and I got into a goofy discussion and began talking about our future and our ultimate ends. In a way the conversation took place over several years and evolved to the position that neither of us really wanted a traditional burial with a gravesite and a stone marker. That seems like a bit of a goofy thing to concern yourself with so early in a marriage, but it led us to discuss other important things like God and kids and life insurance policies. So it worked.

The net result was that my wife left instructions for me on what to do with her cremains. Having long ago opted to carry out the same process of cremation no matter who died first, she suggested we save some of our ashes for "us" so that we could be together.

But my goofball brain still had a little trouble figuring out how to feel when I stopped by the funeral home to pick up my wife's ashes. Carrying your wife under your arm is a surreal experience no matter how you look at it. I sat in the car and cried for a while, not knowing why. I guess it made it all real. Again. I had cried the day before as well, when the funeral home had called and left a message asking me to call them. I knew what the call back would mean. But we get goofy about such things. The indeterminate truth is hard to handle.

My problem with grief is that it really can have a long shelf life. In the Linda/Chris relationship our mutual grief extends back 8 years to when Linda was first diagnosed with ovarian cancer. Right away we felt grief for what once was, a life innocent of cancer. It was like being born into a reality we could not have anticipated, and didn't.

Waves of grief, including a tsunami or two, would wash over us in the years ahead. There was grief over her suffering. Grief over her laments, and mine. Grief over the difficulties of not being able, at times, to do the things she loved best. Grief at the idea that together we needed to sacrifice the activities that originally bound us together.

It was also hard to start anything new in our relationships. Linda tried cycling with me because it was low impact. We bought her a sweet rolling Trek Navigator 2.5, but her feet were so numb from neuropathy she could hardly control the pedals, it turned out. When she did get rolling her eyes would water profusely from the chemo. She had no eyelashes either, so there was nothing to stop the tears. Then her wig wouldn't stay on. Yet she still to tried. So hard at times.

I do recall one fine summer day we rode out to Wasco and back on the Great Western Trail, a distance of about 6 miles. Linda started slowly at first, unsteady on the bike. Then on the way home she picked up speed and ceased to look back to see how close I might be flying. She was temporarily liberated. The wind was in her wig, you might say.

We finished and posed for a photo together at the start of the trailhead. I was proud of her. Grief relented in those moments. It is quite a fine thing to go from grief to relief.

Living with grief is possible. Our little "secrets" of survival became the bonds upon which we based our mutual hope. But as she put it in a "last wishes" letter written in 2011, "This can't go on forever, right?"

And she was right. No human gets out of here alive. Her life was cut short, or was it? It seems to me that everyone's life is exactly the length it turns out to be. It's absurd to speculate any other alternatives. So we deal with it.

On Good Friday I called my brother in Pennsylvania and told him I was attending services that evening. "Whoa..." he replied. He thought it might be "too soon," and he was not the

only one concerned that a Good Friday service could be too "dark" for someone grieving over the loss of a spouse.
I told him. "I want to walk straight into the pain."

He burst out laughing. We both knew it was the best way. Dive into the absurdity. Face death face first.

It was the right thing to do. It turned out the service was cathartic. Both pastors delivered huge insights that helped me greatly. Then came Easter. My gosh, I thought. The whole idea of your wife dying during holy week is so literal it's goofy. What more direct confrontation with death and promise of life could you possibly imagine?

This morning I awoke thinking about the things I loved about her. In that moment I dwelt on the physical. I thought of her head to toe, everything I knew about her. It felt real, not imagined. Then I said a little prayer of thanks for her companionship. It felt right to do.

Chuck The Dog is still a little mystified by it all. So he and I have been in the same sort of mode. He'll sit up in bed and pause a moment, as if he's thinking: Something's missing. But he's doing okay. We both are. We go on, that little dog and I, greeting our friends in our same goofy way. We're both a little hyper and by nature a little anxious and needing attention. So neither of us knows how to experience life--or grief--in any other way. It's our goofy little club. We didn't sign up to be members, but maybe we did by loving someone fully. Life is goofy that way.

Yardwork and Jack Sparrow's Compass

Sunday, April 7, 2013, 6:30 PM

I spent the day cleaning the yard, cutting down the grasses Linda always let me burn in the rickety fire pit we've kept year after year. Stupid thing has three legs but you'd never know it. It leans so far to one side it looks like an upside down R2D2. The old fire pit. On its last legs, as they say.

But some things never change. I cut down the ornamental grasses that are thin as paper and stuffed them deep into the fire pit. A small flicker of flame is all it takes to ignite them. The flame creeps through the gut of the grass and flickers eight feet in the air. A small part of me is a pyromaniac. It seems like everyone likes a little flame in their life. We burn candles and firewood in the fireplace.

My favorite part of a wood fire is when the flames subside and the whole log glows red, orange and yellow.

In absence of human company, fire is a companion. In the presence of other human beings, fire unites us. Love burns too. All it takes is a spark. So it was my consolation and reward to burn the winter grass and touch the spring soil. She was with me there all day.

The neighbors might assume I know nothing of the garden she created, and what to do with it. But that is not true. While Linda was the true gardener, I liked to listen to her plans and help whenever she asked. It was always my job to empty the patio pots in the fall and help carry them back out in spring.

One learns a lot from seeing the dying forms of summer plants. The roots tell a story as well. So does the soil and its condition after a growing season. You see how it layers and how the roots bunch when they have nowhere else to go. Like many things in life, they must content themselves with the space allotted them. Sometimes that's all any of us can do.

Then there are the accouterments of the garden.

It was a strange thing to me that the yellowed thermometer that has been hanging on our tree for 15 years suddenly blew down from its perch and broke last week. Frankly the thing was no longer accurate. Much of the time it only reflected what we wished the temperature would be. It worked almost like the compass owned by Captain Jack Sparrow in the movie Pirates of the Caribbean. In other words, it was a thermometer in name only.

Yet its presence was a fixture of sorts. So the temperature might be 60 and the old thermometer reads 80? We forgave its neglectful ways. It mattered more that it had stuck with us all these years.

We cherished certain things like that. There is a sign of words formed from metal tacked to a tree outside the picture window. It says Miracles Happen. We saw our share. Blessings were fulfilled.

Tonight when the yard work was all done I made a trip down to talk with some of Linda's closest friends about some plans for the Memorial Service this Saturday, April 13 at 10 am. It had to do with flowers. Naturally.

When our talk was through they invited me to dinner. These are treasured friends and their bright eyes and companionship was all I really desired. But some real duty called. I had commissioned work to complete this evening, and catch up. It pays well. So I thanked them for the invitation and came home. But the minute I got here after a stop at the pet store and Jewel (laundry soap!) and an excitable greeting from Chuck the Dog, I felt the tinge of regret. I wished I could have stayed.

The easiest thing in the world is to be strong and stupid. It's much harder to be weak and wise. The first takes determination. The second, real courage. Tonight is one of those nights that seem to fall in between the two.

It's a fact. There is mourning, and then again there is morning. Tomorrow's another day and knowing that you still have to meet your commitments despite your grief falls somewhere between all that strength and wisdom stuff. But sometimes you just feel stupid about your choices. It's worth forgiving oneself on that one.

One does learn that it pays to be weak in some ways, and a little stupid at other times. Believe it or not, letting yourself be a little weak and a little stupid can be some of the most important attributes in working your way through a loss. We don't ask for these things to happen, do we? So why should we assume that we're automatically capable of wishing away the hurt that comes with them? It's going to take time. I learned that by trying some things this weekend for which I was not yet emotionally prepared. It stung. "Okay," I said out loud. I know that's not the right direction, right now. It helps to recall that Jack Sparrow's compass was sometimes wrong as well.

The yard work was the right thing to do, however. It felt like being on the deck of a good ship. The right direction.
And it turns out some others think that's a good ship to sail as well. Some of Linda's friends want to come over and help out with the garden.

But if you can't wait for that and want to help out with something special, this Thursday night we'll be putting live flowers in small plantable pots to be given out to each family at the

Memorial Service this weekend. The whole thing has been organized by Randy and Debbie. So if you'd like to come help prepare the pots this Thursday, meet at the Cudworth house at 7:00 p.m. Call if you'd like to help out or email me at. It won't take that long and wine will be served, as we've got a shelf load to share.

Yard work can be therapeutic. Even in tiny pots.

On honeymoons and funerals

Sunday, April 14, 2013, 4:30 AM

In 1985 my wife Linda and I were married in a church ceremony and then an outdoor reception in the backyard of her parents home in Addison, IL. It turned out to be a picture book day with friends and family in attendance. Yet weddings are dizzying affairs. People from all corners of your life converge in one place. The groom and bride whisk through vows and greetings, toasts and dancing, and then land together in a hotel room to begin life together, perhaps with the honeymoon.

Our choice was to hold off on the honeymoon for a month and make a trip by car to Glacier National Park, a favorite destination of her parents and one of the most beautiful places on earth. We drove 13 hours the first day to camp at the Badlands, a national park in South Dakota. The landscape was moonlike, hot and dry. The wind blew steadily and it was everything this young groom could do to put up a tent in which to sleep that first night. Some fellow wandered over to "help" of course, and I bristled at the inferred suggestion that the tent would not go up under my own supervision. It did get up somehow.

As we were preparing to cook our first meal, the park ranger came by to instruct us that no ground fires were allowed. "We have this small grill, can we use that?" we asked. He told us to put it up on the table. So we did. The small grill heated up fast with coals and we set out some bread on the table in anticipation of cooking up some chicken. The bread quickly turned to toast, literally, in the hot, dry air. Some coals fell down through the grill and we burned a hole in the table. We'd done what we were told, but it was probably a failure of communication all around.

We drove out to Yellowstone next and camped in an area where there had been bear activity. Grizzlies are the glory of Yellowstone and Glacier, but with the glory comes risk. We hiked with bear bells dinging as we went, and wore the plastic rain gear we'd purchased to keep away the rain.

The trip north to Glacier followed the giant spine of mountains leading to the northwest part of Montana. Pulling into Glacier is a dramatic event. It was then and remains today a park with mountains that seem to jump up from behind its own foothills. Romantic and awe-inspiring, Glacier was a perfect spot for a honeymoon.

We stayed in a cute cabin a couple nights and went on dayhikes, learning our way around the park and its cool valleys. Then we hiked into the wilderness to camp overnight at Otokomi Lake, up in the mountains. There were bear maulings at the lake at one point in time, and our bear bells and rocks clacked together seemed like thin protection against the threat of grizzlies. Then my wife informed me that her period was coming on, and that's never good news in bear country.

We managed a meal cooked next to the remote lake. Our belongings were hung in a pack 16 feet in the air and we changed clothes after eating and cooking our meal, because bears smell food and come sniffing if you have any trace on your body.

The little tent was set up amongst rich green fir trees that allowed a peek at the lake. The sky fell to twilight and the trees on the ridge above turned black and jagged. We slept with one ear out for sounds. Years later I'd see a cartoon in *The Far Side* that described how we felt about that night. The cartoon pictured two bears looking at a pair of campers in their sleeping bags. One bear holds a paw up to shield his voice and says, "Look! Sandwiches!"

The final leg of our trip was a drive up to Waterton on the Canadian side of the park. The hotel sits on the far north end of a long lake between two swooping sets of mountains. The very idea that this lake and its bed were carved by ice, glaciers to be exact, is beyond human comprehension, yet there it sits, windswept and bold. "Deal with it," the vistas seem to utter.

Linda and I wandered out with our cameras to take some pictures of the hotel, and of each other. The photo of her in her black top and purple skirt, tan skin and golden hair is one of the most stunning images from our marriage. Behind her the mountains stand like witnesses to our lives together, and the lake. You can almost see the breeze behind her yet she appears joyful and serene in her place.

My son Evan discovered that photo of Linda in our Glacier album and posted it on Facebook the night of her Memorial Service. My daughter noted that Linda always seemed tan, like a coconut when she was young. "I guess that makes me the inside of the coconut," my daughter chuckled wryly. Her fair skin does not tan easily. Linda would always say, "You have beautiful skin Emily. Be glad for that."

Such are the journeys of life and discovery that our experiences converge in intense ways. The eulogy delivered by my son at the Memorial service was so replete with combinations of humor and love that there could be no additions or subtractions without diminishing the message. He captured all the years of our marriage and her motherhood with well-chosen words. In essence he painted a picture all could appreciate; that Linda was a loving and heartfelt mother and teacher, gardener and lover of nature.

Linda at Waterton, Glacier.

You can see that in the picture of her standing in front of that vista looking south to Glacier National Park. She is ready for what comes next, yet time wraps its arms around her. I envision her in such a place now, but what can we really know? It satisfies our urge for eternity. That is enough for me.

What more could a husband and father, son and daughter, sister, mother and friends ask of one person? She gave herself to life, as our pastor said in his sermon remarks, that is a gift indeed, and in deed.

I hope you know this is not just romanticizing a wife lost to cancer. Our lives were not perfect and she would be the first one to tell you that. Yet the untold struggles and the mountains we climbed were what made it all matter. There were bears and fears. The sniff of blood on the wind, it seems, is what even us humans must survive. It was one wild trip, our honeymoon, and our marriage. We would not have had it any other way.

Maybe I'm Still Amazed

Saturday, April 20, 2013, 12:45 PM

At lunch a friend tells me, "I'm so used to seeing you together. I keep expecting her to walk in the room with you."

Another says, most kindly, "I keep hearing her voice."

All kindnesses. Shared experience. Yet a way of moving on, while keeping memories alive. The presence of someone in your life turns out to be, somewhat unexpectedly, more than their physical being. How wonderful. Joyous. Necessary. Real.

The entire scenario of losing a loved one has however gotten me thinking about the similarities between death and divorce. Neither is an easy proposition to face. In either case, there are things to be reconciled. The past. The present. The future, of course. How is it that we are supposed to reconcile the future exactly?

We are forced to re-imagine ourselves as a person with a changed identity. A person no longer part of a couple. Yet a person who still longs for love and acceptance. Affection and commiseration. Conversation and joy.

Sometimes even a fight or two would do just fine, to feel the grit of life. Only a few times in marriage with Linda did I draw the F bomb for pushing her too far on this or that subject. Once she was trying to choke down some horrid medication for a medical test she had to take, and it wasn't going too well. The drink tasted awful. So she went outside for fresh air to try and get it down. When I came out to help and made a suggestion on how to proceed, it was one offer of encouragement too far. F-off! At that moment, you get the message. Marriages and relationships are made of that stuff, too. People standing up for themselves.

But when it all comes down and the separation begins to feel real, and all the grit you once had is suddenly missing, you find yourself thinking, "What the hell is this, exactly? How do I exist in time? Where do I belong now?"

It's like a combination of all sorts of time. The paspresenfuture. All of it comes rushing at you at once. The memorial service for a loved one shines like a diamond, but it reads like a kaleidoscope. Same with divorce or any other sort of separation. By force or by choice, we've suddenly got to reconcile a whole lot we used to take for granted. And look to the future, whatever that might mean.

Caring friends walk you through the process of reconciliation with a death or divorce as if you were taking a tour through a haunted house, yet out of season.

Don't touch this...Be careful where you step...

Scary stuff still pops up. Even when the lights are on. Especially so. Something reminds us of that loved one and a jolt runs through our soul connection. It's hard to part with anything associated with that person, yet to keep too much of it around is to live in a haunted house of sorts.

I knew a woman who lost a husband that happened to have a twin brother. Within weeks of her husband's death she married his twin brother and he moved in, wearing the former husband's clothes, that fit him well of course. Needless to say their kids were just a little freaked out. It was like their dad went into the closet of death and another dad walked back out.

We're used to talking about coming out of the closet to find our true selves. But in cases like that, going into the closet is a weird interpretation of being born again. Occupying that space in a darkened closet it not where most of us need to be. Not those of us grieving, anyway.

And who doesn't recall a not so nice experience with a dark closet of one kind or another?

I used to be scared of the dark. Somewhere along the line, through faith or reason or both, that all changed. One day I was walking up a dark stairway and no longer felt any fear. It didn't make sense any more to be scared. A whole sheath of childhood fell away at that moment. It was liberating.

My brothers used to call that scary sense of being followed in a dark hall or stairway the Gray Ghost. Fear made your ears turn red and your whole body go tense. You'd tear up or down the stairs and burst through a door into the light only to feel suddenly strange at what had just moments before seemed terrifying. You stood there relieved, wondering what the fuss was all about. Darn you, Gray Ghost.

But it's all gone now. No more Grey Ghost for me. What made it go away? That feeling of fear and dread...

The idea of fear can be so powerful you can almost imagine it overtaking you. That was the Gray Ghost. Ultimately, if you believe yourself to be either a reasonable and faithful person, or both, there is enough there to protect you, one way or the other.

One thinks of the biblical passage, "*When I was a child I spoke as a child, I understood as a child, I thought as a child; but when I became a man I put away childish things.*" I Cor. xiii. 11. (NIV)

We are also given a promise, looking ahead. "*For now we see only a reflection as in a mirror; then we shall see face to face. Now I know in part; then I shall know fully, even as I am fully known.*" 1 Corinthians 13:12. (NIV)

So we waltz back and forth between our childish thoughts, our fears and our greatest hopes. That is human existence.

The first night at home alone after the death of my wife, I had taken a shower and crawled into bed only to be awakened by a loud noise from another room. I sat up in bed, alarmed. Then I realized what had caused the noise. During the shower I had turned a bottle of showering gel upside down because the bottle was almost empty. At some point enough lotion flowed to the bottom to shift the weight and make the bottle topple off its perch on the shower ledge. Fear explained. Fear dismissed.

I remember the first time we brought our dog Chuck into the house. He was nervous and scared and didn't know what to make of his new situation. Sitting with Linda and I on the floor, he was calming down when the clock chimed above us. He barked loudly at the noise. Then he looked at Linda and, seeing no reaction to that strange noise, he never barked at the clock again. Would that we all have someone to turn to and calm our fears when needed. I feel that exists through faith. But not everyone does. Rationality is preferred. Of course it works both ways.

But what do we make of the fear of being alone? Frankly even during a marriage many couples spend the majority of their time apart. There are examples of fidelity that stretch our imagination. As once mentioned, the most adoring fact I ever learned about Paul and Linda McCartney was that in all their years of marriage and traveling around the world, they spent just a night or two apart. That is truly remarkable. For someone so famous and so rich to be that devoted and loyal is a great example to the rest of us. We can never know the intimate truth of all marriages, but the symbolism of it is enough for me.

Linda McCartney died from cancer even though she was a noted healthy eater, just like my Linda. It's all so random, who gets cancer and who doesn't. Doctors tell us that every one of us is walking around with cancer cells in our bodies. Hormones or foreign substances like smoke or pesticides or a zillion other environmental factors can set it off. That's evolution at work, unfortunately. It hurts to admit. We pray for healing. Somewhere in between we make the best of it. We gain time through medication and trust and hope and prayer and help. Linda was a survivor for many years past the statistical values assigned to ovarian cancer. Like I said, I'm proud of her. Just like Paul McCartney was proud of his Linda, for sure.

Both did everything they could to stay alive. Lived right. Loved well. Yet while life is finite, the time we spend together expands into experiences that last a lifetime through memories. Also, the people we affect while alive also hold that trust.

That is the basis of Christianity, if you think about it. One life, well-lived and sacrificed for the benefit of billions of people. That's what draws me to the Christian story. That ideal is as important, or more important, than the literal verity and the supposed infallibility of scripture. I don't believe in that. But I do believe in giving hope because we've seen it extended to us. Kept us going. Linda wanted more than anything to give back some of the love we received. I like to think of my wife Linda in that respect. She gave simply, and simply gave.

Somehow, in some ways, I imagine my wife running up the dark stairway of death, bursting through that door to that place we call heaven. She is permanently freed from the fear of the Grey Ghost that is cancer. We cannot know the reality of that, but we can embrace the liberty it implies. Salvation. Rescue or release from suffering. Knowing the joy of oneness with the universe perhaps.

I know life has to go on, and I am prepared to embrace that future. I want to love again and perhaps share life with someone else someday. That is no disrespect to my Linda. Paul Mc-Cartney is a loving example of that, a man faithful to his past while living in the present and the future. Okay, that one wife of his didn't work out so well after Linda. Was he too trusting? That's a harsh deal. Life can be that way.

The loss of my Linda makes me think of a McCartney song written before he lost his Linda to cancer as well. Perhaps you know the song. It is so beautiful. A love song and a confession all at once.

Music to my ears

Sunday, April 21, 2013, 8:00 PM

Kind of an amazing weekend in many respects. We had a little party with friends who shared in some special events and exchanged kindnesses of many sorts.

Ooops, that 'amazing' statement is a bit repetitious following the previous post.

Sorry, I was listening to *Maybe I'm Amazed* (again) because my son Evan sent me a version that he wanted me to hear. It was beautiful and different. And then I listened to McCartney again and was shaking my fists in the air at the sheer intensity of that song.

One of the lyrics talks about *right me when I'm wrong.*

We all need someone to help us out in that category. But I have to tell you something funny about what Linda said to me about a month ago. Something true. Something funny and true.

She was never too impressed with my musical capabilities. It's not my key strength. My son and daughter are far more knowledgeable and musical. My sister-in-law plays for the CSO. What am I supposed to do, compete with that?

Linda also knew a fair number of other musicians earlier in life and I think they actually knew how to play guitar, whereas I only strum and sing, and not all that well at either one of those.

So I'll tell you what she said about my musical efforts, but first there's a little story to preface her advice on music and me.

A few months ago I was looking to buy a simple cross to wear, and of all places I went to Wild Roots in Geneva, Illinois to see what they had. What I picked out might have been a little young in some respects, but it works for me. Just a metal outline and a cord necklace. I like it.

While there I got talking with the owner--as I am wont to do in many retail situations--and we chatted about the Beatles posters in his store and how we never thought our music from youth would last this long. I asked him if he plays guitar and he said, "Oh, I'm not really a guitarist. I just play songs."

That's me too, I thought. It was satisfying to hear someone describe it that way.

I've even written a few songs, which I played incessantly as I struggled to perfect them and never really did. Linda had to listen to that practice through the floor of our house. Sound travels up through the floor with no problem. It's one of the quirks of the Cudworth manse, of which there are many, since as I've told you before, just about everything I've installed from doorknobs to light switches has been put in backwards. Not my strength, those fix-it things.

So about a month ago she told me, "Chris, I have to tell you something. Music isn't your strength."

I knew what she meant. It's not my strength. I don't have a naturally beautiful voice. I've sung in many choirs and have learned to discipline my tone and fit in well, but solo work is not my forte. I'm decent at fitting in, but one time a church choir director asked me to sing the tenor part solo when no one in my section showed up and I barked back, "I think not." The whole choir cracked up. They knew the drill...

Still, while leading a praise worship a few months ago there was one song on which I felt confident to sing the lead part into the microphone and after the service a noted happy critic of the group--husband of one of the female singers--told me, "You should have sung more."

Wow! I thought. That's a triumph of a sort. I've heard my voice on recordings and know there are a few moments when I don't sound too bad. But there are many times when I do miss notes or get out of my range. But I'm smart enough never to have been tempted--if I were much younger--to audition for American Idol, The Voice or anything else. I'm not delusional. I know my limits when it comes to music.

So, in a key respect, my wife's advice was music to my ears. She was never one to give a ton of advice, for one thing. Not her style, really. Usually she tried to encourage me or others in a better direction if it was possible. It took her a long time to come out with something direct like that. In my case, it took 28 years. Ha ha. God Bless Her. She put up with a lot from me.

Yet she did not foster false hopes, either. When the parent of a child in her Pre-K class needed to hear about a learning challenge with their young one, Linda found ways to communicate the need and the truth. It was hard for her, but that's a gift. It's hard to give difficult news like that to someone else, but at the same time it is a gift just the same. I'm not sure how many people see it that way, as a matter of practice. But a great many people suffer through things needlessly as a matter of practice, as well. A certain guy named Jesus was good at pointing that out. And many wise men and women since have helped the human race see clear of their own foibles. Heck, Aesop's Fables used animals to teach people lessons about life. Tortoise and the Hare, anyone. I've always thought the moral of that story was that there might be too much sugar in carrots, but what do I know? I'm just a dumb jock who doesn't eat right. The rabbit and I have much in common.

But getting back to the matter at hand, a husband of a teacher hears many tales of how children acted up that day in school. Some days Linda would come home frantic after having a roomful of kids acting up from too much sugar, the moon, the local flu or whatever else addles their little brains and big hearts. Did you know that little children sometimes turn into holy demons? It's true. Yet Linda loved them nonetheless. I know that most sincerely. Some of her greatest joys were children with the greatest challenges. She started her career teaching the profoundly disabled, no easy gig. Her compassion for those with physical and mental challenges was most profound. But it's all a question of degrees, is it not? What we can do and can't do is all so personal.

That's what I mean about the music thing, and me. She meant her advice most kindly, and I will take it, and what a parting gift, in a way, delivered with love and affection. Okay, so I'm not the greatest singer or guitarist. I can deal with that. But honestly, I'm going to keep on singing. She knew that too. What are we practicing in that regard, hope or foolishness? It's hilarious, in a way, yet serious business to the soul.

As you can tell, I really do love to write, and thank you for your patience in receiving all these messages over the years. It's been our way of coping and sharing in the process.

Linda understood my need to write but found it confounding in some ways. She claimed to hate writing yet was so succinct when she did write that I would sometimes grow frustrated when she begged me to help her write a note to the preschool parents or address some other communication. Usually if left alone she'd come out with this nugget in that handwriting I love (it's Linda!) and read it aloud, yet apologetically.

I'd usually say, "It's perfect" and she'd groan, walking around the kitchen like she'd just spoiled a cake. I'd take it and tweak it if she liked but usually it was fine the way she wrote it. It just took some re-arranging on occasion.

That makes me think about her gardening, where I'd try to help, not always helpfully. I'd pushed her once to take her skills to a commercial level because she was really good with plants. She read them like books and people often begged her

to come analyze their gardens and fix what they'd done. Over the years she'd read many magazines on the subject. She knew her stuff but didn't want to turn it into a vocation. I get that.
This weekend some close friends and I were discussing Linda's ability with plants, especially in pots, and I told them I was going to try to replicate her efforts. "Good luck," they chortled. "We've been trying for years."

Indeed. They are good gardeners. But they appreciated that Linda had a gift and an eye for what needed to happen. She also kept a secret stash of cash to support her love of gardening. We all laughed that she would emerge come spring with that wad of cash and go shopping in the most interesting and distinctive gardening greenhouses across our area. I can tell you I never, ever questioned where that money came from. For all I cared, it grew on trees. I wanted her to be happy and I knew, after all, that I ranked #5 or so on the list. God. The kids. Her garden. Chuck. Then I rolled in. And was happy to be there. She smiled at me. We laughed together. She was a good cook, and I'm not. And those gin and tonics on summer nights. The fireflies looked brighter, for sure.

Her gardening was distinctive for a reason. She could even walk through Home Depot or Menards (both gross commodifiers of garden plants, she contended, but necessary, she guessed...) and find the one strange little plant that might fit into her plans. In that way she was a Ghandi of the Garden. Full of peace and wisdom, yet not afraid to wade through the awful truth of life to find the good stuff.

That's why her words of advice about my music were music to my ears. In some sense, she was simply trying to save me trouble, help me concentrate on what was most important. Not spend too much time on things that were destined to go nowhere. But damn I still like to pick up that guitar now and then, and try my hand and voice at making music.

So forgive me darling. I did listen to you, and heard your good intentions. I know my music career isn't going anywhere. But it was never meant to be a career anyway. I'll leave that to others. Now it's time for bed and the sound of Paul McCartney singing "Maybe I'm Amazed" is still running through my head. Again, music to my ears. Still worth my singing for no other reason than it makes me feel better about life in general.

Well, I know she liked that. She often told me so. Anyone want to sing along?

Medically speaking

Tuesday, April 23, 2013, 3:00 AM

Between 2005 and 2013, there were long periods when my wife Linda enjoyed triumphs over cancer. We cherished periods of remission. The cancer community calls these times "Dancing with NED," with stands for *No Evidence of Disease*. It is a medical term cancer patients have co-opted for their own purposes.

It can be tough when one must move from Dancing with NED to another Tango With Treatment. There is the shock of knowing what is to come, and knowing not at all what might happen.

Then there is the gradual immersion into an elective illness, punctuated by the inevitable new side effects as well as problems that never seem to leave. Linda had numbness in both her hands and feet called neuropathy that made it hard to do normal activities of all sorts. She laughed it off the best she could. Then with Doxil last year her hands and feet blistered so badly she could hardly function. Yet she went out into the drought and heat and gardened for all she was worth. That is real courage. She had real courage.

It became medically absurd by the time eight years was over and ibrain surgery became necessary to remove a cancer tumor in her brain. "That's not supposed to happen," the doctors told us. *Medically speaking, anyway.* But we went through brain surgery together. Then came a crazy day of radiation treatment involving a giant metal ring around her head to help aim the beams.

She endured that day with aplomb, I can tell you, being positive despite her lack of hair and a heavy crown of metal worn to calibrate the radiation treatment. The metal tray had small spikes that poked into the bare skin of her scalp. I could not help thinking of the crown of thorns Roman soldiers jammed on the head of Jesus Christ. This was crown was for healing, not torture. But you'll note that even the Passion story breaches those two concepts. From torture came the ultimate healing. Sacrifice. A gift of tremendous insight and love. Life itself. In our case we took some photos and had a laugh at the absurdity of it. That was our way. It is what it is.

The month following radiation treatment was a time of euphoria for Linda. The steroids prescribed to handle swelling of the brain lifted her mood. We lived as if there were no tomorrow. Honestly it did not matter if there was. Medically speaking, she was cured of the cancer in her brain. That was a miracle of sorts. So we went with it. I did not attempt to slow her joyful spending on whatever tasks or joys she desired. We even bought a new car. I had the sense that all this was important to her.

Ultimately the cancer in the rest of her body had the final say. Lungs. Liver. We'd hit that cancer with round after round and years of chemotherapy but it was too persistent. The first six years of engagement we were able to stave it off. But then the cycles of treatment came closer and closer together. Finally it made no sense to do chemotherapy. Her blood counts simply would not allow it. So we came home and watchfully engaged in what care we could embrace. Her stomach swelled with ascites. That made her sad and frustrated. At one point it was a question in my mind whether we should have the ascites drained as we'd done years before, removing 6 liters of fluid at the time. But in her condition with low counts there was too much risk of infection or other complications. So we went the natural route. We were never gamblers by nature.

It was tough for my son and daughter, her mother, sister and brother to see the strong soul we know as Linda become unable to do the things she loved to do. Know this: there were no regrets in my mind or hers. We discussed the fact that we had done everything we could over the years and made the absolute best of it. Of that there is no doubt. No gambles. Our choices were good ones and as a result, we had 8 more years.

The hospitals and doctors were many; Lutheran General Advocate, Rush Copley and Cadence Health System all did their part as we bounced around a little thanks to medical insurance, HMO and PPO. That's a whole different story, insurance. If you want to hear it someday, let me know. America could learn a lot from our tale. As for our opinion, the fact that a law has been passed preventing health insurance discrimination on basis of pre-existing conditions is the most important piece of legislation to have passed in the last 20 years. Seriously, it should be a basic human right to have access to health care, not an actuarial judgment on profit and loss.

Yes, there were tough moments toward the end. No one likes

to face the end of life. Even in that fearful passage we found humor in the moment with Linda. She kept her character in so many key respects, and we admired her for that.

At last her fears flowed freely and we did our best to field them and offer comfort back. It was received. She talked at length with her children. We were all a bit unstable emotionally because when the medicine changed from trying to produce a cure to trying to keep her comfortable, the very nature of relationships begins to change. That left us to share the care, and each one of us pitched in.

Linda asked for some quiet moments as she moved through long days perched on a medical bed out in the living room where morning sunshine flowed in and illuminated the many flowers delivered to our door. We respected her need for quiet yet craved to be with her while also taking care of the necessities of life.

It was a blessing that my son and daughter and I were all there together when she moved beyond this life. There is nothing medicine can do or should do in those days when it is right to seek comfort and care rather than intervention. We'd all also been through the passing of my father-in-law just a year before. It is a passage of rites for everyone.

We know how to sit by the bedside. We know how to love in the moment. We're learning what it means to miss those we love while finding joy and comfort ourselves from our network of friend and family.

We all try to limit our gambles in those respects. Phone calls help. So does saying "I love you." All the time.

Because it's true. In the end, love really is the best medicine. Or is that laughter? Do we have to choose? I think not.

Angel Benefits

Friday, April 26, 2013, 2:45 PM

Yesterday I got home from work and did some quick calculations in my head to decide whether to try to squeeze in a run before a meeting at church at 7:30. Life has been busy though, and I decided not to rush around. Instead I grabbed the dog leash and took Chuck for a walk. That was merciful frankly, because he had not gotten out all day and really, really had to go. Really. Had to go. Good dog, for waiting.

With business finished and picked up, we continued on our little neighborhood loop where we encountered a pair of sweet little children playing in their front yard with their father watching over them. Chuck loves kids and he started pulling on the leash but I held him back to see how everyone would react. Not everyone appreciates an overeager dog, especially little children.

As we approached it was evident what the children were doing, picking up sticks and placing them on a little pile by the curb. Just then the little girl walked over to her father and said, "Daddy, I found these in the grass." She handed him something and he looked down at her and said, "These are prescription glasses, honey. It's good you found them because someone must really be missing them."

I was only a few feet away and recognized the glasses he was holding. "I know this is going to sound weird," I told him. "But those are my glasses."

What were the odds? He looked at me funny and handed them over for inspection. The lenses were spotted from rain and a bit muddy, but otherwise the frames and lenses appeared unharmed even though they had been sitting in that yard for over 3 weeks. The family had even mowed that day, and the glasses escaped harm.

I'd lost those glasses just three nights after Linda passed away. It was a blustery cold March evening when I'd rushed out of the house with my pockets full of glasses, contact cases and other things I'd been carrying around during the week. The glasses had apparently fallen out when I'd hurriedly bent over to pick up after Chuck that night.

That next day I realized the glasses were gone and I searched the whole house and the car and the sidewalk leading into the house, but no luck. It was a little depressing to lose something so valuable right at that moment.

Accepting that I would not likely find the glasses again, I went about the process of getting quotes on a new pair from a couple optical shops and the price was always between $600 and $800--as expected. Apparently my prescription requires that my lenses be ground from minerals on Mars and manufactured by Santa's Elves or something. They're always so expensive.

Yet I held off buying the new specs and used an old pair of glasses until my head could clear and it was possible to make a good decision about what to do. I also wanted to find out if our company offers one of those programs with vision discounts. It does.

Suddenly all that turned out to be unnecessary. Getting my glasses back was a little like greeting the prodigal son. "Welcome home, eyeballs! I've missed you so much! Come, let's kill the fatted calf and hold a party!" After the church meeting that night I had a beer instead.

No word on whether the old glasses that had come out of retirement to rescue my dizzy eyes were bitter or sad at being second fiddle again. I'm thinking I'll throw some ordinary lenses in there as an alternate pair. Loyalty deserves respect.

Being genuinely grateful and bit taken aback by the serendipity of arriving on the scene at the exact moment that little girl found my glasses, I thanked the man yesterday and offered him a few dollars to buy the kids ice cream or something.

"Not necessary," he smiled. "Just bring your dog by now and then." He pointed to the little girl and said, "She really wants a puppy but it's not in the cards right now."

Just as he said that, our dog Chuck flopped down in the grass next to the little girl, chewing on a stick she had offered him. As he's wont to do, he nudged up against her knees and she looked up at her dad with pride. She petted his back and with a smile said, "Nice puppy." Oh. My. God.

Everything seemed to fit a strange and perfect order. Chuck seemed content. I was grateful for the return of my specs. The man seemed happy to be part of some small miracle in the spring sunshine.

Random? Not really. The odds of walking by with Chuck at the precise moment when that little girl found my glasses were more than coincidental. I'm convinced of that.

There have been many little miracles like that in life, and for years. I choose not to take them for granted. The fact these little miracles continue to happen is a sign to me that while it's good to grieve for Linda it is also okay to prepare for the life ahead. This might even have been a nudge.

My model in this regard comes from her. Through all her challenges, she kept her eye out for little miracles and expressed thanks for those that came along. So do I. Neither of us went in for hookey-spookey stuff like *The Secret* or other commoditized spiritual tricks. There are enough miraculous things going on the world without trying to manufacture them out of your own head. Better to pay attention than to pay $29.95 plus shipping and be disappointed that the meaning of life can't be gleaned from a best seller.

In other words, I won't go so far as to say that Linda's spirit handed those glasses to me. But it sure felt like something of that order was going on.

Of course, there's also a bit of humor to be found in all this. Linda got really disgusted whenever I lost things--and there were more than a few lost items over 28 years of marriage. Car keys. Cell phones. Probably a few forks or spoons thrown away in the trash. I even put her contacts in my eyes one morning and went for a run. Returning home loopy and weirded out, I put them back in the case and told her what I'd done. She shook her head and said, "Serves you right." But I heard her laughing when she told the tale to a friend later on. She forgave me these faults. Thank God.

Over time I've become much more disciplined about my habits but things still happen. The glasses are just such an example. Under stress and emotional burden we are all prone to mistakes and errors in judgment. It's human nature. If you studied it close enough, there's a great chance that evolution plays a part in the absent-mindedness of some human beings. We either evolve better behaviors or we won't. Those who claim not to believe in evolution simply aren't paying close enough attention to note that subtle changes lead to major shifts in the world. Mountains get pushed up over billions of years, and continents crawl over the surface of the earth. Topography and climates get changed as a result. It's just too slow and subtle for some people to appreciate. But they're missing the real miracles of creation as a result. I truly believe that.

There is spiritual tectonics as well. That's what the Bible covers. If Linda does happen to be an angel now, trotting behind to keep me out of trouble, she's done a pretty good of it.
If neither one of us were that big on angels as a rule, people still gave us angels for the garden and our home. It happened again for me this past week when the Confirmation class at Bethlehem Lutheran gave me an angel birdbath for which I've picked out the perfect spot where I'm installing a new water feature in the back yard. The angel will hold still waters for the birds that come to visit. And it won't move much. That thing is heav-ee!

On a practical note, it seems you can only ignore angels so long before they sneak up and bail your ass out of trouble whether you think you need it or not. It's pretty certain we've cashed in a few Angel Benefits these past 8 years and more. So my new lawn decoration will be a reminder that even if you don't know you're being watched, sometimes you are.

But angels of a different sort are in operation all around us. For example, I just got a $100 ticket from a Red Light Camera at an intersection in Downers Grove. In the photo I think I can see what appears to be an angel seated on the lamppost above the camera, pointing at my license plate with what looks like an expression of glee on their face. A joke like that can turn out to be a benefit, especially from an angel. So thank you, angel. That's $100 I won't spend on other mischief. Lesson learned.

We Sort Ourselves Out By How Hard We Try

Monday, April 29, 2013, 8:30 AM

A familiar figure ahead on the road. Strong calves. Vee-shaped back. A quick pedal turnover on his black hybrid bike. I recognized my old friend Pete, a high school cross-country teammate, pedaling out of town headed who knows where.
It was 5:00 on a Sunday. Light was getting dim due to a flat overcast sky. No threat of rain. Just lack of light getting through. So Pete looked almost like a black and white photograph on his bike. Some friends are like that anyways.

A little history

Pete was a tiny kid in high school, standing only 4'11 as a freshman. Yet no one could wear him out. His endurance and commitment to running was admirable. With a running style that was more churn than burn, his short torso seemed carried along as if he was the Roadrunner from cartoon fame. But again, long distance, not speed was his forte.

Sometimes we'd come in from a run and Pete would show up later only to tell us, "I went a little longer." That was his thing. If he couldn't be first, he'd do more than anyone else.

You can see it in his eyes

All those thoughts came through my mind as I drove past. Wanted to pull over, park my car and stop and talk but Pete seemed focused on his effort. Actually, that hardly describes it. The expression on his face, that I could see in the rear view mirror, was 'eyes ahead and don't slow down.'

Last I saw Pete was a year ago. He was on a walk on the river trail in the company of his mom, who turned 80 recently, and she really looked fit. She hadn't seen me in nearly 40 years, not since I was a 16-year-old kid, yet her eyes brightened right away. Runner Moms never forget a former teammate either. That special bond that comes from watching kids torture themselves to exhaustion through the woods and rain and cold and heat burns a face into your memory. Runner Moms are the best that way.

Catching up

Runners and cyclists just "get it" when it comes to living with difficulties.

As I pulled into the forest preserve where I'd driven to walk the dog and check out spring flowers, I wasn't expecting to see Pete again. Yet minutes after I'd pulled in and entered the woods to walk the drive looping 7/10ths of a mile around and over a prairie kame--along came Pete on his black hybrid bike. He must have been hauling ass to get out to the preserve that quickly. I'd seen him more than 5 miles back! Yet here he was. Some people amaze you that way.

Pete came rolling around a curve on the woods drive and I smiled and called out "Pete!" at which a flash of recognition came over his face and he came to a rolling halt. Smiled that big smile. He's compact now, not small. His marine arms and shoulders bulged under a tee shirt with the word Performance on the front. He wasn't breathing hard despite what must have been 8 hard miles of cycling. Not a whit was he breathing hard, in fact. Instead, the first words out of his mouth were,

"I'm so sorry."

He was speaking about the death of my wife March 26. "Was it sudden?" he asked.

I explained that it was not sudden, not for a long time. She'd not given in despite eight years of alternately tough existence given chemotherapy and surgeries and side effects that might have brought other people to their literal knees. I told him that I was proud of the time she'd given to all of us.Many blessings were fulfilled as a result. That is how I really feel.

There was no need to feign vain or superstitious ideas about her courage. Of course a cynic might retort, "What the heck As a runner and now power-cyclist he'd know what I meant. Living with suffering is a way of life for most runners. It gives you an insight into things other people either seek to avoid or don't understand such as perseverance and dealing with inconvenience, and even how to control your nerves in difficult situations. Thinking on that, in many ways my wife was more of an athlete than I will ever be. Sometimes I would compare her struggles through cancer to competing in a marathon, or training for one at least.

Effort and Recovery

"Honey," I'd tell her. "You have to think of these days after chemo like you'd just run a marathon. It takes time to recover."

She'd grunt and go outside to work as long as she could by the garden. Yet sometimes I'd find her plopped in an Adirondack chair exhausted and sweating, flush in the cheeks and pissed as hell. Outright pissed. "This sucks," she'd say. But she wasn't speaking about the cancer. She was speaking about the limitations it put on her. I don't think I ever heard her complain directly that she had cancer. Not in a resigned sense or in some whining way. That was not her style.

What really pissed her off, right to the roots of who she was, is that she could not sometimes do the things she enjoyed. That made her mad. Disgusted. Frustrated. Disappointed mostly. But not always. In fact not most of the time. She wanted to live, and keep on living. She lived that philosophy to the end. That is not to lionize her in some romantic way. I admired her courage and grew frustrated with her stubbornness. But you can't necessarily have one without the other. Ask Winston Churchill. FDR. Martin Luther. Martin Luther King, Jr. Muhammad Ali. Joe Frazier. Jon Stewart. Steven Colbert. She liked those two guys. Stubborn and funny. Justice and humor.

That's one of the tarsnakes in life. You sometimes can't separate the good from the bad.

Meaning of life. Meaning in life.

Life is all about overcoming limitations. Dealing with failure. Accepting success with grace rather than Lording it over others. My old friend and running partner Pete understood all that in a heartbeat. I could see it in his eyes.

Bloodroot. A perfect Sunday flower.

We walked along as I pointed out flowers along the path. Dutchman's breeches. Bloodroot, which almost always blooms in the weeks following Easter. A perfect Sunday flower. When you break off the plant, red sap flows from the stem. Hence the name.

Linda and I would journey to that hill in all seasons. Sometimes to walk the dog. Also just to "be" somewhere.

It was a test of cancer fitness if she could walk the hill. She did it many times. Strava recently told me there is a 9% grade in the middle of that hill called Johnson's Mound outside Elburn, Illinois. There is a Strava Segment on that hill and I'm amazed at how fast some cyclists can go up that grade. I ranked somewhere around 100 when I rode the loop the other day. Not thinking about the Strava segment. Only wanting to incorporate it as part of my 40-miler. But I will return. And ride it harder. I have to now.

An old school measure of fitness

I also knew I was very fit back in competitive running days when I could cover the portion of the loop from the woods-opening to the top of the hill in 3:00. You had to be in 31:00 10K shape to go that fast. I know from experience, because that was how it worked for me. The flats had to be covered at 5:00 mile pace or under. The hill had to be traversed without pause. It was both training and a measure of character. It was back in 1971 when I first ran it as a high school freshman. And it still is. Hills don't change. How we view them sometimes does. That can change.

Reading a book of passage

Pete and I walked slowly up the steep sections of the hill with him pushing his bike and me pulling my dog away from the pee trees. Lots of people walk their dogs in those woods. There are lots of pee trees as a result. Probably Chuck was reading a book about other dogs.

Pete and I were reading aloud from a book about the present and the past. He asked about various running teammates we knew and I filled him in. His curiosity was both genuine and not too possessive. Pete is one of those people who doesn't cut too deep a groove in the air through which he passes. Sometimes it pays to act small in that respect. You maintain a better sense of self that way. It doesn't mean you don't think of the important stuff.

We talked of sons and daughters and I realized that Pete and everyone else on earth faces the same sort of wind resistance no matter how fast or slow we're going, or how big or small we are. It's all-relative. The universe offers our pleasure and pain in the same way that sunshine hits us evenly, or rain. You can't outride the sun or run between the raindrops. Yet we sort out who we are by how hard we try.

How hard we try.

St. Dominick's Rain

Thursday, May 2, 2013, 9:45 PM

I am not a man who does not know his way around the grocery store, and I have my preferences. For some reason the layout of Dominick's has always appealed to me. *(Author's Note: this grocery chain has since gone out of business.)*

Probably there is some primeval logic to this. The way the vegetables sit so patiently for attention. The deli meat counter faces west. Who knows?

As you move through the grocery store it is impossible not to notice the people. Women walking through the store with their families in mind. Men with their ball caps on, walking with that distracted look on their face that men get in grocery stores. What am I forgetting? What did she/he say? Hope I'm remembering everything.

They don't put mirrors in grocery stores for all the above reasons. People don't want to see themselves when they're shopping for food. For those of us with comfort food issues and a few pounds to lose (it's all relative, people) mirrors remind us of the struggle.

So what do we do? We look at other people. Quickly inspect their carts. What looks good in there that I should or should not have?

They do play music at the grocery store. As I was walking past the last stretch of the meat bins with hamburger and chicken laid out in shiny packages. I was moving toward the milk and orange juice in freezers, a song came over the loudspeakers. A song I know so well from youth, when I was 10 years old and putting models together with glue. The memory is very specific and real to me. Time bends when I hear it. *Nowhere Man* by the Beatles. It was the real thing too, not some Muzak version.

I sang along, and then heard another voice singing in front of me. I smiled and said to her, "It's still a great song, isn't it?"

She took off her glasses and said, "Is that Chris Cudworth?"

We exchanged quiet smiles and she told me who she was. The older sister of a girl I'd dated a few times when I came home from college. I always like that girl. She had twinkling eyes. She knew how to kiss. That was enough for both of us at the time.

"I'm so sorry about your wife," the woman in the grocery store told me. "Susie's been crying for you too. She's always had a soft spot for you." What a sweet, meaningful thing to say at that moment. Then the woman in the grocery store felt compelled to tell me a story.

"I work in Real Estate, you know. And all this week I've been crying about Father Bob, from St. John Neumann. He just died a bit ago. So they asked me to go through his place and get it ready for sale. So I was walking through the house and came to a point upstairs where there was a T in the layout. Most people would have used that spot in the house for a play area for the kids. But as I walked into the T, I found there was a small altar at one end, and a cross at the other. It stunned me to realize this is where he would hold his own daily mass. It was such a private and beautiful space, with a kneeler in front of the flimsy wooden altar. And I told them they should make sure that altar goes to a young priest. It is all worn and such. It was just so special to see."

I stood leaning over the cart listening to her tell the story of how much that space meant for her to see. To witness that precious aspect of someone's life is special indeed.

We parted ways with a simple goodbye and I turned up the cereal aisle to face the ugly music of how cereal companies lie to us and manipulate us. Cereal boxes are evil incarnate, and so is the pricing of such cereals. You cannot possibly tell if you are getting a so-called "good deal" or not. You might see a price that says 2-for-1 for $4.99 and realize you're still only getting 3/4 of the cereal contained in one box that says $3.99. Cereal boxes really symbolize everything that was once good and may now be wrong with the world. Twisted logic. It used to be cereal companies competed to deliver the most value. Now it's the opposite. It signifies that we can't seem to be honest about anything, lest we learn the real value, or lack of it, incarnate in the things we consume. It's horrific really.

Standing there among the sexily clad cereals in their skimpy boxes I looked up to see a partially hunched figure passing by with her own little cart pushed ahead of her. The woman's hair obscured her face, and some malformation of her hip caused her to limp. She was talking to herself a little as she passed by, adding up some equation in her head whilst trying to figure out what she was going to buy next.

When my shopping was finished, I headed to the checkout line and found myself in line behind the woman I'd seen just a few minutes before. She was jabbering happily to the checkout woman about how her cat no longer needed insulin and how the groomer was going to patch up the animal's fur. She also owned a dog apparently, and was obviously proud of her pets. The checkout woman literally threw me a grocery separation bar so I could start loading my groceries on the belt. I smiled to let her know there was no big hurry. We were the only two people in line.

While waiting for the rather long process with the woman cashing in coupons and pulling out cards to pay for her groceries (which by the way seemed sensible enough) I looked outside and noticed that the rain was again coming down quite hard. It had begun to pour the minute I stepped into Dominick's and I stopped at the door to look back at the rain. I was staring out the door with another man who was standing there silently watching rainy cats and dogs popping up from the parking lot. I remarked, "It's really something how much rain we're getting, huh?"

The man said nothing. Just stared at the rain. Perhaps he was waiting for someone. I heard him breathe a little sigh. Obviously he did not wish to be bothered. I walked away. Now it was raining again, and just as hard. It was obvious the walk back to the car would be a wet one. You could see the fluorescent streetlights reflecting brightly on the parking lot.

I nodded to the checkout gal as she also made note of how hard it was raining. Then I realized that the woman in front of me in line was talking about walking home to her house by the Fire Station off Fargo in Geneva. "Excuse me," I asked her. "Are you going to walk all that way with your cart?"

She looked up at me then. Her face was made up in the most marvelously dramatic fashion. Too much mascara. Bright red lipstick. The upper part of her smile was somewhat broken. But she smiled broadly and said, "It wasn't supposed to rain until later on!"

I glanced at the checkout gal and turned back to the woman with her little cart and her groceries. "Let me drive you home, if that's okay," I told her. "There's plenty of room in my car for your cart. That way you won't get all wet."

"That's nice," the checkout gal said. But a compliment was not necessary. There was no way any human being, upon thinking about that woman walking home in the rain, should do any differently.

I pulled the car up and loaded her nifty little cart in the back. Then I threw my own groceries in the back seat.

It didn't take but a few moments inside the car to realize the woman smelled pretty strongly of cat urine, or so I hoped. Oh well, I thought. It's not the end of the world. The end of the world does not smell like cat urine or anything like that, I figured. I am told the end of the world smells of fire and brimstone if you trust a literal interpretation of Revelation. The end of the world probably smells like cosmic horse shit if the Four

Horseman of the Apocalypse legend is true. Either that, or it's your own pants that will stink at that point, because a sight like that is sure to scare the shit out of you.

And such a concept! Some even say it is all coming to fruition soon. One radio preacher even predicted the day, but proved himself wrong, once again. I don't choose to believe in all that crap. I'm sorry for the bad language, but not really. Some things are not better left unsaid.

The basic facts are what matters: just because someone stinks it is not the end of the world.

The woman's name was Patty. And she repeated the story about her kitty cat and the vet or groomer or whoever else was taking care of her prized pet. She directed me to drop her off at a very nice townhome near the west side Fire Station. Then she said thank you while carefully pronouncing my name. "Thank you, Christopher."

I don't share this story as some sort of self-aggrandizement or because I want you to think I'm sort of saint. St. Dominick or something. I share it because I know that many of you do kind things for others too, and to encourage you to keep doing that. It all comes flowing back, you know. But that's not the motivation for doing it.

The motivation for doing it is because St. Dominick's Rain falls on all of us at some point in life. And if someone can be there for you, I wish it to be true. And if you can be there for someone else, I wish that for you too. Because you'll find the experience to be equal, in terms of rewards. Gratification at helping others is its own reward, whereas being helped by others sometimes requires a heap of humility. But we all get wet when we walk in the rain together.

St. Dominick's Rain is the price of living, with all its flaws. Our cereal costs too much. People lie and deceive. But the saint who appreciates that these things are not the end of the world can find ways to make the world a better place. Through kindness to each other we overcome what the world throws at us. Then when the rain comes when we least expect it, we do not panic.

As the beneficiary of so much kindness over the years from so many, including strangers, I just like to share that gratitude if at all possible. And the kind woman whose sister I once dated, singing Nowhere Man in the grocery store and not caring one whit if someone else heard her, that was a gift given and received. Kindnesses and a great story were exchanged. She got to tell someone about her experience in the home of the recently deceased priest and his little altar and the sanctified space she will never forget. You could tell she wanted to share.

When she walked out into St. Dominick's Rain that evening it might have felt a little different. Perhaps she didn't even care if she got wet on the way to the car. Sometimes that's all we can pray for. A little perspective as the rain falls. On all of us.

The Island of Widowhood

Monday, May 6, 2013, 12:15 PM

You might think the term "widow" the worst thing a man or woman could utter. But as you know, it is my humble little mission in life to redefine for myself, and possibly others, what it means to have lived through something so significant as cancer with someone you love.

After all, we did it. We lived through it. We lived in it. We lived for it, in a way, because you really have no choice in some respects. The fact that Linda finally died from cancer has little to do with how much life was drawn from the experience. As I've said before, many times, blessings were fulfilled. Miracles happened. We Thank God and our friends for that.

Unless two people time their deaths to a precise, chosen moment in the future, or luck out like that sweet old couple in that movie *The Notebook*, dying in each other's arms so that a nurse finds them together in the morning light, one person is going to be a widow while the other folds into the arms of eternity.

There are sad moments. Like walking through Home Depot the other day. I had hoped to swing through and look at flowers but instead it was raining and the stupid house sparrows were chirping away up in the rafters that magnifies the sound and the whole scene overtook me. Profundity hit me like a wall of water. Linda was not there like she usually is, sifting through the common flowers to find the good ones.

I wound up leaning on a giant stack of mushroom compost bags crying in the rain. Some burly dudes were moving wall stones and bricks around and were either kind enough to ignore me or thought my face was just wet with rain. I didn't care. Why should I care? I care enough to cry. That's the most important thing to me.

By contrast there are days when I'm filled with joy at the thought and memory of my late wife. I was doing just that, when I said out loud, "I miss you Lover Girl," to no one but myself, and a strange yet interesting thing happened. Chuck was lying next to me on the chair and his ears perked up when I spoke those words He jumped from the ottoman and looked out the window at the mention of those words, "Lover Girl." It was my pet nickname for Linda, you see. Pun intended.

Chuck must have associated my use of those words with Linda. We couldn't get him to put 2 and 2 together with her actual name. He knew EMILY and EVAN and THE KIDs and would run to the window when we spoke their names, but Linda would laugh at me when I would say, "Where's Linda?" To Chuck, that wasn't her.

But he knew the words Lover Girl somehow, and it's the first time he's acted like that. I must have said those words often enough that some little synapse in his doggie mind decided to respond. At least that's what it seemed like the moment. He's been pretty good about not being mopey and sad overall. Sometimes he finds something that smell like her and he spends a few moments sniffing. That gets me of course.

His new friend Mona across the street takes him over to her place each day and she loves Chuck's company. He loves her too. In fact while I was taking the garbage out on Thursday night he slipped out the door and ran over to her place across the street (not good, doggie) and stood there staring at me until I called him home.

It was like looking out across the bay at a fuzzy little sailboat crossing the water through the misty haze. Everything seems a little distant, and yet so near you can touch it.

So it's like the big waves of grief have settled down into wavelets that lap up on the shore of the Island of Widowhood. Some people say it can get a little lonely way out on your own with no one to talk to. But the coconut telegraph is alive and well in my life, and I use it frequently, reaching out to friends. It's like stepping onto a boat for an afternoon or evening of sailing. Then it's back to the Island of Widowhood. But it's okay. That's the way it all works.

Perhaps you'll recall that movie Castaway with Tom Hanks. He's a busy executive for Federal Express and heads off on a trip only to have the plane crash in the ocean. He's forced to make his way stranded on an ocean island and basically befriends the only companion he can find, a Wilson volleyball with a bloody handprint on its face. By the time he works up courage to depart the island it is a bittersweet thing, made even more bittersweet by the ensuing loss of his good friend Wilson, who drifts off on the Pacific and out of sight. Out of sight.

When the Hanks character gets back to civilization it is a strange thing for him to adjust. After having to catch and eata raw crab at one point during life on the island, the proliferation of food including cooked crab meat at a banquet in his honor is an embarrassment of riches. He thinks back to the strange journey of survival he's been through and wonders if anyone can comprehend his thoughts. It appears that he decides they cannot. Not completely. His loneliness is something that will accompany him forever. Yet he knows that the future calls as well.

Then he gets in touch with the woman he once (and still) loved only to find out she has married another man. Their love is rekindled in some form, but ultimately she must choose the live she's built because to do otherwise would be a dishonor to herself and her values. The whole thing just hurts. Hanks accepts the verdict however and realizes that life itself has become an island of sorts.

Yet he's got one more mission to fulfill, delivery of a FedEX box to an artist somewhere out in the waysides of Texas. He unwittingly meets her at a crossroads on the road out from her house to the main highway. She is intrigued by this seemingly lost soul. She also doesn't know that he's actually returned something precious to her. One wonders for a moment if there is a new destiny awaiting Hanks. The romantic solution might be for him to find love in an out of the way place. But reality is different.

In the final scene he stands looking at open roads in four directions. There's no GPS. No maps. Just the Hanks character and the big-ass island called Texas offering up its expanse. Then he drives off.

The message is that we are all widows of a sort. Even when we are possessed of the knowledge of a certain person we love who may still be alive. Or they may yet be gone. They may be a past love, or someone with whom a relationship never worked out. All are losses of a sort. Our gains in life really are hard won. Like Tom Hanks in *Castaway*, survival means using an ice skate to knock out an infected tooth. Our God hides behind the stormy pinnacle that shrouds the island bay. The water changes color with the sky, affecting our mood, but why? It is the reflection of our inner selves we sometimes see. The light is benign, as is all of nature. Our emotions bounce back to us from everything we see, and do.

We all live on the Island of Widowhood. The waves of memory are lapping at our feet daily. We are grateful when there are no storms to suck us out to sea. That is why the concept of a tsunami is so powerfully etched into human consciousness. The idea of the ocean coming ashore to get you is beyond our imagination.

Yet it happened in a sense to Linda and I. The tsunami of cancer rushed into our lives and forced us to swim, together, for years, in hopes of reaching those islands of cancer-free existence. And we did it. Repeatedly, actually. Those are blessings to be cherished. Accomplishments to be held close. Our children joined us on those islands of remission, as did all of you.

I recall a day when Linda and her sister and the kids and I were fortunate to be swimming in Lake Michigan when the wind was blowing in toward shore from the east. The waves grew to six feet tall and there was real surf in which to play. It was a happy day bouncing around in those giant waves. When we all got home you could still feel the rhythm of the waves in your muscles and blood. The water itself seemed to rock within you. We were feeling the world from the inside out.

That's what I'm doing right now, or trying to do. Feel the world from the inside out. They say that cancer has the power to change people, to make them appreciate the world and the life they have. Big changes. Some vow to not sweat the small stuff. Others vow to love others more fully, repair damaged relationships and clamber onto the shore of a different island, away from the hubbub and madness of normal daily life.

I can honestly say the whole experience changed Linda and I in significant ways. We learned not to worry so much. We learned to trust people more, and hopefully be more generous.

Those changes came with a price. Now it means standing in a garden center shedding happy/sad tears while picking out bright new flowers to celebrate new growth. Missing her, yet finding a good way to look ahead.

Like the Hanks character in Castaway, given up for dead and returned to a world where nothing seemed quite the same, there is a time to move on. A demand even. It is the sound of the ocean in the distance, like the hiss you hear in a conch shell when you hold it up in your ears. So familiar and within your grasp, yet just an illusion, it turns out, of the mind.

Perhaps that is the voice of the oceans beyond this world in which we'll someday swim. But for now we stand on the Island of Widowhood missing mothers and fathers, spouses and pets, holding the conch shell up to our ears so that we don't forget the sound of the ocean even if we don't get there often enough.

Present in Spirit

May 25, 2014

Recently a friend sent me a link to a story about a scientist that believes he has evidence that the world we live in is not the only dimension possible. His book is titled "Biocentrism: How Life and Consciousness Are the Keys to Understanding The Nature of the Universe." The author, Dr. Robert Lanza was actually voted the 3rd most important scientist alive by the NY Times.

An article about Dr. Lanza posted on wakingtimes.com states "...the scientist became involved with physics, quantum mechanics and astrophysics. This explosive mixture has given birth to the new theory of biocentrism, which the professor has been preaching ever since. Biocentrism teachers that life and consciousness are fundamental to the universe. It is consciousness that creates the material universe, not the other way around."

The fact that 'real' scientists continue seeking ways to determine evidence of spirit and consciousness is compelling testimony that many of us sense "something more" than what we can see or feel in this world.

In our experience this "something more" manifested itself in tangible little miracles that seems to come out of nowhere. Yet each had enormous significance in our lives. Those sensibilities echo on.

A few weeks after my wife died a friend of my daughter came to visit our home. The young woman studies astronomy at a leading university and is in love with science. She respects and admires the rational world. Her intellect is obvious upon first meeting her, an impression that only grows deeper as you get to know her. But she is not without sensitivity to the energies of the universe.

On a previous stay at our home we invited her to sleep in the guest room at the front of the house. But this time she refused. "I don't sleep well in that room," she told us. So she slept on the couch in the living room.

She awoke that evening to the feeling that someone was with her in the living room at that moment. Then a tile hung that by a wire on an angled nail popped off the wall and fell on the top of a cupboard between the dining room and living room.

It startled her of course. But the room was silent and she credited it all to things that happen in a house on occasion. Still, she shared the experience with my daughter and I the next morning. We then inspected the tile and realized it would have been necessary for it to rise vertically by a quarter of an inch to actually lift off the angled nail that held it in place. Emily and I stared at each other. All we could do at that moment was shrug.

Two nights later our guest woke up again with a feeling that someone was with her in the room. She was lying on the couch with her feet pointed at the center of the room. When she lifted her head from the pillow, she noticed that the space at the other end of the couch seemed to twist and three lights or orbs appeared before her. One was green. One was red. One was white.

This time a stronger feeling of presence overwhelmed her. Then the lights faded and disappeared. She literally pinched herself to make sure she was not dreaming. She was fully awake. The experience she'd just had was just so strange. Yet she fell back asleep.

The next morning I was the first one to rise. After having breakfast in the kitchen to avoid disturbing our living room guest, I stepped into the dining room to put the newspaper in the recycling bin near the back door. She sat up and called me over.

As she related the manner in which the lights had appeared the night before, I looked at the end of the couch, I turned to her and said, "That's exactly where Linda was lying in bed when she passed away. That's where her head would have been."

When my daughter got up from bed later in the morning we shared the story again. Emily said, "I believe it. Earlier this week I was in the bathroom working on my hair when I heard the hall closet close. It takes a lot to close that door so I went out into the hallway and our dog Chuck was just standing there, freaked out. I was freaked out too."

Listen. We're not a hooky spooky family. Nor is my daughter's friend. But we all felt we'd experienced something unusual those few days together. Later Emily asked a friend online what the orbs could have meant. They related the meaning of the colors. Red for high energy. White for protection or shielding. Green for healing and fertility.

While you obviously can't trust everything you read on the Internet, there are some fascinating takes on phenomena similar to what we experienced. A website titled eternea.com provides this perspective:

"Orbs exhibit consciousness and can respond to requests by appearing in meaningful places at meaningful times. A growing number of people are experiencing the orb phenomena as a spiritual, transcendental or other worldly event that occurs after the death of a loved one. When photographed by a grieving family member, orbs can give a sense of solace unlike any other during a time of loss and adjustment."

"Orbs are mentioned in literature across many genres and have been captured in traditional film, digital photography and video. There is a growing body of publishing information, videos and websites discussing this phenomenon. With a simple camera anyone can learn to take pictures of these incredible light beings. Though generally not visible to the naked eye, people can see them while others are able to "feel" their presence.

Orbs are a beautiful demonstration of manifesting physical reality through consciousness. They are the most readily available proof of the existence of life beyond our third dimension. As the veil things between our worlds, we are afforded the opportunity to connect with the magic and beauty of spirit. We have been given a window to the divine. Thanks to the digital camera, we now have a visual experience that quite possibly validates for the first time what mystics, spiritual leaders, and religious doctrine have expressed for millennia; that we truly are eternal beings."

Well, we did not get photos of the orbs witnessed by our house guest. But if nothing else, such phenomena hold fascination about dimensions we may not clearly conceive or recognize. Eternea suggests this is a familiar experience to many:

I'd had experience with some sort of light phenomena earlier in my life. Years ago while riding with a friend on a country road, I was gazing out the window at the twilight sky on a summer night when a white light appeared across the expanse of an alfalfa field. At first I assumed the light was actually a reflection of something inside the car because it moved along with us at the same speed as the vehicle. Then I realized my window was actually down and the wind was blowing in. At that moment the light made a pointed dash toward our car and came along beside us. It moved in concert with our vehicle, seemingly free of the influence of the wind. Then it flashed briefly and disappeared up above the roof of the car. It was gone.

I turned slowly to look out the windshield. After 10 seconds or so I turned slowly to my friend whose eyes were wide. "Did you see that?" we both exclaimed at once.

Again this friend was a very scientific person. His stern science-teacher father had raised him to know about science, especially biology and forestry. Yet we'd both seen something that was well outside our joint realm of rational experience.

So despite my own firm belief in material science and evolution as foundations for knowledge, there have been experiences where normal explanations do not suffice to cover the light of being.

It would not surprise me to someday learn that the force of

consciousness is so strong that someone like my wife would continue to live on. There is something hopeful in the notion that someone we love lives on in some way. Perhaps that's enough to know. For now it seems we're on a "need to know" basis with the universe. Or so it seems. Eventually we may be able to see the light.

More than a painting

June 6, 2014

The Limestone Coffee Shop is a small establishment on the main street of our town. It used to be situated down the block in a historic building made from local limestone, hence the name. Apparently the landlord jacked the rent so Limestone had to find a new home.

The new interior is beautifully done in that way that only local coffeehouses can seem to muster, homey and interesting. It's a welcoming place.

Coffeehouses. Where so much talking gets done. I sat down this morning to wait for a fellow I know who wants to change the world using his Real Estate acumen. This theory has to do with finding new ways to fund a non-partisan government. Another friend had been invited to join the discussion. He's a fellow that has been engaged in social progress and business change for years. But he wasn't really buying the change the world schtick. I get antsy in those situations.

Then it occurred to me that breakfast had worn off so I wander to the counter for a piece of Amish cinnamon cake. I won't do coffee, but coffee cake is just fine.

While waiting for the order I complimented the woman next

to me on the pattern of her skirt. She looked me in the eye and asked, "Don't I know you? Perhaps from Water Street Studios?"

That's a very successful local art coalition that hosts shows and supports the arts in our area. I realized that she and I had met a couple years before during an open house. As a water-colorist myself I had admired her intriguingly liquid paintings. They speak of a place somewhere in the mind or an imagined beauty that is also quite real. Good art is confusing like that.

I told her that I actually own a piece of her work. Her eyes grew wide. "Your wife purchased a painting..."

True. Just over a year ago, before my wife passed away from cancer, we had visited an art show opening with friends. At the time my wife was taking steroids as treatment following an operation on her brain to remove a tumor that had metasta-sized from the ovarian cancer that was taking her body down one week at a time.

The steroids made my wife fearless and attentive to so many details in life. She purchased new lights for the kitchen and we installed them. She bought a new car with the insurance mon-ey we received from the car that was totaled while my daugh-ter was driving it. Money was no object to my wife when she was on steroids.

I decided not to fight her lack of fear. We'd been through a lot together and money simply lost its significance at some point. When I first saw the painting on the gallery wall I knew she might like it. You could tell by the look in my wife's eyes when she came across the gallery floor to tell me about the painting that something deeper was going on. This was about much more than a painting. This was about us. And life. And the art of life.

We purchased the painting and hung it in the living room. We positioned a light on the floor to illuminate it. It was perfect. Even though I paint as well there is something wonderful about bringing the work of another artist into your life. That's especially true when you get to know the artist.

However the night we purchased the painting the artist was not in attendance at the show. That meant my wife would never have the opportunity to meet her. She died the very next month.

So it meant something to stumble into the greeting with the painter that produced the work that now hangs above my bed. I shared the story with her about how much the work meant to us, and what it means to me now. The art of living is that we recall so many of our experiences in the manner of water-color fauvism. Many of our experiences are similarly blurred by time and events glazed over events.

Yet the connection in meeting the artist and sharing the story of my wife's gravitation to her work was clear as day. Her friend was standing next to her as we made the connection. We all got tears in our eyes. We all shared a hug right there in the Limestone Coffee House.

That is also the art of life. Being open to coffee house connections can make all the difference in how you process your experiences, your memories and the present. We all bear a brush with which we paint the day. We simply need to be open to the signs the universe is trying to send us.

Butterfly ranching

July 8, 2014

This summer the rains have come consistently and the garden is lush if a bit weedy. In our household we have "ranched" butterflies for years. That means finding the eggs or caterpillars on milkweed and dill plants in the garden. Linda used to bring them inside to an aquarium stocked with clippings of their host plants. The caterpillars would feed until they grew to full size and then convert into a chrysalis stage lasting a couple of weeks. Then they'd hatch and we'd release them into the wild.

In peak years we raised and released up to two dozen monarch butterflies. But in the past 5 years or so the numbers of monarchs visiting the garden dropped to near zero. It pained Linda to see so few monarchs. But what pained her worse was watching the butterflies we did ranch tumble out of their chrysalis stage too weak and sick to fly. It broke her heart and it made her sick to think that life could dissipate like that.

In many ways she had also cocooned like those moths and butterflies we ranched. It was hard walking into the three-season room with her during those days of dying butterflies. It seemed to shred some sort of hope, deep down.

These days my daughter Emily has continued the tradition of

ranching butterflies. She even had a monarch tattoo placed on the back of her shoulder in honor of her mother. This year she added two bees to the design as well. Emily has a strong sense of social justice when it comes to environmental concern. She also has a strong sense of recollection about her mother's dedication to the insects in our garden.

To some degree raising kids is just like ranching caterpillars. It seems like you pluck them out of the cosmos, nurture and protect them. As teens teens they huddle up in a cocoon of self interest for a time, then if you're lucky they're ready to emerge into the adult world and you let them go for their own sakes.

This summer the butterflies on our dill and milkweed are finally doing quite well laying eggs. We've let the milkweed essentially take over the garden path. Emily has been harvesting eggs and caterpillars and her boyfriend built a brand new frame with screen so they can thrive. We've come to terms with life through their emergence.

The symbolism seems a little obvious but it is not. That instinct to ranch butterflies and release them in honor of mom is as direct and true as the pain we felt on losing her. There is an emotional component to all of nature. It feeds us and challenges our existence at the same time. For my son that connection has come through fulfillment of his goal to start his own business, which would definitely have made his mother proud.

It's like this. When you hold up your hand and allow a butterfly to fly free, into the unknown, it works the other way as well. Something goes to work within us. It's a hope that circles back, calling us to fly as well. That's the spirit. Raise your wings. Aim toward the sun. Go where you need go. Trust your instincts. Have faith. And fly. It's what you must do.

CHAPTER FOUR

Perspectives on what we learned

The 3Cs: Character. Caregiving. Community.

While there's no magic formula to facing cancer, it can be helpful to have a mental construct to organize your thoughts and actions. What follows is a description of three categories, Character, Caregiving and Community. Each can serve as a template in understanding the ways in which people respond and work together in facing cancer.

We could call them the 3Cs of cancer survivorship.

Character is the personality and value system of the individual facing a challenge.

Caregiving is the philosophy and actions of people providing physical and emotional support during survivorship.

Community is the network of support arranged to provide support of all kinds for survivorship.

CHARACTER

Our character is what drives our decisions and gives us strength to make choices. It also helps us accept the consequences, be they good or bad, in the choices we make.

In order to understand better how and where character develops it helps to consider its root meaning. Character is defined as "the mental and moral qualities distinctive to an individual."

That means character comes from two sources. First is our genetic makeup, what we might label our inherent source of character. Our other source of character is the knowledge we derive from experience. These two sources of character intertwine to form what we might call our character DNA. It's what drives us to be the people we are.

Common cause

In fact all human beings share a genetic heritage that provides the very foundation of our being. Our lineage extends all the way back to the source of human awareness. In that regard we're all related. Of course that dictate that we we are all alike in terms of personality or character. Our individuality makes us special and our diversity makes us unique as people.

For these reasons we delve back into human history and literature to encounter stories about people of great character because they inspire us to hold fast in times of trial and to fulfill our calls to service, joy and community in life. The manner in which they individually respond or provide leadership to other people is inspiring. It helps us face our own challenges by teaching us that our individual gifts have value.

Many kinds of character

Whatever the nature of your character, what really matters is how it comes into play when facing any number of life's challenges. Some people face the injustice of a disease like cancer with relative equanimity. They choose calm in the face of a storm. Others get angry or fight back, throwing themselves at their treatment with fury and determination. Still others go the rational route, trying to figure out the best and most efficient way to deal with a disruption in their lives that in some cases threatens life itself. There are all illustrations of how the nature of character comes into play. All are valid in their context. There is no predicting how you or anyone else may respond when going through challenges in life.

Character tests

We might grow to think of our character as something fixed or insoluble. Just as character can be built through time and experience, it can also change suddenly or be altered by events or in the face of adversity. Moods may shift and hopes my waver. A normally happy person may become dour. A seemingly rational person can throw caution out the window. These apparent changes in character are all natural responses to unnatural circumstances. It is important when providing support to anyone facing a life challenge that we take these possible changes in character into account. Cancer survivorship depends on working with the character of the person facing the disease.

When we say that a person is acting "out of character" we recognize that they are under stress or behaving in some manner not in keeping with their typical response to life. Character is the rock of our being, but we must remember that the sand on the beaches was once solid rock. Nature tempers our character and sometimes it changes its form to adapt to circumstances.

People going through something so profound as cancer, that includes caregivers and all those engaged in survivorship, often declare themselves changed by the experience. It can feel like you're turned inside out at times. Values sort out into new channels. Formerly worrisome attitudes about the world modify or entirely change. Some describe a feeling of liberation while others feel imprisoned or are simply glad to get through it all.

There is nothing wrong with any of these emotions. They do illustrate the potential for character to change.

Those of us called to walk beside people whose character is being put to the test may find our own character changed by the experience. Cancer is not contagious, but compassion, courage and fortitude in helping some face cancer can be. Even our shortcomings teach us things to know about our character, conscience and dedication. All these things build character even when we're not aware it is happening.

Baselines

Because people arrive at their position in life with a lifetime of character-building experience behind them, they may hold fast to what might seem like the wrong focus at times. So be patient, always. Show respect and patience for another person's character no matter how obvious their flaws might seem to you at the time, or how much you may disagree with their approach to life.

At the same time, do not be surprised if people unleash emotions, fears or needs that seem a little out of context, even with strangers, during survivorship. They might be baring their soul in reaction to circumstances about which you know little about. Discretion is always appropriate. So is listening.

It can also happen that a person under duress will inspire you with their apparent courage. But be careful when taking these efforts at face value. Know that people often adopt (or adapt) a dialogue of courage when in truth their insides are roiling with doubt and fear. So again, always be patient.

When it comes to observing and supporting the very personal character found in everyone, watch and listen for the role you are called to play. Look for the subtle signs of character evident in everyday actions. If you so choose, make it your job to support their character even if they're one of the most unpredictable characters you've ever met.

Let's admit it, even people of great character can be characters at some level. If you or someone your know faces cancer or some other challenge in life, it is important to respect both the quirks and quality of a person's character. Those are the foundations of individuality. They are the keystones of survivorship.

We can never fully predict what aspect of our personalities will become most important when life demands our all. For some it may be a sense of humor. For others it may be having the character to not worry whether they're now bald or go through life-changing surgery and an entirely new body image. All take character to address, ideally supported by caregiving and common

CAREGIVING

The first time many of us find ourselves in a position as primary caregiver there is an almost instinctive response to deny such deep involvement and the additional burden of a caregiving assignment. That can be true even when you are joined by the bonds of marriage or a long term relationship. It is hard to assume the responsibility of care for someone. It does not come naturally to everyone. For some people caregiving is the hardest thing they will ever do.

But care you must, because nothing is so important as recognizing the needs of others and then responding to that need the best way you know how.

Caregiving crosses a broad spectrum of activities. So let's take look at what it is and how caregiving occurs.

The basic definition of a caregiver is as follows:

Caregiver: An individual, such as a physician, nurse or social worker, who assists in the identification, prevention or treatment of an illness or disability.

Also; an individual, such as a parent, foster parent, or head of a household, who attends to the news of a child or dependent adult.

Front lines

We might wish (or like to think) that professional caregivers can provide all the assistance required (or requested) by a person in need. Often however, the care just begins when leaving the doctor's office or hospital. Be aware that is true even with medical treatments that seem like they should be confined to a hospital or medical setting. Caregiving can teach you things you never thought you'd know or want to know. But you can and will survive and even thrive with the right kind of pride, commitment and attention.

You might find yourself opening and closing pick lines and cleaning them with antiseptic fluids to clear out the tubing. You might be called to dispense expensive medicines or learn how to treat sores, rashes or nausea. The entire enterprise of caregiving can be unpredictable and sometimes scary, especially to those without medical backgrounds. That's most of us.

Untold benefits

Caregiving can also be intimate and life-changing. Sure, the responsibilities may be humbling. Helping someone take a bath, shower or to go to the bathroom is difficult at first. Few people are used to assisting others in such intimate tasks. With time, objectivity usually replaces discomfort. You find yourself operating like a nurse on call, able to perform tasks with positivity and support that were previously scary or abhorrent. Activities that initially felt like chores eventually become part of the 'dialogue' that goes with caring for another person's needs.

Open books

People in genuine need cannot afford to distinguish the difference between professional and personal caregivers. That means as a volunteer or personal caregiver you might be asked to do things for people in strange situations that seem way off the normal playing field of existence. If you can't handle it at first there is nothing wrong with saying so. "I just need time to prepare," is sufficient to go off and prepare yourself. Retreat to a quiet place and consider your feelings or pray for guidance. Take a moment to figure out how best to handle the situation and determine whether you truly need to call in professional help. These are not failings as a caregiver. They are normal human response to caregiving challenges. That it why it is important to establish a Big Picture perspective in your head.

Big Picture caregiving

If you are the primary caregiver, your responsibilities often do not end with physical needs. There are phone calls to make, bills to pay and family needs to address. At times the pressure does not seem to relent. You can wind up stressed, burned out or ambivalent. Some situations can even lead to chronic anxiety or depression.

The classic caregiving advice is that you must take care of yourself as well as the person for whom you are providing support. That means finding time for yourself and doing activities that you like to do. If that means calling in a substitute to provide care of your loved one or friend it is wise to do that.

That's easier said than done sometimes, but don't give up. You must also be firm in your caregiving role. Get things in order and communicate the need for a time out. Escape and read for a while if that's all you can do. At times it is fair to ask that only critical needs be communicated so that you can recover your sense of balance. Both sides of a caregiving equation need to offer respect.

If you can afford it or find the resources, there is nothing wrong with calling in professional caregiving support or assistance. That is especially true while tending for a parent or someone with cancer or other condition requiring 24/7 care. There are caregiving resources available through local churches and other non-profits that can provide safe, trustworthy support so that you can do shopping, go for a run or walk or even get out with friends.

Feel no guilt in that. Big Picture caregiving takes your personal and mental health into account. Make room for your life so that you don't collapse into a black hole of caregiving gravity.

One of the most unique resources now available to caregivers is online support such as ShareTheCare or Lotsahelpinghands. These online organizational tools can be set up to coordinate everything from meals to driving or any other caregiving needs that may occur. Your local church or cancer support center through a hospital can often guide you in these processes.

Caregiving benefits

Helping someone through health challenges or through elder years may be a burden at times. But you are giving them a gift of support that also gives back to you in ways that may be difficult to see in the short term.

Giving time and energy to someone else is a sacrifice that can temper your spirit in vital, meaningful ways. You learn patience and tolerance and hope in the face of setbacks. All these life skills have practical and emotional value and are applicable to many other goals in life. As a result of your caregiving you might find yourself a better, more patient performer at work for example. Your new perspectives on character can give you a better appreciation for people in general. That opens doors in networking, collaboration and teamwork.

If you are the recipient of caregiving it can feel awkward to be at the center of so much attention. Some people feel (or react) as if they've been forced to give up their old life in favor of a new life they never requested.

You might really want your old life back. That's natural. But we are called to consider all of life's changes in context. Learning to live in the present with all its changes, new people and routines is ultimately life-sustaining for everyone. It's helping ourselves or other people over that hump that is so hard.

The inner light of caregiving

There is a yin and yang relationship between caregivers and the people receiving care. That dynamic depends on communication, with emphasis on the root word, which is to "commune." That leads us to the importance of Community in supporting Character and Caregiving.

COMMUNITY

Definition of Community

1. A group of people living in the same place or having a particular characteristic in common.

2. Feeling of fellowship with others, as a result of sharing common attitudes, interests and goals.

The notion of community really is a beautiful concept. It helps us define our social and work lives so that we can create cultures needed to foster creativity, support and trust.

With those definitions in mind there are hundreds of ways to consider creating a caregiving support community that works for you. Even if you don't appear to know a soul in the world who can help you, there are people who care, who will pitch in and who will respect your character while helping you gain access to the caregiving needed to support your survivorship.

From Simple to Complex

Some communities truly are simple, just two or three people

willing to stand with someone in need. We find such communities throughout history. Even the biblical concept of "two or three people gathered in my name" communicates a bond of community in the name of a cause or purpose.

The concept of community has become enormously diverse over the ages. Now, with the world available to us through the Internet, even national or international boundaries do not hold back the notion of communities. Community is a powerful tool in all cases because the leverage of many people acting on behalf of the few produces results that seem almost miraculous at times.

So let us consider how communities form and why it can be so important to have some sense of community at work for you.

It starts with caring

A friend recently posted this message to a social media site after her the woman she called a friend and a sister passed away:

"On Saturday several hundred of us celebrated the beautiful life of Maria. I was so very proud of how strong and faithful my brother and niece and nephew and his wife were, and how powerfully healing it is to see so many family and friends holding each other up as we mourn. As Patrick stated during the service, Maria's basic directions for life were to tell those you love "I love you" as often as possible, and to treat every person you meet with kindness and respect. Maria did this with ease, and they are wonderful words to live by."

There are hundreds of tales of inspiration and care behind those words, especially in the "I Love You" philosophy Maria shared with all those she encountered in life. Expressing love is an important sign of character. Love reaches out to create communities wherever it goes and reaches beyond our ability to grasp its depth and breadth, both temporal and eternal.

We must take love into consideration with all we have now measured. Character. Caregiving. Community. With love we bring out the best in all these ways.

FOR ALL PRACTICAL PURPOSES

What follows are some simple guidelines and perspectives to keep in mind as you examine the benefits of character, caregiving and community in cancer survivorship:

Keep your mind and heart open to possibilities

There is nothing in life more valuable than the grace of trust, hope and love. That's true when you find it in yourself and when you receive them from others. Also, reality is not limited to that which we can physically touch. We know that emotional pain is real, so why ignore the healing strength of emotional joy and the hope of possibilities? Our dreams, imagination and creativity drive so much of our motivation. Take time to place them at the forefront of your survivorship.

Communicate the best way you know how

While the practical need of protecting your medical privacy is important, sharing your basic needs can help you cope with challenges in a number of ways. First, it can help you balance the emotional burden. It can also be a great stress release to have people with whom you can consult and compare experiences in order to gain perspective on your personal situation. It is also much more possible for people to discern your true needs when everyone is in open, regular communication.

Listen To Your Doctors. But don't be afraid to ask questions.

Sometimes it seems there is very little time to actually engage in conversation with your primary care physicians, surgeons and oncologists during cancer care. That means it is very important when you do have an opportunity to discuss your condition with doctors to listen carefully to what they have to say. Take note when you are receiving news. It can be hard to recall later on exactly what was said. Doctors often see dozens of patients per day. They may focus on details that matter medically but not get to the simpler questions like how long you might be staying at a hospital or other such details. Write down your questions, and ask them.

It is your responsibility to prepare questions for that moment when they walk in the room. If necessary, dismiss other people from the room to allow your "core team" of caregivers, family or friends to also carefully listen to what the doctors have to say. If you are one-on-one because it is early in the morning or late at night when the doctor comes, don't be afraid to ask if you can turn on a cell phone and record your discussion. Some doctors may frown on that, but it never hurts to ask.

Reach Out To Cancer Communities. National and local.

There are tremendous support groups and online resources where you can share your experience and get vital feedback from people around the world going through similar experiences in cancer treatment, caregiving or relationship management with doctors and other resources. Usually caregivers are welcomed in these circles when you identify yourself and your purpose in being there.

Find Resources As Close to Home As Possible.

Medical groups and systems around the world have begun to establish localized cancer resource centers offering support in areas such as financial or insurance advice, stress management and mental health, support groups and advocacy. Ask at your treatment center or doctor's office if an organization like that exists near you.

Set Up a Care Giving Group

Web resources such as Share The Care and Lotsahelpinghands now exist online to help cancer patients and their caregivers coordinate groups of people willing to help people through their cancer journey. It generally costs little or nothing to set up a care group. You can list your needs and a group leader can manage the assignments if you like.

Listen To Your Own Instincts

Some people find inspiration in big events and organizations dedicated to wiping out cancer. Others find a quieter approach more effective. Perhaps you're a very private person who prefers to keep your cancer quiet and personal. These instincts are all normal and all are correct.

Share Your Journey If You Like

You don't have to be a great writer or communicator to benefit from sharing your journey. Simply write your thoughts in the best way you know how and help people understand your needs. There are many resources online to help you do so.

Don't Let Cancer Define You

Cancer and other diseases can be demanding on your time, your health and your goals. Finding ways to exist outside that bubble of focus on going through treatments is important to your long term health. If you can't manage "big" activities for a time, strive to thrive on smaller pleasures. Take joy in simplified versions of things you like to do if necessary. If you're a gardener, grow some things indoors. If you're an athlete, be satisfied with simple progress like walking for health rather than running. Most of all, don't beat yourself up over having to change. There is often purpose to be found in any challenge.

We also believed that keeping cancer in perspective was key to managing things whenever difficulty came along. Our chosen phrase "It Is What It Is" was not meant as a sign of resignation but as a method of keeping cancer in its place as we worked and played and live to its fullest extent.

Pay Attention To Your Spirit

Even if you are not a religious person, you have spirit. Spirit is motivation. Spirit is hope. Spirit is keeping faith and hope through adversity. Spirit is what lives in side you, gives you life and helps you appreciate being part of a wonderful world and what may lay beyond. Pay attention to your spirit. It can help you see miraculous things at work.

Emily Cudworth, Chuck, Linda Cudworth, Evan Cudworth and Christopher Cudworth

The Journey Blogs

CHAPTER FOUR

Photography credits: Christopher Cudworth, Emily Cudworth
Book and Cover Design: Christopher Cudworth

To view other writings and artwork by the author visit:

www.werunandride.com (running and cycling)
www.naturesymbol.com (artwork, photography and writing)
www.genesisfix.wordpress.com (theology)
www.3ccreativecontent.com (business)
www.behance.net/christophercudworth (writing and marketing)

Find the author on social media:

Twitter : @gofast

LinkedIn: www.linkedin.com/in/christophercudworth/

Facebook: <u>www.facebook.com/pages/Christopher-</u>
<u>Cudworth-114949008603738</u> (Christopher Cudworth Artist)

About the Author

Christopher Cudworth was born in the Finger Lakes of Upstate New York and moved to Lancaster, Pennsylvania at the age of 5. His family migrated to Illinois in 1970. He currently resides in the town of Batavia, IL.. He attended Luther College in Decorah, Iowa majoring in Art with an academic emphasis in English and Biology. He was a team All American in NCAA Division III cross country and went on to compete post-collegiately in road and track racing.

An accomplished painter and designer, his work has been featured in prints and posters. He has sold more than 2000 original artworks to collectors. His running poster design was named to the Runner's World Cream of the Crop Top 5 competition. An avid birder and naturalist, Chris often writes and paints about nature.

As a writer Christopher has published thousands of articles and feature stories and earned the Best Article of the Year award from Yahoo! Associated Content in 2008. He is professionally employed as a content marketer with his own business, 3C Creative Content. The author is available for speaking engagements at 3Ccreativecontent@gmail.com or <u>cudworthfix@gmail.com</u>.

Postlude

Linda Cudworth was not only a person of great character and strength, she was also one to find humor and reason to celebrate life. We also enjoyed the serendipitous nature of life together.

The Game Ball

While attending a Chicago Cubs vs. Houston Astros baseball game, Linda was careful while walking up the many steps leading to seats in the 2nd balcony on the third base side. She had recently had bunion surgery and her right foot was tender from the surgery. We found our seats and in the middle innings Ryne Sandberg came up to bat against Nolan Ryan, a Hall of Fame pitcher. Sandberg fouled off a pitch and the ball sailed up into the stands. Dozens of fans scrambled after the ball and Linda bent down to protect her foot from all the hubbub. Finally the hectic search ended but no one had come up with the ball. "I wonder what happened to it," I asked. "I'm sitting on it," she said, and reaching under her lap she pulled out the prized baseball. "It rolled into my hand while I was protecting my foot," she grinned. We kept that ball for 30+ years. It was recently given to the Pastor of our church, an avid Cubs fan and the person who served as our spiritual guide in the last weeks of Linda's life.

Notes:

CPSIA information can be obtained at www.ICGtesting.com
Printed in the USA
LVOW04s1808150914

404141LV00018B/1298/P